REPRODUCTION
AND
SUCCESSION

Books by Robin Fox

The Keresan Bridge

Kinship and Marriage

The Imperial Animal (with Lionel Tiger)

Encounter with Anthropology

Biosocial Anthropology (editor)

The Tory Islanders

The Red Lamp of Incest

Neonate Cognition (edited with Jacques Mehler)

The Violent Imagination

The Search for Society

REPRODUCTION
AND
SUCCESSION

Studies in Anthropology, Law, and Society

ROBIN FOX

Transaction Publishers
New Brunswick (U.S.A.) and London (U.K.)

Library of Congress Catalog Number: 92-13207
ISBN: 1-56000-067-8
Printed in the United States of America

Library of Congress Cataloging-in-Publication Data

Fox, Robin, 1934-
    Reproduction and succession : studies in anthropology, law, and society / Robin Fox.
        p.   cm.
    Includes bibliographical references and index.
    ISBN 1-56000-067-8
    1. Kinship. 2. Kinship (Law) 3. Human reproduction. 4. Law and anthropology. I. Title.
    GN 487.F7 1992
306.83--dc20   92-13207
                                                                    CIP

To
Michael, Julian, and John

That they might revere the law enough to keep it, but always be
critical enough to want to improve it.

Contents

Preface

Those looking here for anything resembling the traditional anthropology of law will be, at least initially, disappointed, if what they expect are detailed disquisitions on the legal systems of specific tribal societies, or something like that. Of this there is nothing. Chapter 4 certainly deals with tribal laws and customs, but not in the way that anthropologists of law have usually tackled them. Similarly, the first two chapters are within the scope of the sociology of jurisprudence, or even of the study of legal reform. But the first takes an exotic case—Mormon polygyny—to which, perhaps, only an anthropologist (and one interested in history) could do justice, and the second—surrogate motherhood—goes much farther afield than even sociologists of reform would care to tread. Not many of them would want to discuss the evolution of breast-feeding or the ethology of the mother-child bond. The third chapter—Greek tragedy—takes yet another turn, and could well be seen as contributing to an anthropology and literature enterprise—for which indeed it was originally written, or even an anthropology and history symposium— to which it has been read. But it is in fact about the same issue as the first two chapters: the great shift from what I choose to call "kinship law" to "state law" that parallels what Sir Henry Maine immortalized as the shift from "status to contract." The final chapter—on the role of the maternal uncle—moves into what appears to be the more usual exotic sphere of the anthropologist in the strict sense. But it ends by discovering—at least to the author's satisfaction—a cultural/biological universal that may be more significant than either of those two old anthropological chestnuts, the nuclear family and the incest taboo.

The link is there between the seemingly disparate subjects: Antigone's stubborn insistence on burying her brother despite the "law" to the contrary; the maternal uncle's ubiquitous if sometimes shadowy presence in all systems of succession; the Mormon assertion of the right to polygynous marriage as a religious obligation; and Mary Beth Whitehead's insistence on the superiority of the rights of motherhood over those of contract. The war between kinship and state, between kinship and contract, and between kinship and rampant individualism, is one of the great movers of history; perhaps more so than the war between the classes or between the colonizers and the third world. Indeed, it may well encompass these. All history is the history of reproduction and succession; in other words, of kinship (Mary Beth is fighting the same battle as Antigone). Anthropology seems to have forgotten this, although it once made the study of kinship central to its enterprise. Sociology never did quite grasp it, getting bogged down in something called "the family" and an enterprise of "family sociology" that was indeed the pursuit of a cultural construct rather than a cultural universal. Psychology and economics have not helped.

If this book is "about" anything then—as opposed to the obvious subissues that it can be seen to be about—it is about Maine's great shift from the law of status to the law of contract, with this twist: Maine was right to see this as a shift in ideas; but, below the ideas— the ideology—may rumble some intractable biological givens of the peculiar species that we are. So, no matter how much we shift our ideas about how the world ought to work, these atavistic, limbic, subrational motives may continue to surface, like sinister social coelacanths, in ways that are either a discomfort or a disaster to our neat social constructions of modern (or even postmodern) reality. Law is supposedly our most rational attempt to impose order on nature and society. But law equally must grapple with such matters as reproduction and succession, which seem to defy rationality in ways that law itself cannot handle. We have to go beyond the law to help it in its ever-evolving task, and to help it to understand better what that task is and what its possibilities and limitations are.

This book is an attempt at such a constructive approach to the law. It does this by using four case studies of a deliberately varied nature and by discussing their particulars rather than by preaching a general theoretical position. I am not sure, except in a vague sense, what that position would be or how easily I could describe it within the existing intellectual constructions of behavioral science. I think of it in a very broad and even old-fashioned sense as "anthropological" in the way our forefathers meant it, and that is why I have put "anthropology" firmly in the subtitle. But I suspect this is a growingly idiosyncratic position. For that I am sorry, since I envision an "anthropology of law" as something more than just the ethnography of tribal courts. Perhaps the readers will be better able than I am to articulate just what this anthropology might be. For the moment I can only warn, "watch out for the coelacanths!" and take it from there.

ROBIN FOX
Princeton, New Jersey
June 1992

PART I

REPRODUCTION

Introduction
Empirical Knowledge and Legal Theory

Scientists have their delusions of grandeur just like ordinary mortals. They know best about how the world works and figure they should be making the decisions on how to work it.

But they rarely get to do so. They don't have the stuff dictators are made of, and if they are really busy being scientists they don't have the time to get elected, where this is possible. What is more, there is no specific "scientific" platform, except that they are all agreed that ever more generous portions of the GNP should go to scientific research.

Social scientists have perhaps more delusions than others since sociology, political science, economics, and anthropology are the "policy sciences"—they are directly concerned with the social world and its ordering. Some purists among them may affect a disdain for the practical applications of the fruits of their labors, but few can resist the invitation to meddle. This is usually from the very best of motives. These are good people with an honest desire to be of some use.

The problem comes when trying to decide what in their findings is certain enough to be safely "applied." For, as we know, while most social scientists lean to a liberal-left, reformist-progressive position, they are by no means agreed among themselves as to how their knowledge fits the world of policy. They are not even agreed among themselves about what they know and how they should go about finding anything out. In fact, most social scientists today would prob-ably repudiate the appellation "science" when applied to what they do. This is on the surface strange since their forebears labored mightily to be included in the scientific fold, one reason being that they wanted to qualify as "experts" in order to be called upon to influence policy. The economists succeeded earliest and continue to be most in demand, and most other social scientists openly envy them. It is the economists who are emulated, with their advisory positions in government, and even the high offices to which they can aspire. Their effect on legislation can be direct, if not always happy. But it is the direct influence on legislation that is seen as the model. Plato's philosopher king haunts the imaginations and ambitions of the social scientists.

Thus, the most usual tactic for the social scientist addressing the relationship between his subject matter and the law is to state some basic and sound scientific facts or principles and to suggest that these be made the basis of benign legislation aimed at improving the human condition by bringing statute law more into line with scientific knowledge. This is a worthy aim, but the trouble with it is that the proposals are usually vague suggestions of basic principles, and even if they find their way into statutes, their translation into action is often problematic and fraught with unanticipated consequences. The fascination of scientists with statute law is understandable, since their model is indeed that of the Platonic philosopher king whose business is to search for the proper basis of legislation. Such philosopher monarchs are naturally impatient with and usually indifferent to—and certainly largely ignorant of—the more mundane processes of the common law. Their attitude to social policy is derived essentially from the Enlightenment and is, like that of the *philosophes*, enamored of the Continental legislative "code." In the English tradition, the Utilitarians (or philosophical radicals), the Fabian Socialists, and the Disraelian Tories have similarly concentrated their efforts on influencing legislation to ameliorate social conditions.

The main thrust of British sociology, for example, with the development of the social survey and the accumulation of data on poverty, housing, educational opportunity, health conditions, and the like, has been to overwhelm governments with statistics showing how bad things really are, thus pushing them into legislative redress. It is perhaps not surprising that the very un-Disraelian Thatcher Tories (in fact, buccaneer, laissez-faire liberals) have started something of a vendetta against sociology, even to the point of taking "Science" out of the title of the Social Science Research Council. Anthropologists at least understand how important these symbolic gestures are. But anthropologists, now that there is no longer an empire to govern, are rarely called upon for anything except ethnographic filmmaking for the BBC. The public is always open to movies of half-naked people of dark complexion doing odd things. This is not, however, what anthropologists have in mind when they pontificate on the relevance of their endangered discipline.

They once did indeed ride high and proud as the advisors of viceroys, governors, and colonial secretaries, and they have a good track record. They did influence colonial legislation, and usually for the better. Given the initial wisdom of indirect rule (not an anthropological invention, it should be added), they were needed by the colonial governors to describe what the native laws and customs were that should be left in place. This they did superbly well. And, on the whole their influence was a good one. They were almost without exception on the side of "their" natives, and they respected the indigenous cultures. Cynics might say they had a vested interest in keeping these cultures pristine anyway, but that is a little hard, and from my own experience I know of very few in the fraternity who did not genuinely have their subjects' welfare at heart. But, like the sociologists back home, they were seduced by the business of legislation. If not philosopher kings, then at least they could be philosophical grey eminences.

American social scientists, and for that matter their Continental brethren, have never had the same degree of legislative influence as their British cousins. The history of why this is so would be inappropriate here; a moment's reflection on America's turbulent capitalist history and its system of government will suffice to remind any reader of the unlikelihood of intellectuals' getting that much influence. When they came near to it—as with the eugenicists and the progressive movement, for example—they were the wrong intellectuals. Again, economists almost monopolize such influence as social scientists managed to exert. But it is superfluous to point out that America has never had a socialist government that might have been receptive to sociological input. The nearest thing was the New

Deal, but even here the input was minimal, with perhaps only the TVA employing sociological expertise to any extent. Still, the aim of most social scientists who still consider themselves such (scientists, that is) is to "be in Washington"—they want to influence, propose, evaluate, and generally be involved with legislation. Anthropologists are rarely called upon by anyone except for occasional testimony in Indian land disputes. (Even if they got to legislate Indian affairs they would no longer be welcomed by the very Indians who have been their bread and butter. Paternalism is out; Indians want to legislate their own affairs these days.)

The American tradition, however, provides an interesting alternative to the philosopher-king pose of the social scientist. Because of their unique position under the Constitution, American courts have been almost as active and influential in social reform as has the legislative process. And, given their powers of judicial review, they can often either extend, change, or thwart legislation in a manner not as available to their English counterparts. Whole areas of American life have been altered not by legislation but by court-ordered action: busing to achieve racial balance in schools; abortions at the volition of the mother; affirmative action in college applications; quotas of low-income housing in every township (New Jersey); and so on. Another possible approach to the relationship between science (in the broadest sense) and law, therefore, could be to consider intervention in case law. This is of course done every time a scientist is called as an "expert witness," But the scientist usually only intervenes in this particular capacity—as a witness. To intervene more systematically, the scientist would have to become a student of case law, and the lawyer a student of the relevant sciences.

Such an approach would truly bring scientists and lawyers (qua lawyers) together, more so than the legislative approach which largely conjoins scientists and politicians. This can best be illustrated by taking cases actually in progress and showing how the law can benefit from scientific intervention and how the scientist can best intervene if he knows something of the law in question.

The first case here considered—the specific injunction against polygamy applying to the state of Utah—first came to my attention in an abrupt fashion when I applied for a visa to study in the United States in 1957. Among the many questions about possible unsavory associations and indulgences was the following: "Do you practice, or advocate the practice of, polygamy?" I was considerably baffled by this at the time since I had no idea why this was being asked of me or anyone. That immigration should frown on my possible membership in the Society for Cultural Relations with the U.S.S.R. I could perhaps understand. But polygamy? Why bother? My attempts to enquire further were cut short by the bored consular officer at the London embassy. "Just put No, son," he said wearily. "Don't give me a hard time." So I put No, which was the correct answer anyway.

Later I learned that the question had been put on visa application forms as a result of various acts of Congress in order to discourage Mormon recruiting in England—recruiting that was very successful in the mid-nineteenth century. Most historians have explained its continuing presence there by legislative inertia. All these questions (including the strange "Do you suffer from ... sexual deviation?") require an act of Congress for their removal. It is easier just to let them pile up and have people put No than waste congressional time in removing them. Perhaps. After my experiences with this case I am not so sure. The polygamy issue is not and never has been a rational one in this country. It is rarely discussed with disinterested intellectual curiosity, and most everyone seems to wish it had not been raised and that it would just somehow go away. This includes scientists and lawyers as well as politicians and laymen. The deep prejudices and even deeper hypocrisies that this attitude betrays are curious to an observer. But the observer is not from a country or culture in which the issue has raised its hoary head, at least in the form in which the Mormons—to everyone's embarrassment, including today their own— have raised it.

However, our business will not be to examine all the fascinating issues raised by polygamy and by attitudes to it in (nominally) Christian monogamous cultures, but to examine the specific arguments used by the Supreme Court to declare constitutional the antipolygamy legislation of 1862, and specifically the famous argument in the 1878 case of *Reynolds v. U.S.A.* This has become necessary as a result of a recent court case in which I was asked to be the proverbial "expert witness" and which presents a rather unusual but instructive instance of the kind of "intervention" I have advocated above. The case was ultimately lost, but the issue will not go away; and to deal with it the "expert" will have to understand some constitutional law, and the lawyer will have to understand the expert. Whether the judges will heed either is open to doubt; but the caution of the courts serves to force us to make the best case possible.

The second case, that of the famous "Baby M," where a "surrogate mother" contracted to deliver a baby to its biological father and then refused to give it up only to have it seized from her by a court order, was not something I intended to get involved with. But I had presented a paper on my Mormon findings (as detailed in chapter 1) to a symposium at the Gruter Institute for Law and Behavioral Research in California. Since this was a foundation concerned with the relationship between law and behavioral science, I was happy to be involved. They wished to follow up the Baby M case since the issue of surrogate mothers was clearly going to be a hot one. Because I was based in New Jersey where the case was pending, I was asked to look into it. The aim here was not to be an "expert witness" (although I was invited) but to see to what extent we could get lawyers and scientists to cooperate on asking the right questions about such an issue.

I had no feelings one way or another to start with. The case seemed murky and the facts were obscure. Who had done what to whom? There was a "contract," but what did this mean? No one seemed to have seen it except the parties and the judge who made the initial ex parte order. Even so, what intrigued me was that before the issue came to court, before even the barest minimum of information was available, everyone with whom I discussed the subject had made up his mind—usually passionately and usually anti the mother. "A deal's a deal" was the answer from many people to any doubts expressed. Mary Beth Whitehead had made a promise and she should keep it. That was one side of the response. The other was just as passionate and said that the baby was better off with the father and should stay there. This opinion was rife among my middle-class, white, educated colleagues, neighbors, and friends. I was surprised by the passion in both positions, and then surprised by my own surprise. Why should class and contract *not* be matters of passion in this country? The case took on a larger meaning and I determined to pursue it.

In an attempt to find something out I went to a public meeting at the Rutgers Medical School where several doctors, some divines of the compulsory three faiths, and the lawyer for William Stern (the biological father) were speaking. It was a strange gathering. Any statements to the effect that contractual parents should take precedence over natural parents were greeted with loud applause. The Catholic priest, who looked as if he had come straight from the seminary and was desperately trying to remember his moral theology lectures, confused everyone with a long discussion about whether or not semen might be gathered in a donor's condom provided said prophylactic had been pricked with a pin, thus avoiding the sin of artificially preventing birth—or something like that. The doctors spoke seriously about the "new birth techniques" that were becoming available, and a layman told his own story of obtaining a child by in vitro procedures with a surrogate in England and having himself and his wife declared the legal parents in the United States.

Then Skoloff, the lawyer representing the biological father, spoke on the Baby M issue. He maintained that his case would rest on the contract and predicted that it would devolve into a custody battle that he would win for the middle-class Sterns as the "better parents." This again was roundly applauded. Some technical questions were asked, and then, wishing to elicit some information from Skoloff, I innocently asked why a surrogate mother who changed her mind should not be given the same privileges as a mother who had promised her child for adoption. In most states, and certainly in New Jersey, a mother who promised her child for adoption had a specified period of time in which to change her mind. I was not prepared for the response. There was uproar. There was booing and catcalls and shaking of fists. Above the noise, Skoloff shouted that it was an outrageous suggestion since the "father" had a contract. I wanted to point out that a mother who had promised the child for adoption had a contractual obligation too, but I wasn't allowed to speak. Of course, an obvious objection to my objection was that in this case there was a "father" who wanted the child. I would have objected in turn that in adoptive cases—of teenage mothers, for example—there was also a "father," but he was rarely consulted. And so on. But debate there could not be. I only discovered afterwards that this had been a meeting sponsored by an association of infertile couples, who comprised 90 percent of the audience. I felt like Salman Rushdie at a gathering of the Islamic faithful. But I realized more than ever that to get involved with this issue was not going to be easy. No one was dispassionate about it.

Still, my brief then, as it is now, was to try to assess, with the help of colleagues, how the scientific information we had at our disposal bore on the legal issues qua legal issues. While sticking to that brief, I shall wander occasionally into comment on the remarkable furor this case caused, and make some suggestions as to its origin and meaning. What should have been a private matter between two essentially well-meaning people turned into a public, legal brawl and an international cause célèbre.

The two cases—Mormons and surrogate mothers—might seem at first blush unrelated, but a moment's consideration reveals that they are both about our rights to reproduce in a manner we choose, without state interference. And they are curiously both about "plural marriage," or at least plural mating and its legality. Both raise the same deep questions about reproduction, morality, and the laws and customs of an avowedly individualist culture—something explored further in part 2. In the dry issues that follow we should not lose sight of the deeper questions raised, even if we cannot resolve them.

1

The Case of the Polygamous Policeman

Though the law may never become a completely logical system, it can never entirely dispense with the effort in that direction. For that helps men to know what they may or may not do.

— Morris Raphael Cohen
Reason and Law

Potter v. Murray City: Three *Is* a Crowd

On 1 December 1982, Royston E. Potter, a police officer in Murray City, Utah (a suburb of Salt Lake City), was fired from his job. The reason given was his admitted marital liaison with two women (later a third "wife" was added). I stress "admitted" because many fundamentalist Mormons have more than one wife yet suffer no legal disabilities even though they are technically breaking the law, and mostly they keep these "marriages" secret. In Mr. Potter's case the marriages were an open secret. I stress "liaison" because it is hard to construe in what sense the second union was legally a "marriage" since it was only sanctified by an unrecognized Mormon fundamentalist sect not licensed to perform marriages. But Mr. Potter was not fired for practicing bigamy per se. Indeed, while he might have been guilty of "fornication" or "unlawful cohabitation"—two

11

crimes no longer prosecuted in Utah (or anywhere else for that matter)—it would have been hard to prove bigamy insofar as, legally, there had been no second marriage. It could perhaps have been argued that the second marriage constituted a common-law marriage, except that Utah does not have common-law marriage. But it is important to note that Mr. Potter was never charged with anything; he was simply dismissed from his employment.

The grounds for dismissal were as follows: as a police officer, Mr. Potter had sworn to uphold the constitution of the state of Utah and to arrest offenders against its statutes. However, one of the basic statutes—the one that had "enabled" the then territory of Utah to join the Union—is the one forbidding plural marriage and forbidding it forever:

> The following ordinance shall be irrevocable without the consent of the United States and the people of this State:
>
> First:—Perfect toleration of religious sentiment is guaranteed. No inhabitant of this State shall ever be molested in person or property on account of his or her mode of religious worship; but polygamous or plural marriages are forever prohibited. (Utah Constitution of 1890, art. III)

The Utah Enabling Act was passed by the U.S. Congress on 6 July 1894 (ch. 138, §20, 28 Stat.).

This statute was intended to apply not only to legal forms of marriage (prosecutable as bigamy) but to any other form of "marital liaison" even if unconsummated, clandestine, or performed by unauthorized persons. To make this quite clear, the Utah Criminal Code specifies that the antipolygamy statute applies to those who, knowing they have a husband or wife, purport to marry another person (Utah Code Ann. 76-7-101[1]-[2]-1990]). This makes polygamy, like true bigamy, a third-degree felony. Since Mr. Potter, a Mormon fundamentalist convert, was living openly in such an illegal liaison, he was held to be in contravention of his oath to uphold the constitution, and so fired. He was offered his job back on condition that he renounce all but one of his "wives" (decision of the Murray City Civil Service Commission, 18 February 1983). This he refused to do. It is known that many Utah officials, elected and appointed, live in such unions with impunity (one mayor has ten "wives"). But, for whatever reasons, Murray City decided to apply the letter of the law and act upon it.

Mr. Potter decided to sue for reinstatement on several grounds: that his First Amendment (freedom of religion) rights had been abridged since polygamy was required by his religious beliefs as necessary to salvation; that his right to privacy had been abridged; that he had been denied due process since no criminal charges had been brought against him; and that the statute requiring Utah to ban polygamy forever in order to be admitted to the Union was unconstitutional anyway (for various reasons), so he should not be required to enforce it.

This suit, brought initially against Murray City and the state of Utah, represented the strongest challenge to antipolygamy legislation since such legislation had been declared constitutional by the U.S. Supreme Court in the landmark case of *Reynolds v. U.S.A.* in 1878. The Utah District Court (Central Division) dismissed an application by Mr. Potter for summary judgement (*Potter v. Murray City et al.,* 585 F. Supp. 1126 [D. Utah 1984]). The problem was passed to the Federal Appeals Court (Tenth Circuit). The state had insisted that the United States be included as a defendant since, its attorney general argued, Utah was bound in this matter by an act of the United States Congress. The Federal Appeals Court, in upholding the decision of the district court, excused the United States as defendant on the grounds that any state may amend its own constitution by a two-thirds vote of its legislature. That Utah had never done so on the "perpetual anti-polygamy" clause, the judge argued, implied that it acquiesced in the restriction (*Potter v. Murray City et al.,* 706 F.2nd. 1065 [10th Cir. 1985]). So the United States was off the hook at this level but remained open to challenge in the Supreme Court, since it was a decision of this court that had affirmed the constitutionality of the congressional ban on polygamy in the first place.

However, when the case was appealed to the Supreme Court in 1985, the Court, in its wisdom, denied the application for a writ of certiorari, as is its right and its wont when it reckons the potato is too hot to handle. Polygamy is still illegal. There for the moment the matter rests. But, as we shall suggest at the end of this account, recent developments in common law are bound to reraise the issue, probably under the rubric of the "right to marry" principle. In the meantime, let us look briefly at some background on the Mormons and their contentious polygamy.

The Mormons and Polygamy:
Useful Revelations

For those not familiar with Mormon history, a few background notes are in order; others may skip to the next section.[1] The Mormon story begins in the 1820s during the ferment of religious activity in New England that eventually produced Shakers and Owenites, Christian Scientists, Universalists, Seventh-Day Adventists, and a welter of breakaway Baptists. Utopian experiments, like the Oneida community with its "omnigamy" (everyone married to everyone), flourished and failed.

Joseph Smith, born in Vermont but raised in Palmyra in northern New York State, was a religious boy confused by the embarrassment of sectarian options. He prayed for guidance, and God answered him directly in the form of an angel—Moroni—who presented him with sacred books written on tablets of gold. These books described the second coming of Christ to the new world and the fate of its original inhabitants. Translated under the guidance of the angel, they became the original *Book of Mormon* and were then buried.

Smith was ordered to found a new religious order that would avoid the deficiencies of the other Christian churches and restore the true intentions of God. Thus, the Church of Jesus Christ of Latter-day Saints was born, with a program of anticapitalist, agrarian, communist, utopian reform. How it became transformed into an urban, Republican, capitalist, conservative, all-American, and eventually worldwide church is one of the more fascinating chapters in modern American history. But this is to run too far ahead.

In 1831, Smith initiated the first of several moves his community had to make to cope with the paradox of increasing success coupled with increasing persecution. At first, Mormons would be welcomed for their industry and capacity to improve barren areas; but once established, they would become inevitably the object of envy and suspicion and the attacks of more conventional neighbors. So they moved to Ohio, to Missouri, and to Illinois, where in 1839 they seemed to be well established at Nauvoo.

Many Eastern immigrants and dispossessed farmers were attracted by the Mormons' promise of land and the support given by the system of communal farming and sharing. But it was just these features that attracted the wrath of capitalist, individualist neighbors, and eventually real violence broke out, with Smith being killed by a mob in 1844.

Fortunately, Smith had a worthy successor in Brigham Young, who led the famous trek westward in 1847 to the arid desert of Utah, where he set up the Mormon state which was to flourish for forty years, sending colonies out as far as northern Mexico and California. During this time, the whole of the Great Basin west of the Rockies was under Mormon control, exercised from the capital in Salt Lake City. A benevolent theocracy ran a communist, agrarian state, whose basic principles ran as counter to those of American capitalism as the denunciations of Karl Marx. A clash was as inevitable here as it was with the agrarian, aristocratic, and slave-owning South. The northern Republicans pilloried, with the insistence of Cato, the "twin relics of barbarism" that must be destroyed: slavery and polygamy (*Congressional Globe*, 1860, 1410). Unfortunately for the Mormons, the polygamy issue gave the Union just the excuse it needed to smash this rival economic utopia.

Polygamy had not been in Smith's original program, but he was bound to have been influenced by the sexual experimentation going on in the New England communes. More to the point, Mormon recruiting had been extremely successful with women, who soon began to outnumber the male converts—by as many as two thousand in 1856. These women had been promised homes and families, so clearly there was only one logical way to provide them: plural marriage.

Smith had conceived the idea while still in Nauvoo, and the practice began with a few of his chief lieutenants in 1843. As a "prophet," the Mormon leader could receive direct revelations from God, which gave them absolute authority. Polygamy was one of these useful revelations, and for a time it contributed mightily to Mormon success. But it was in the end to backfire. Although visitors like Sir Richard Burton and Sir Charles Dilke praised the sobriety and decency of the polygamous families, the victorious Union government after the Civil War moved to destroy this unacceptable center of rival power in the West, with destruction of the evils of "barbaric" polygamy as its excuse.

Acts were passed by Congress; the *Reynolds* decision was rendered by the Supreme Court; troops were sent to the Utah border; Mormons were deprived of the vote and subjected to a carpetbagging administration which expropriated church property; and federal marshals began twelve years of "polyg hunts" which jailed more than twelve hundred men (including Mr. Reynolds for a year and a half) and forcefully broke up the families. By 1890 every Mormon leader was in jail, in hiding, or on the run. The fourth president of the church and therefore reigning prophet, Wilford Woodruff, had another useful revelation, and declared that God had told him that Mormons should obey the law of the land as regards marriage.

This might have got the Mormons off the hook legally, but it left many outsiders still suspicious, and many of the faithful unconvinced. What had started as a pragmatic move had become an article of religious faith. Even though perhaps only about 5 percent of Mormon males had ever practiced polygamy, it remained an ideal. Fundamentalists continued to practice in secret, particularly in the Mormon colonies away from too much federal scrutiny, while the federal government continued with its special clauses in the Utah Constitution and its general harassment, including the addition of polygamists to the list of prohibited immigrants (1891). This is where matters stand today, with polygamy officially banned by the Mormon church as part of its amazingly successful adaptation to the very civilization it had set out to oppose, but with plural marriage, or "living according to the principle" still revered by many members as the only way to live according to God's word and achieve salvation. Officer Potter stood squarely, then, in a good Mormon tradition, only he chose to do it openly and had to face the consequences.

The Dominance of *Reynolds*:
Bad Facts Make Good Law

Four acts of Congress, aimed specifically at the Mormons, established the illegality of polygyny (usually referred to as polygamy) in the United States: the Morrill Act of 1862, the Poland Act of 1874, the Edmunds Act of 1882, and the Edmunds-Tucker Act of 1887. The last of these was the vicious legislation that broke up Mormon families and dispossessed the Church of Jesus Christ of Latter-day Saints, thus effectively destroying the Mormon state. The Morrill Act essentially banned "polygamy" in "all states and territories" of the United States. Thus, when the Utah constitution was being drawn up in 1890, the special clause was inserted into the state constitution to make assurance doubly sure: the Mormon state could not say that it had not assented specifically to the conditions of the Morrill Act. (The claim that this clause was invalid because it was entered into under duress was dismissed in *State v. Barlow* [107 Utah 292 (1944)], but it became an issue in the Potter suit, which claims that it was always invalid since conditions for entry to the Union must be the same for all states.) The constitutionality of the Morrill Act was affirmed by the Supreme Court in the landmark decision of *Reynolds v. U.S.A.* (98 U.S. 145 [1878]), and this decision was reconfirmed as recently as 1946 in *Cleveland v. U.S.A.* (329 U.S. 14 [1946]). Thus, legislation passed in 1862 and confirmed in 1878 is still the law of the land, and it is this that Mr. Potter's suit sought to challenge.

The *Reynolds* decision did more than just confirm the law against polygamy. It established an important legal principle that still, in general, holds: that while the First Amendment protects religious belief, it does not necessarily apply to religious action if that action can be shown to be "subversive of good order."

This was recently modified in the case of *Wisconsin v. Yoder* (406 U.S. 205 [1972]), where Mennonite petitioners sought, on religious grounds, to withdraw their children from public schools after the age of fourteen. The court ruled that a state, if it is to interfere with religious action that flows from sincerely held religious beliefs, must show a "compelling interest" in so doing. That is, the burden is on the state to prove that the public welfare would be in danger from the practice in question. The court was also enjoined to determine whether there exists a "less restrictive method of regulating the religious practice" than the outright banning of it. Various judgements had in part anticipated the *Yoder* decision,[2] which was recently reconfirmed in *Thomas v. Review Board* (101 S.Ct. 1425 [1981]) and *United States v. Lee* (102 S.Ct. 1051 [1982]), where Justice Burger restated the opinion.

A related issue is the so-called "right to marry," where again a series of cases (e.g., *Meyer v. Nebraska* [262 U.S. 390 (1923)] and *Skinner v. Oklahoma* [316 U.S. 535 (1942)]) have established that if a state interferes with the right to marry, in whatever form it takes, its interference is subject to the doctrine of "strict scrutiny": it must demonstrate an "overriding and compelling interest" in so doing, and that interest must be tested against the constitutional rights of the parties rather than against some lesser principle such as the convenience of state administration. In the key case of *Loving v. Virginia* (388 U.S. 1 [1967]), the Supreme Court, in striking down Virginia's antimiscegenation laws, affirmed this right based on the Due Process and Equal Protection clauses of the Fourteenth Amendment. The equally important case of *Zablocki v. Redhail* (434 U.S. 374 [1978], Justice Stewart, concurring) confirmed that this "right to marry" doctrine was not confined to cases of racial discrimination but applied to any "unwarranted encroachment upon a constitutionally protected freedom." The encroachment could only be warranted if the health and welfare of the individuals, or public safety, could be shown to be endangered.[3]

These doctrines of "compelling interest" and "strict scrutiny," as they apply to religious action and the right to marry, opened the way for a fundamentalist Mormon to plead that the state of Utah can show no such compelling interest in the case of polygamy. This was indeed Officer Potter's plea to the District and Federal Appeals Courts, and was rejected on strange and illogical grounds, which we shall examine later.

In the meantime, our mandate here is to look at the reasons advanced by the Supreme Court in two crucial cases—*Reynolds v. U.S.A.* (1878) and *Cleveland v. U.S.A.* (1946)—to determine the status of the factual evidence and the reasoning that was held to show that polygamy, even if held as a sincere religious belief, is in action "subversive of good order" or "in violation of social duties," and so properly banned by the U. S. Congress under the Morrill Act of 1862.

I here set out the relevant portions (paras. 164-166, written by Chief Justice Waite) of the *Reynolds* decision so that readers may judge the fairness of my criticism. (The rest of the decision was concerned with legal technicalities stemming from the original trials of Mr. Reynolds, which were part of the appeal and with which, we might add, the court dealt crisply and apparently quite fairly. It should be added here that Mr. Reynolds was a secretary to the Mormon leader Brigham Young, and his case was deliberately brought to test the constitutionality of the Morrill Act.) I take up the decision after an interesting discussion of Thomas Jefferson's remarks, during the debate on the Constitution in 1785, on the right to the free exercise of religion. Jefferson opined that "legislative powers of the Government reach actions only, and not opinions," but added that while the Constitution should "restore to man all his natural rights," said man "has no natural rights in opposition to his social duties." The court, heeding the authority of Jefferson, concluded that:

> Congress was deprived of all legislative power over mere opinion, but was left free to reach actions which were in violation of social duties or subversive of good order.

Applying this doctrine to polygamy, it continued:

> Polygamy has always been odious among the Northern and Western Nations of Europe and until the establishment of the Mormon Church, was almost exclusively a feature of the life of Asiatic and African people. At common law the second marriage was always void, 2 Kent, Com. 79, and from the earliest history of England polygamy has been treated as an offence against society. After the establishment of the ecclesiastical courts, and until the time of James I, it was punished through the instrumentality of those tribunals, not merely because ecclesiastical rights had been violated, but because upon the separation of the ecclesiastical courts from the civil, the ecclesiastical were supposed to be the most appropriate for the trial of matrimonial causes and offenses against the rights of marriage; just as they were for testamentary causes and the settlement of the estates of deceased persons.

> By the statute of 1 James I, ch. 11, the offense, if committed in England or Wales, was made punishable in the civil courts, and the penalty was death. As this statute was limited in its operation to England and Wales, it was at a very early period re-enacted, generally with some modifications, in all the Colonies. In connection with the case we are now considering, it is a significant fact that on the 8th of December, 1788, after the passage of the Act establishing religious freedom, and after the convention of Virginia had recommended as an amendment to the Constitution of the United States the declaration in a Bill of Rights that "All men have an equal, natural and unalienable right to the free exercise of religion, according to the dictates of conscience," the Legislature of that State substantially enacted the Statute of James I, death penalty included, because as recited in the preamble, "It hath been doubted whether bigamy or polygamy be punishable by the laws of this Commonwealth." 12 Hen. Stat., 691. From that day to this we think it may be safely said there never has been a time in any state of the Union when polygamy has not been an offense against society, cognizable by the civil courts and punishable with more or less severity. In the face of all this evidence, it is impossible to believe that the constitutional guaranty of religious freedom was intended to prohibit legislation in respect to this most important feature of social life. Marriage, while from its very nature a sacred obligation, is, nevertheless, in most civilized nations, a civil contract, and usually regulated by law. Upon it society may be said to be built, and out of its fruits spring social relations and social obligations and duties, with which government is necessarily required to deal. In fact, according as monogamous or polygamous marriages are allowed, do we find the principles on which the Government of the People, to a greater or

lesser extent, rests. Professor Lieber says: polygamy leads to the patriarchal principle, and which, when applied to large communities, fetters the people in stationary despotism, while that principle cannot long exist in connection with monogamy. Chancellor Kent observes that this remark is equally striking and profound. 2 Kent. Com., 81, n. e. An exceptional colony of polygamists under exceptional leadership may sometimes exist for a time without appearing to disturb the condition of the people who surround it; but there cannot be a doubt that, unless restricted by some form of constitution, it is within the legitimate scope of the power of every civil government to determine whether polygamy or monogamy shall be the law of social life under its dominion.

In our opinion the statute immediately under consideration is within the legislative power of Congress. It is constitutional and valid as prescribing a rule of action for all those residing in the Territories, and in places over which the United States have exclusive control.

The decision in *Reynolds v. U.S.A.* was in large part based on what was assumed, at the time, to be established fact. That this "fact" was agreeably in tune with established prejudice made the task of the justices easier, of course, but as in all such cases it left open the question: what if the facts should prove to be wrong? On the assumption that good law should never be based on bad fact, it surely follows that if the facts are shown to be in error, then the law must be changed. The principle can of course be reaffirmed, but it will have to be on the basis of different facts.

What is offered here, then, is an opinion as to the present state of knowledge concerning the ethnographic distribution, history, and social implications of plural marriage and plural mating as these bear upon that decision.

I have distinguished plural marriage from plural mating, and this becomes important in the argument that follows. By "marriage" here I am adhering to the conventional meaning of a legally sanctioned arrangement between a man and a woman concerning cohabitation, property, offspring and their legitimacy, etc. Plural marriage then would involve either a man or a woman in several such arrangements. We should get the terms out of the way: polygyny is the marriage of one man with several women; polyandry is the marriage of one woman with several men. Polygamy, strictly speaking, refers to any form of plural marriage, but is commonly used as a synonym for polygyny.

"Plural mating" is my own term for plural unions that are more than casual liaisons (which would simply constitute plural sex) and that imply some continuing relationship between the parties and the offspring, whether or not the unions are recognized as legal marriages (the offspring, e.g., while perhaps technically illegitimate will receive some consideration from the "father"). In many cases, even if only one legal marriage is recognized, secondary unions can become so established by custom and social (if not legal) sanction that they approach de facto marriage. Sometimes, when they are legally recognized (e.g., if illegitimate heirs are given rights of inheritance), these unions can better be termed secondary marriages, but often the law will not recognize as legal the union of the parents, even though it allows rights to the children. Part of the argument here will be that in almost all monogamous systems, such plural mating is practiced. Thus, plural mating is the more inclusive concept, of which plural marriage is an instance. The major difference then between polygyny and monogamy could be stated thus: while plural mating occurs in both systems, under polygyny several unions may be recognized as being legal marriages while under monogamy only one of the unions is so recognized. Often, however, as we have seen, it is difficult to draw a hard and fast line between the two.

I shall not in the following two sections be concerned with the various legal issues that are debated in the *Reynolds* judgement, especially the important First Amendment considerations that arise from it and the related arguments in *Cleveland v. U.S.A.*. I shall be mostly concerned with the historical and anthropological "facts" cited therein, and shall pay particular attention to Mr. Justice Murphy's interesting dissent in the *Cleveland* case.[4]

Reynolds and History:
Higamous, Hogamous, Who is Monogamous?

The *Reynolds* decision, then, established firmly that while the First Amendment applied to "opinion," Congress and the courts had been "left free to reach actions which were in violation of social duties or subversive of good order."

The court obviously therefore had to argue that polygamy (polygyny) is thus subversive. We should note that it did not do so by presenting evidence that plural marriage among the Mormons was "in violation of social duties" or "subversive of good order." Clearly it was not—among the Mormons. The court therefore had to argue that it was and always had been "odious among the Northern and Western Nations of Europe" and "almost exclusively a feature of the life of Asiatic and African people."

We should pause here to note this issue. By its own argument the court has to hold that the actions (polygyny) are "in violation of social duties" or "subversive of good order." At this point, however, it argues simply that they are "odious" to a certain racial group. (It goes on to argue that this "odiousness" is long established.) At this juncture of the argument, then, we can only suppose that, being "odious," these actions will be "in violation of social duty," because to do something that is odious to the majority is such a violation, and that since the said majority will be offended, the action is "subversive of good order." As it stands, this is simply a doctrine of the infallibility of the majority, which clearly, even in 1878, could not be sustained. The court had to go further, then, by establishing the "long standing" of the odiousness and its tendency to be associated with unsavory social circumstances.

To do so, it attributed polygyny (almost) exclusively to "Asiatic and African people"—thus ignoring large areas of the globe[5] and glaringly omitting the Semitic peoples (unless it considered them "Asiatic" or "African" or both?). This omission is all the more startling since of course the "Northern and Western Nations of Europe" derive their religion directly from Semitic sources and, as the Mormons argued so embarrassingly, from a holy book of the Semites in which polygyny is given full sanction. Indeed, these same Christian nations regarded this compilation of Semitic texts as the revealed word of God! Perhaps the court felt it wise to sidestep this issue. It certainly failed to address it.

The implications of even this passage are astonishing. The logic of it is that polygyny among the Asiatic and African peoples is synonymous with "lack of social duty" and "subversion of good order"—which presumably is all right for them but odious to the Christian nations. I say astonishing because today it *is* astonishing. But it was part and parcel of the quite overtly racist thinking of 1878 when the idea of social evolution dominated educated thought, and it was commonplace to regard white, monogamous, Christian civilization as the top of the evolutionary ladder. I shall not expatiate on this point, but leave the readers to ponder it.[6] I shall return to this brusque dismissal of the marriage customs of the rest of the world later, because the court itself chose this moment in its argument to turn to history.

It turned to its "proof" that "from the earliest history of England polygamy has been treated as an offense against society" and to the correct demonstration that bigamy laws were specifically reenacted in the colonies.

In fact, what the court showed is that, as of the reign of James I, polygamy was a civil offense (*Statute of 1 James* I, ch. 11). Before that time it had been tried in ecclesiastical courts. The court's hasty insistence that having the trials take place in ecclesiastical courts had been because the ecclesiastical courts were the "most appropriate" is, I feel, a deliberate attempt to skirt the fact that, until 1603, the taking of a second wife was largely a concern of the churches, as was marriage generally, the state taking little or no interest. What the court's hasty comment conceals is the whole history of the church's attempts to bring marriage under its control, and the subsequent continuing struggle of church and state for jurisdiction over it.

In general, marriage, including plural unions, had been slow to come under ecclesiastical jurisdiction. This unwillingness of the populace to submit to such jurisdiction persisted down into the nineteenth century in parts of England and Wales. The early attempts of the Christian church (working on a still part-pagan population) were to have at least the "wed" (the customary betrothal ceremony) performed at the church door and presided over by the priest. The full command of the church over marriage (for example, the calling of banns, etc.) was not established until the Hardwicke Marriage Act of 1753, and then was as often as not ignored.[7]

This ongoing attempt of the church to wrest control of marriage, not from the state but from customary and pagan-based usages, has to be seen against the background of the evolving Christian position on marriage. "It is better to marry than to burn," said St. Paul, and his sentiment was echoed by many theologians and fathers in what became a general "anti-sex" position in the church (see the works of Origen, Chrysosthom, Augustine, Aquinas, etc.). Sex was equated with sin, and the only possible lawful sex was therefore that guarded by the church's sacrament of marriage—and by implication monogamous marriage. Monogamous marriage, sanctified by the church, became the lowest common denominator that allowed procreation while avoiding sex. (Celibacy, of course, was the holier state.) After the conversion of Constantine and the establishment of the Roman version of the Christian church (circa 330 A.D.), and later, after the creation of the Holy Roman Empire under Charlemagne (800 A.D.), this doctrine became codified and enforcement was attempted.[8]

But we must ask two questions: was plural marriage always "odious" to these Northern and Western peoples before the enforcement of ecclesiastical monogamy (initially by Gregory the Great, circa 600 A.D.), and did this enforcement work? The answer on both counts is no. An extended history is impossible here, but we know, for example, that both kinds of plural marriage (polygyny and polyandry) flourished among the Celtic and Germanic tribes—both are reported among the Britons by Caesar. Glendon in her excellent review of the history of marital law and practice states clearly:

> Among the early Germanic peoples, marriage was different from other sexual unions only in that the wife and children of the marriage enjoyed a more secure position in relation to the husband and his kinship group than other women with whom he cohabited and their offspring. The distinction between marriage and other unions which, though not disapproved, are of lower status appears in Roman Law and in Pre-Tridentine canon law, and in the civil law of France until the 16th century. (See note 7.)

Among the Anglo-Saxons, the "hold-fast wife" and the "hand-fast wife" shared uxorial duties and favors. The nobility and royalty were openly polygynous, and the Frankish dynasty, the Merovingians, which ruled before the usurpation of the Carolingians, was completely polygynous. It was this dynasty (under Clovis) that concluded the "concordat" with the papacy that eventually led to the Holy Roman Empire.[9] Yet its members never renounced their polygyny, nor was that ever required of them. (It is worth noting that the Merovingian era was one of high culture and literacy. After its end and the establishment of Christian monogamy under the Holy Roman Empire, Europe sank into the Dark Ages, and no such standards were achieved again for many centuries.) The church was busy at that time converting the mass of semipagan peasants. Charlemagne himself practiced plural marriage and had many concubines. Most of the "old nobility" of Europe is descended from these, and the Merovingian pretenders to the French throne are descendants of "plural wives."

If it was not then "always odious," did the advent of the new church power render it so? Was Christian monogamy ever wholly established? The state, as we have seen, was, until the reign of James I, not only indifferent but often hostile to monogamy in that kings rarely took monogamy seriously in practice no matter how much they paid lip service to the institution for the sake of the church. If the church had not been so keen on monogamy, the Reformation might never have occurred in England.

Here we must turn back to our distinction between plural marriage and plural mating. No one would question that since the establishment (in the literal sense) of Christianity, monogamy has been the only legal form of marriage. A brief exception occurred in Germany after the Thirty Years' War when the state/church did legalize polygyny in an effort to repopulate the devastated nation. (Similarly in Russia, immediately after the Revolution of 1917, the concept of illegitimacy was abandoned and plural mating not discouraged for the same reason.) The question is, was plural mating always "odious," and did it continue to be so? The answer of course is no, but this was clearly not an acceptable answer to "respectable" Christian monogamists and guardians of "social order" in 1878, themselves heirs to a particularly puritanical version of a puritanical religion.

The facts, however, are that various forms of plural mating always existed and continue to exist to this day. Various utopian sects of the seventeenth century, as brilliantly described by Christopher Hill, proposed polygynous versions of heavenly harmony on earth. This kind of thinking was submerged in the rationalist eighteenth century, but reemerged in the nineteenth with even greater strength. In the Middle Ages, the ideal of courtly love (the knight with his married "Lady") was platonic, but many historians doubt that the ideal was uniformly realized, which produces an interesting version of mediaeval polyandry, a form debased but continued by the cicisbeos and gigolos of later ages. The institutionalization of concubinage; the keeping of mistresses; the taking of secondary common-law wives; the droit de seigneur; the routine exploitation of servant girls, and, in Russia, e.g., of the daughter-in-law in the extended family—all testify to the strength of plural mating.[10] (I am not here including the persistence of prostitution. This is simply plural sex, which is commonplace even in wholly polygynous societies.)

The most notorious examples of plural mating are of course among

European royalty and nobility. This was the rule rather than the exception. (And we should note that this is always the case in polygynous societies: the rich and powerful are most likely to have the most mates.) Even in the heart of Victorian respectability—the court of Queen Victoria herself—plural mating flourished. Edward VII as Prince of Wales openly kept mistresses (Lilly Langtry the most notorious) who were accepted at court and befriended by his wife. This was not an isolated instance but part of a long tradition. The Hanoverian kings had "official" mistresses, except the supposedly "despotic" George III, who was impeccably monogamous! The keeping of mistresses, their ennoblement and enrichment, was a firmly established tradition. In France and England—and indeed most of Europe—this was, in the seventeenth, eighteenth, and nineteenth centuries, a firm and honorable tradition, and continues to this day in some circles.

It is important to note that this was true plural mating according to my definition. There was one legal wife; but there were many, often "official," mistresses who were themselves given titles, had court positions, and had their children fully accepted into the nobility (viz., the Bourbons in France, Charles II in England). These children had the right to heraldic devices quartered with the royal insignia and the "bend sinister" to indicate their origins. In England, the offspring of royalty and nobility not ennobled could still bear the mark of their origins with the prefix "Fitz-" (derived from the Norman French "fiz de"—son of). It is one of the charming ironies of history that the fundamentalist Christian, prudish, and upright captain of the *Beagle*, who was so shocked by Darwin's opinions, was surnamed "Fitzroy"— a name that showed his illegitimate descent from Charles II but that he bore with great pride since it indicated his royal blood.[11]

It cannot be overemphasized that these extensive forms of plural mating were not clandestine, that they conformed to strictly regulated social and sometimes legal usages, and that they persisted over many centuries without effective opposition from the church (in fact, *with* its tacit support) or, as far as we can see, any dereliction of social duty or subversion of social order. The church went through alternating periods of sexual repression and relative indifference. Even within the church, polygynous and promiscuous "heresies" had their day, and numerous theologians and commentators, as Cairncross (see note 10) shows in such detail, defended the concept of "christian polygamy."[12] Several popes and many cardinals, in fact, kept mistresses.

This is not to say that everyone involved in plural matings was happy, as the works of Colette attest. But that is not the issue. How many people in monogamous unions are entirely happy with *them*? Not more than half, to judge by divorce statistics. The question is not whether these extensive systems of plural mating were satisfactory to those concerned, but whether they were "odious" to society at large, and they clearly were not. When the court insisted (in *Reynolds*) that "polygamy was always odious," it was referring to legal marriage and hence to what was "odious" to the law. It cited the bigamy statute as evidence, which only showed that polygamy was illegal—which is not in question—not, as was implied, that plural mating was generally repugnant. Of course, plural mating was not so readily available to the poor. But the poor had their own means of plural mating that were curiously prophetic: they simply stayed outside legal marriage and hence were free to rotate mates, or to practice plural cohabitation, which was not bigamy since it was never legal or solemnized. This was rife in English cities in the nineteenth century, as the official Blue Books, on which both Engels and Disraeli drew so copiously, bore eloquent witness.[13]

It would be easy to go on multiplying examples, but the point is to establish the principle. Christian monogamy was a misogynistic intrusion, invented by fanatic religious celibates, into societies accustomed to plural mating. These societies only half-heartedly accommodated to the intrusion. The fear of the fires of hell, or the real fires of the Inquisition, no doubt kept large numbers of the populace in line. But those at either the top or the bottom of the social scale who could avoid monogamy did and practiced plural mating of one kind or another. It was the Calvinistic bourgeoisie, heirs of the Jansenist, antisex tradition, which stuck closest to the "ideal" and which dominated moral thinking in the late nineteenth century. It was this audience which found even the suggestion, much less the practice, of any form of plural mating "odious," and through the medium of its judges projected its prejudices onto history. In this "tradition," plural sex, as long as it was furtive, was tolerated; but what could never be tolerated was the institutionalization—the obvious and honest profession of sex with more than one woman at the same time. With the brilliantly inventive hypocrisy that has always characterized this class, however, it went on to invent its own form of plural mating via easy divorce and serial monogamy.

Reynolds and Ethnography:
The Polygynous Persuasion

We must now return to the more strictly anthropological questions raised by the *Reynolds* and *Cleveland* judgements. In *Reynolds*, as we have seen, having first established the (fictitious) long-standing "odiousness" of plural marriage to those pure "Northern Nations," the court had to bolster its case by "proving" that polygyny *eo ipso* was socially deleterious. It was not enough, even for these casual racists, to dismiss it as a characteristic of "African and Asiatic people." They had to show that it was undesirable even then.

To do this they embarked on a dangerous excursion into ethnography. First, they established a sociological principle:

> Marriage, while from its very nature a sacred obligation, is, nevertheless, in most civilized nations, a civil contract, and usually regulated by law. Upon it society may be said to be built, and out of its fruits spring social relations and social obligations and duties, with which government is necessarily required to deal.

Apart from a perhaps tendentious quibble with what counts as a "civilized nation," there is not much to quarrel with here. That every society is of necessity "built" out of marriage might seem a little extreme. But certainly no anthropologist would quarrel with the assertion that the regulation of reproductive life is central to social systems.

The argument proceeds, however, rather alarmingly, from this point:

> In fact, accordingly as monogamous or polygamous marriages are allowed, do we find the principles on which the Government of the People to a greater or less extent, rests.

That they unqualifiedly regard the "extent" as "greater" tells in what follows:

> Polygamy leads to the patriarchal principle, and which, when applied to large communities, fetters the people in stationary despotism while that principle cannot long exist in connection with monogamy.

It cannot be too strongly stressed that this dubious proposal was the heart of the court's case against polygyny. As we have seen, it was not enough to attribute polygyny to the racially inferior; it had to be shown that polygyny is in and of itself a cause of the "subversion of social order," etc.

In fact, it was not shown to be this at all! Polygyny was "shown," on no authority whatsoever, to be the basis of "the partiarchal principle" and "stationary despotism"—both of which are incompatible with monogamy!

Even without anthropological evidence we can ask immediately "why is the partiarchal principle incompatible with social order?" Indeed, there must be many feminist historians who would be quick to point out that the Supreme Court of 1878 didn't need any lessons from polygamists on "the patriarchal principle."[14] And where is the evidence that "stationary despotism" is incompatible with "civilization" or "monogamy"? Hitlerian Germany was almost prudishly monogamous, as was Franco Spain and the U.S.S.R. In short, there is not a scrap of evidence that there is any direct connection between the number of legal mates a society allows and any form of civil constitution. And are we to infer that all the "African and Asiatic people" are in a state of "stationary despotism"? Quoting Chancellor Kent's approbation in the *Reynolds* case of Professor Lieber's unfounded assertion adds nothing to the argument.

No specific reference is given, but the professor in question is Francis Lieber (1800-1872), a prolific writer on ethics, law, and political science; editor of the *Encyclopedia Americana* from 1828 to 1832; and a professor at Columbia University from 1858 until his death. His major works, including *A Manual of Political Ethics* (1838) and *Legal and Political Hermeneutics* (1837), were written before this date and are almost eighteenth century in character. Stray references to polygamy appear throughout his works, and, as a self-confident Christian monogamist who believed he was living in the most ethically advanced society in the world, they were obviously unfavorable. He was an ardent antisecessionist and regarded the Mormon state, with its polygamy, as a threat to the "moral basis of government."

The court was probably here alluding to his most outspoken statement: "The Mormons: Shall Utah be admitted to the Union?" published in *Putnam's Magazine* in 1855. Lieber adhered to all of the standard prejudices of his time, and, of course, was as limited in his knowledge of polygamy as everyone else. Indeed, he scarcely bothered to quote even what little was known, taking his assertions to be "self-evident." He did express unease over the numerous examples of polygynous and promiscuous cults in the twelfth, thirteenth, and fourteenth centuries (citing Chateaubriand), but comforted himself by dismissing these eras as lower rungs of the ethical ladder, the highest being of course the United States (Northeast) of the 1830s. There is no point belaboring the issue that such opinion is hopelessly out of date and almost totally uninformed by real facts—ignoring as it does 90 percent of the globe—were it not that Lieber's 1839 to 1855 opinions are still allowed to stand as the basis of law in 1985.

To be too harsh on what appears to be simply silly is to be unhistorical. Lieber's opinions were, as I have said, part and parcel of the evolutionist thinking of the time and were undoubtedly taken more or less for granted by the justices—as surely as we would take their opposites today. But the fact remains that current law is still based on them. That despots and despotisms can be legally (and even in practice) monogamous is now obvious. If so, this crucial link (that polygyny *causes* despotism) in the *Reynolds* arguments has to go.

It becomes more urgent when one looks at the *Cleveland v. U.S.A.* case, which was decided in 1946, when there was less excuse for misjudgement. After quoting with approbation the statement in *Reynolds* on "odiousness," the court goes on to quote *Mormon Church vs. U.S.A.* (136 U.S. 1, 49 [1890])

> The organization of a community for the spread and practice of polygamy is, in a measure, a return to barbarism. It is contrary to the spirit of Christianity and of the civilization which Christianity has produced in the Western World.
> ...
>
> The establishment or maintenance of polygamous households is a notorious example of promiscuity.

And so on in the same vein.

Is what was admittedly prejudiced and erroneous in 1878 still admissible and forgivable in 1946 and still the basis of law today? Are we to conclude, as the obvious logic of *Cleveland* leads us to assume, that the Supreme Court of the United States of America regards the African and Asiatic peoples to be, because of their practice of polygamy, sunk in barbarism and promiscuity and condemned to stationary despotism? This opinion would have to embrace, of course, many Native American peoples who allowed (and allow) polygynous marriages. It would be interesting to hear the court today reaffirm this position!

What are the facts on polygyny as a social practice, and its results and concomitants? They are as varied as the facts associated with monogamy. There is this difference: polygyny is allowed or enjoined in the overwhelming majority of societies, and plural mating of some form or other is virtually universal.

As a starting point we can do no better than quote Mr. Justice Murphy's dissenting opinion in *Cleveland*. Mr. Murphy, unlike his colleagues, was not still living in the unthinking social evolutionary atmosphere of 1878. He disagreed most strongly with the belief that taking a woman across state boundaries to enter into a polygynous marriage could possibly be equated with "prostitution and debauchery." He was not, he insisted, "defending polygamy," but claimed that we must "understand what it is, as well as what it is not." What it is, is a form of socially sanctioned, institutionalized marriage. (He included "group marriage" among those forms, but most modern anthropologists would not concur, there being few if any authenticated instances. But there had been much anthropological discussion of the possibility, which shows that Mr. Murphy was well read in the subject.)[15] Polygyny, he insisted, is "one of the basic forms of marriage." "Historically," he said, "its use has far exceeded that of any other form. It was quite common among ancient civilizations and was referred to many times by the writers of the Old Testament." We must recognize, then, that polygyny, like other forms of marriage, is basically a cultural institution rooted deeply in the religious beliefs and social mores of those societies in which it appears. "Polygyny is a form of marriage built upon a set of social and moral principles. It must be recognized and treated as such."

One could go on with quotations from this remarkable opinion, but these will suffice to show that as of 1946 at least one U.S. Supreme Court Justice had conscientiously caught up with the facts and was not content simply to reiterate and reinforce the racist platitudes of the 1878 decision. The case is crumbling. Polygyny—whether one likes it or not—is not historically odious or foreign to Western European civilization; does not automatically lead to barbarous or despotic government, even if it has been associated with such governments in the past; is not in any sense equated with promiscuity; is a recognized, legitimate, institutionalized form of marriage where it occurs; and is in fact the form of marriage approved, encouraged, or enjoined by the overwhelming majority of societies known to history and ethnography.

Could it be that the brief historical episode of Christian monogamy with its curious antisex bias is the anomaly? The answer is the proverbial yes and no: no, because obviously there are other monogamous cultures (even if they are a decided minority); yes, because the peculiar theological basis of this imposed monogamy is unique. We tend to lose sight of this because the technological dominance of Christian monogamous cultures is so obvious— particularly their spread across the globe during the period of colonial expansion—that we take them as the norm. But this is purely a value judgement. China had achieved a level of civilization before the arrival of Marco Polo with which Europe was extremely slow to catch up—but it was not reflected in an extensively industrial technology. There is no rule that says it should be. And China was, until the advent of its own version of communist totalitarianism, extensively polygynous. Now it has achieved "despotism," it is of course legally monogamous!

The earlier anthropologists, even in the 1870s, knew that polygyny was practiced in more societies than was monogamy.[16] But they were also responsible for reinforcing the idea of the technological evolutionary ladder with industrial technology and Christian monogamy at the top. Once this notion is abandoned and cultures simply treated as alternative lifeways, then the automatic "dominance" of monogamy fails.

One of the first attempts at simple quantification was that of Hobhouse, Wheeler, and Ginsberg, published in 1915. Between 1878 and 1915 considerable new ethnographic evidence had come in from North America, Africa, and particularly Australia. The authors divided their sample of 443 societies into seven "grades," from "lower hunters" through "highest agriculture." They divided polygyny between "occasional" and "general," and found that this accounted for 378 cases. Their conclusion:

> It will be seen at once that the permission of polygamy is by far the most general rule, but (a) the extent of polygamy is much more variable, (b) there are scattered cases of monogamy in all grades except the higher pastoral, while (c) indissoluble monogamy is most exceptional but occurs in four grades (out of seven). (L. T. Hobhouse, G. C. Wheeler, and M. Ginsberg, *The Material Culture and Social Institutions of the Simpler Peoples* [London: Chapman and Hall, 1915], pp. 159-60)

Hobhouse, et al. could only "conjecture" about this distribution—associating poverty negatively with monogamy (i.e., poor people can't practice polygamy). But otherwise it was not positively associated with any grade.

Their problem, of course, was that they stopped at "higher agriculture." Monogamy is positively associated with "industrial technology," and the reasons tend to be either economic or religious. On the one hand, high industrial mobility favors small units, and the monogamous nuclear family is the smallest viable unit. (This applies also in impoverished areas with only foot transportation.) On the other hand, the advanced industrial technological societies, until the rise of China and Japan, were Christian and monogamous, and were monogamous (legally) because they were Christian.

It has been argued that the overwhelming preponderance of polygyny means that monogamy is either an artifact of ecological restraints or an ideological imposition.[17] In the latter case the imposition is usually a church and/or state combination of suppression of potential centers of rivalry, especially as they appear in large and powerful kinship groups.

Studies since that of Hobhouse, Wheeler, and Ginsberg have used more refined samples—including, for example, societies from the "advanced industrial" grade—and corrected for the overrepresentation of particular cultural areas. They tell the same story. Murdock in 1949 showed 17 percent monogamy and 83 percent preferred or prescribed polygyny (N=238). In his ethnographic sample of 1957, based on 565 societies, the percentages were 77.5 polygynous and 21.4 monogamous (1.6 polyandrous). Ford and Beach (1951), using 185 societies, found only 29 to be monogamous. In the largest sample used so far, that of Bourguignon and Greenbaum (1973), 854 examples were examined, and again 16 percent were found to be "exclusively monogamous" while 83 percent were occasionally or fully polygynous.[18] The conclusion is overwhelming: polygamy is legally practiced in 77 percent to 83 percent of human societies.

It should be emphasized that in all these cases we are measuring legal marriage; that is, we are looking at plural marriage, not necessarily plural mating. In many of the societies listed as preferring or prescribing monogamy, including our own, various forms of plural mating are common. Thus, in many of the "lower agriculturalists," where Hobhouse et al. found monogamy rather more common, anthropologists have noted what they used to call "easy and frequent divorce." This is of course to beg a lot of questions and again to wish our own values onto alien systems. I prefer the more neutral term "rotation of spouses" or "turnover of spouses."[19] In yet other cases, while the state/church laws may demand monogamy, this is simply not reflected in customary behavior where, for example, female-headed families subsist without constant males, and marriage is often a late event in the life cycle, after considerable "rotation" (e.g., Brazil, Caribbean, Mauritius). Our own system, which allows fairly easy divorce and remarriage, and in which 50 percent of marriages end in divorce, has been dubbed "serial monogamy" since, while multiple marriage is permitted, only one legal wife at a time is allowed. Despite this, however, it has to be considered a system of plural mating, and if one looks closely at many of the cases in the 16-24 percent "monogamous" category, one or other of the forms of plural mating are legally possible or customarily practiced. (A notable exception is the Irish, as represented by the Farmers of County Clare.[20] But this is of course the postconversion Irish, not the pagan Celts.)

The clear societal preponderance of polygyny is obvious then, and that of "plural mating" almost overwhelming. But we must remember that in *Reynolds* and in *Cleveland* it was argued that, whatever the quantitative situation, polygyny was less desirable on moral or political grounds. The latter we can immediately dismiss. The equation of "polygamy" with "barbarism" and "despotism" was no doubt conjured up by pictures of the Caliph's harem guarded by eunuchs and the like. But we have seen that, as the state or the church/state alliance grows more powerful and despotic, it is in fact much more likely to impose monogamy. The church prefers celibate clergy, and the state prefers meritocratically or politically recruited bureaucrats. Both church and state resist the formation of powerful kin groups. The British smashing of the Scottish clans, and the growingly arrogant Union government's destruction of Mormon polygamy are but two latter-day examples of a continuing process that finds the imposition of monogamy by totalitarian, despotic regimes a virtual commonplace today. (A not inconsiderable amount of anti-Mormon propaganda gleefully equated polygamy with the practice of slavery. That the Southern gentry both kept mistresses and had slave "bed wenches"— that is, indulged in plural mating of an often intensive kind— obviously helped to inspire this equation.)

As to the moral degeneracy of polygyny—its equation with prostitution, debauchery, promiscuity and immorality—this is, as Mr. Justice Murphy so eloquently pointed out, quite ridiculous. In cultures where plural marriage is practiced, it rarely bears even the remotest resemblance to these irregular practices. It is a thoroughly institutionalized and integrated form of marriage playing a central role in the economic and political life of the peoples concerned. It is often so integral a part of their social structure that nothing of their kinship, of their political and economic lives, of their systems of succession, inheritance and land tenure, or of their relation to their ancestors in religious worship, makes any sense without it.[21] It is as carefully regulated as monogamy in our own society, and in most cases far more stable and responsible in its care for children, old people, relatives, etc. People in most polygynous societies known to ethnographers would be as shocked by debauchery, prostitution, or promiscuity as the Supreme Court Justices! Adultery is usually severely punished, for example, and the whole marital process, including the rights of wives and children, carefully guarded by law and custom. To document this would involve citing many hundreds of careful ethnographies compiled since 1878, and would be an encyclopedic effort out of place here. (A few representative studies are mentioned in note 22 for ease of reference.)[22]

This is not to say at all that in every polygynous household peace and harmony reign! This would be far from the truth. All that is being asserted is that, as a legal institution, polygyny stands in exactly the same position in these societies as does monogamy in our own. Of course, not everyone in polygynous households is happy with the situation, any more than are at least 50 percent of the members of monogamous households, according to divorce statistics. But this is not the issue. A form of marriage has never been banned because some individuals may not be happy with it. Were it to be, the Supreme Court would have no alternative but to ban monogamy, which is clearly, on these terms, a failure. If anything, ethnographic evidence shows polygynous families to be more stable than monogamous families. A large variety of arrangements are made to ensure a minimum of quarreling and jealousy between cowives, and they may be summarized as:

1. Marriage of sisters (sororal polygyny). Sisters seem to cooperate better when under one roof than do unrelated wives.
2. Separate living quarters for unrelated wives, and equal sharing of goods,etc.
3. Strictly enforced equal rights among wives in relation to sex, economics, prestige, etc.
4. Strictly enforced hierarchical rights among wives, such that senior wives have greater prestige and privilege, thus compensating them for loss of attractiveness in which they cannot compete with the younger wives.

Many cases of successful polygyny could be cited, but well-known examples include sororal polygyny among the Crow Indians, separate living quarters among the Plateau Tonga (Africa), strict equality among the Tanala of Madagascar, and strict seniority among the Tonga of Polynesia.[23] The arrangements do not always work—these are, after all, fallible human beings—but that cannot be a basis, as we have seen, for banning a form of marriage.

As far as the bulky ethnographic evidence goes, then, there is absolutely no warrant for concluding that polygyny in and of itself is an undesirable form of marriage from the point of view of stability, satisfaction of the parties, responsibility to members, etc. In fact, the evidence would seem to be the other way round. Frequent divorce and remarriage, the separation of children from their parents, the multiplication of step relationships (responsible for many child abuse cases),[24] the total breakdown of paternal responsibility (80 percent of divorced fathers at some time default on child support)—all suggest that our own institution of serial monogamy is in serious trouble, not its polygynous counterpart. Most polygynous people of my acquaintance, in fact, regard us as immoral and deeply irresponsible. In 1861, that most famous of experts on the sexual practices of

"African and Asiatic peoples," Sir Richard Burton, concluded his interesting account of Salt Lake City by contrasting the sobriety, probity, and responsibility of its inhabitants with the debauchery, prostitution, and human degradation of the cities of England.[25]

If the court is to find against polygyny, it cannot be on the grounds that the institution per se is degrading, immoral, or anything else. It can be rendered so in practice, of course—but so can monogamy. This, therefore, cannot, and never should have been, the basis for an adverse judgement. While we can perhaps forgive past misjudgements on the grounds of ignorance, no court today has that excuse.

Objections to the Objection:
The Nature of Polygamy

It cannot be too strongly stressed that it is not incumbent on us to prove that polygyny is perfect (which it isn't) but to show that the court has not demonstrated its point that unsavory social circumstances (despotism, debauchery, etc.) are of necessity associated with polygyny and that these same circumstances "cannot long endure" under monogamy. This is simply not true, and that is that. But let us anticipate some criticisms in the event that the court eventually looks for other "facts" to reaffirm the antipolygamy decision.

It has been objected that under polygyny women are treated as chattels. Sometimes they are, but so they have been under most monogamous systems, as feminist historians are quick to point out. It is not then polygyny *eo ipso* that is responsible for the low status of women. In many polygynous societies, it could be argued, the position of women is and has been better than in many monogamous societies.

It is also objected that polygyny is practiced for the advantage of males and to the detriment of females. This is a hard point to prove since, again, monogamous systems are not noticeably weighted in favor of females either, and in many polygynous cases it is clear that women have a distinct advantage in some respects. It depends on the criteria one is using.

It is objected that polygyny is usually the privilege of the rich and powerful males in the societies where it is practiced. In many cases this is true, but it is also true of legitimized plural mating in nominally monogamous societies. Those with the means to do so will usually take more than their fair share of whatever is going, including reproductive capacity or paternal investment. And this latter is important, since women often wield considerable power and influence in both types of society, particularly over the reproductive fate of their offspring. To assume they are always merely the dumb chattels of their husbands is itself a male chauvinistic underestimation of female intelligence as ridiculous as Professor Lieber's (see note 14). The "polygyny of the powerful" is not the fault of polygyny itself; polygyny is the result rather than the cause in this instance. It should be observed that in many polygynous societies—and not only the small and relatively unstratified ones—a fairer distribution of wives is assured over a lifetime by reducing the age of marriage of females and raising that of males. This ensures that there is a constant supply of wives for any cohort of males, and that any male who lives long enough will be able to be a polygynist.

We have seen how the *Reynolds* judgement uses a version of the above objection in linking polygyny with "static despotism." We suggested that the justices had in mind a version of the "polygyny of the powerful" known chiefly through the large-scale harem polygyny of various "oriental and African" rulers: The Emperor of China, King Ismail of Morocco, The Kings of Ashanti and Zululand, the Nizam of Hyderabad, the Turkish Pasha, and so on.[26] But this excess of polygyny was just that—excessive; a runaway version; almost a parody of a polygynous system. These rulers were excessive in everything, and mate collecting was included. King Ismail had 800 concubines, but he also killed 30,000 people personally (and mostly gratuitously). To take these examples as representative of polygyny, as the court does, makes about as much sense as to take Henry VIII or Catherine the Great as representative of monogamy. They bear no relationship to the mass of polygynous systems, and, as we consistently argue, do not establish any causal relationship between type of marriage and type of polity. It is true, however, that democratic societies tend to favor legal monogamy since this is more compatible with "fair shares" and the ideal of legal equality. However, as we have seen, it may not be compatible with the equally democratic ideals of "freedom of the individual" or "freedom of religion."

It is also argued that in polygynous societies women have no choice in the matter of marriage. It is a moot point whether men can be said to have a choice either, given that polygyny may be a moral, legal, economic, status, or religious obligation. But the point surely is that this is also true in most monogamous societies known to history and ethnography. If people (not just women) have gained freedom of choice in marriage, it is not a result of monogamy, which has a poor track record in this regard, but as a result of advanced, industrial, democratic institutions. That these usually go along with monogamy does not imply a causal relationship since monogamy is quite compatible with advanced, industrial, totalitarian institutions as well.

In the same vein, it has been put to me that feminism could never arise in a polygynous society. But this again misses the point that feminism has not arisen in monogamous societies because they are monogamous but because they are advanced industrial democracies. In preindustrial monogamous societies, feminism did not do too well either. Civil liberties in general are a product of advanced industrial democracy, not monogamy per se. Insofar as modern societies that allow polygyny become industrial democracies, it will be interesting to see how civil liberties and women's rights fare (in the Moslem countries, for example). In several of these there has been a move to make the taking of a second wife conditional on the consent of the first. But it is worth noting that in many traditional systems this was already a rule that was observed. And anthropologists have reported that in many cases it was the wives themselves who urged their husband to take extra and younger wives to spread the burden of household labor.

A more subtle objection has been raised in this form: sociologists and social historians have established a functional relationship between the highly mobile monogamous nuclear family and the labor requirements of a modern industrial society. Could not the *Reynolds* court then be seen as in fact asserting the "protection" of this necessary relationship in preventing the spread of the "dysfunctional" polygynous alternative?[27]

There are several responses. For one, it should be firmly noted that Justice Waite (and the *Cleveland* majority after him) makes no such claims, nor does he seem aware of them. His rejection of polygyny is based solely on its moral odiousness and its causal relationship with despotism, etc. But, granting that the functional relationship does exist, could we not argue that the court was implicitly responding to this fact—that polygyny is "dysfunctional" in modern industrial society. Maybe. But we should note that Mormon society itself—a mixture of industry and agriculture—seemed to work very well with its limited polygyny, and that this is what was at issue in 1878. Also, as we have noted, the rich and powerful, in any kind of society, practice plural mating with impunity. If one can afford it, it doesn't seem dysfunctional at all. Further then, with the increase of female participation in the work force and the growth of commuter employment with modern transport, what has hitherto been a privilege of the very rich could become the practice of the merely well-heeled. The famous "two-income family" could easily become the "three-income family" and afford the housing and other appurtenances of a polygynous lifestyle. I know many New York lawyers with wives and families in New Jersey or Connecticut who have working mistresses with comfortable apartments in the city.

The breakdown of monogamy suggests that it is its own worst enemy, and that if it needs protection it is not from legalized polygyny. What is more, rather than treating this breakdown as a pathology, we might see it as a normal response to the change from an industrial to a postindustrial society; from a labor-intensive economy to a service-intensive economy; from a situation requiring the monogamous nuclear family to one that could well accommodate a variety of extended-family patterns, including the polygynous. But in any case we should ask ourselves: to what extent we must bow to "functional necessity" in the first place if in doing so we abridge constitutional or human rights? It was often and cogently argued that black slavery was a functional necessity to the Southern economy, or child labor to the British mills and mines. This did not prevent our societies from going to great and often terrible lengths to change these "functional necessities." I do not find the sociological argument particularly persuasive.

Judicial Reasoning:
Not-So-Compelling Interest

This might be the place, however, to look at how a version of the functional necessity argument has been used by the courts to dodge any reappraisal of the soundness of *Reynolds*, an evasion that will give us another chance to examine further the strange nature of judicial logic. In the Potter case, the district court stressed that the compelling interest doctrine did not require the court to look at "empirical or testimonial evidence as distinguished from matters of precedent, principle, concept, history, legislative determination, or public policy of which the court may take judicial notice." In further rejecting consideration of "supposedly comparable practices suffered by modern society, if not approved," Judge Christensen claimed the argument "misses the point of the compelling state interest in the prohibition of polygamy as opposed to monogamy which cannot be accommodated by mere regulation of the former." The appeals court agreed and made the telling comment that:

> Monogamy is inextricably woven into the fabric of our society. It is the bedrock upon which our culture is built. Cf. *Zablocki v. Redhail*, 434 U.S. 374, 384 (1978) (marriage is foundation of family and society; "a bilateral loyalty"). In light of these fundamental values, the State is justified, by a compelling interest, in upholding and enforcing its ban on plural marriage to protect the monogamous marriage relationship. (*Potter v. Murray City et al.*, 595 F.Supp. 1126 [D. Utah 1984])

I hope it is clear what I mean when I say that this is a kind of legal restatement of the "functional necessity" doctrine. But it is given an interesting twist by the assertion that since monogamy is the status quo, and since the status quo is what it is for good reason, then the state has a "compelling interest" in maintaining it. Given this argument, the court can ignore the factual basis of *Reynolds* as well as any other evidence that polygyny need not be subversive of good order, etc. In fact, it can ignore everything except the fact that monogamy is established by a "network of laws," and assert that the state has a compelling interest in maintaining these.

But note that, in the same way that in *Reynolds* it was never explained exactly how polygyny was in fact subversive of good order, in *Potter* it is never explained how polygyny is a danger to "the monogamous marriage relationship." It may well be so, but it is surely incumbent on the courts to explain what they could possibly mean. The assertion that "whatever is, is right" has never been taken seriously. As the plaintiff's petition to the Supreme Court stated:

> It used to be the public policy of some states to require separate facilities for blacks, to require poll tests and to require blacks to ride in the back of the bus. To

> discharge Mr. Potter because his conduct is not in accord with an unconstitutional
> public policy is itself unconstitutional.... An unconstitutional law cannot be valid
> public policy.

All the above-mentioned public practices, it was claimed at the time, were "inextricably woven into the fabric of our society." This did not stop the court from ripping that fabric apart in the name of constitutional rights.

The district court decision contained an even stranger apparent contradiction on the same issue. Judge Christensen argued firmly against two "compelling interest" claims by Murray City and the state of Utah. First, he refused to allow the city to claim a compelling interest "in having its police officers comply with the criminal law and their oaths of office." This was, he said,

> an oversimplification or begging of the question. To discharge an otherwise
> qualified and efficient officer because he forthrightly resisted an unconstitutional
> law, would itself be unconstitutional.... The controlling question is whether the
> law plaintiff violated as applied to him was constitutional.

So far so good, and one erroneous "compelling interest" claim on behalf of the status quo is sternly rejected on the grounds that the constitutionality of the status quo is in question.

Judge Christensen proceeded even more emphatically to what appears to be a total rejection of the status quo argument:

> Insufficient also in and of itself is the position of the State that there is a
> compelling state interest in prohibiting polygamy because of the many other
> adjustments that would have to be made in state laws to accommodate that
> practice. Such cases as *Brown v. Board of Education* 347 U.S. 483 (1954), and
> *Miranda v. Arizona* 384 U.S. 436 (1966), teach us that the bother of responding to
> constitutional mandates does not justify their disregard.

"The bother of responding to constitutional mandates does not justify their disregard"—this would seem, succinctly and eloquently, to put to rest the status quo argument once and for all. The compelling interest cannot be that the state would find it even intolerably difficult to comply. It found it so with desegregation, with busing, and with affirmative action, but it complied.

However, when Judge Christensen comes to spelling out the compelling state interest that he believes does exist, and that, as we have seen, requires no facts external to law in its establishment, what *is* it? After summarizing the problems attendant on exceptions for religious belief, and what exactly religious belief is, he concludes:

> There appear to the court to be no reasonable alternatives to the prohibition of the practice of polygamy to meet the compelling state interest found in the maintenance of the system of monogamy upon which its social order is now based. Any broad exception to that prohibition in cases of polygamy sincerely practiced as a "religious" belief would engulf the prohibition itself with ever extending and complicating exceptions based largely on subjective claims, irremediably eroding the police power of the state and its compelling interest.

First of all, the issue of "subjective claims" to religious belief (albeit one raised by the plaintiff's First Amendment stand) is a red herring since there is no reason why, if the state cannot find a real compelling interest against the practice of polygyny, it should not be practiced regardless of religious belief. But note the assertion of the compelling state interest here. It is found in "the maintenance of the system of monogamy upon which the social order is now based." But no evidence is given to show that the state of Utah has indeed a social order based on monogamy, or that if there were alternative marriage forms this social order would disintegrate. Rather, the following is stated:

> The State of Utah, beyond the declaration of policy and public interest implicit in the prohibition of polygamy under criminal sanction, has established a vast and convoluted network of other laws clearly establishing its compelling state interest in and commitment to a system of domestic relations based exclusively upon the practice of monogamy as opposed to plural marriage.

Thus, it is not so much a whole "social order" that is "based on" monogamy that is at issue but rather a "vast and convoluted network of other laws" none of which are cited! The appeals court, probably embarrassed by this lack, put in a footnote that cited nine. "Vast and convoluted network?"—none of the laws, as it happens, are so convoluted that a minor adjustment of wording ("wife or wives," for example) would not easily accommodate polygyny. But the facts, as the courts have agreed, are less important than the principle: that while the bother of responding to constitutional mandates does not constitute a compelling interest in disregarding them, if the state has established a (vast and) convoluted network of laws that would be extremely bothersome to change, said state has a compelling interest in disregarding constitutional mandates that would cause this bother.

An outsider to the subtleties of legal reasoning may, of course, be missing some vital bit of argument here. But to plain common sense, nothing could be more blatantly contradictory than the district court argument and the hasty attempt of the appeals court to shore it up (and implicitly the Supreme Court's refusal to consider the issue). Vague rhetoric about monogamy being "the bedrock upon which our culture is built" is no substitute for evidence that allowing the practice of polygyny would be harmful. And if the rhetoric is, coincidentally, true, then the "fabric of our society"—to say nothing of the bedrock of our culture—is in deep trouble. The courts themselves, as well as the legislators, in making for easy divorce, have helped to hasten the demise of the monogamous nuclear family, which seems to be as much in need of protection from the law as from the practice of polygyny. The law in promoting easy divorce and divided families, has dealt a far more severe blow to the "bedrock of our culture" than have proponents of polygyny, who are, after all, asserting the seriousness and sanctity of marriage and the family.

All the above legal gymnastics are interesting as attempts to dodge the issue of the soundness of *Reynolds*. The judicial fondness for *Reynolds* borders on the perverse. Judge Christensen, in the district court decision previously cited, notes that only Justice Douglas has ever dared to suggest it might be outdated:

> Action, which the Court deemed to be anti-social, could be punished even though it was grounded on deeply held and sincere religious convictions. What we do today, at least in this respect, opens the way to give organized religion a broader base than it has ever enjoyed: and promises that in time *Reynolds* will be overruled. (*Wisconsin v. Yoder* 406 U.S. 205[1972] at 247)

Both the district and appeals courts list at length the cases in which *Reynolds* has been cited with approval (including, of course, the notorious *Cleveland*, described previously), as though sheer repetition of an error somehow renders it respectable. Judge Christensen allows that *Reynolds* has some little problems:

> Disregarding its suggestion that polygamy should be barred as subversive to good order for the same reason that human sacrifice and Suteeism would, its oversimplification of a proper belief/action analysis of First Amendment problems ... and its seeming insensibility in passing moral judgement on the sincerity of religious belief. (Ibid.)

Disregarding all this (to say nothing of the objections advanced in the body of this chapter), *Reynolds* is still, he argues, "good law." Why? Because it states that "it is within the legitimate scope of the power of every civil government to determine whether polygamy or monogamy shall be the law of social life under its dominion."

So it is. And having established nine laws to this effect, would it be presumably within the court's power to maintain that it would be too bothersome to dismantle these, and that it has therefore a compelling interest in suppressing the free exercise of religion or the right to marry? Yes, insofar as this relieves their honors of the task of looking at any "facts" other than precedent, principle, concept, and so on.

Thus is *Reynolds* preserved like a dusty trophy in a Victorian museum, never to be critically examined since "facts" have ceased to be relevant to the determination of compelling interest, and judicial rhetoric and social convenience can easily substitute for truth. "At no time has *Reynolds* been overruled by the Supreme Court," the Federal Appeals Court proudly announces. And, one might conclude, given the state of judicial reasoning in the lower courts, there is little chance it ever will be.

Conclusions:
The Dangers of Honesty

We could take up more possible sociological and legal objections to polygyny, but it must be repeated that in order to counter the court's arguments in *Reynolds* it is not necessary to prove that plural marriage meets any kind of utopian standards, which would be impossible, but simply to show that polygyny cannot of necessity be held to cause unsavory political or social conditions and hence lead to the violation of social duties or the subversion of social order. Polygyny can certainly be abused and lead to abuses, but so can monogamy, and therefore the possible abuses of polygyny cannot be used as an argument to privilege monogamy when the latter is equally open to abuse and unsavory associations. All these arguments, in any case, have a somewhat academic air with regard to the current case, since no one is suggesting that we go over to wholesale polygyny, i.e., require it of everyone. It is only being argued that the court has not made a good case for preventing those who wish to practice polygyny from doing so. And this of course applies to men and women equally. No woman can be compelled into polygynous associations, and the court's decision makes no good case for restricting their freedom of choice in this matter. The doctrine of compelling interest requires that it make such a case if it is to interfere with the constitutionally guaranteed "right to marry."

I have not here gone into the vexatious question of whether or not polygyny is "more natural" to our species than monogamy, since it is not relevant to the particular issue of the decision in question. The problem tends to get confused because in "nature" there is no "marriage," and when we talk of polygyny or monogamy we are talking of legal institutions, not of human behavior. I have contended, however, that *plural mating*, being ubiquitous in our species, can be considered natural behavior.[28] But this will occur, as we have seen, regardless of the specific, legal rules of marriage. Like so many of the "great questions" of anthropology, therefore, this one is usually wrongly posed. It should be: is plural mating more natural to our species than single mating? These terms would then have to be carefully defined in order to make a determination. Is single mating mating for life, or does it include serial mating? Should not the latter really be included under plural mating, or is it a hybrid case? What about cases where there is a single major mate but some latitude in extracurricular sex? Is this to be construed as single or plural mating? This matters because, while neither monogamy nor polygamy is universal, adultery certainly is, and has to be accounted for.

It can all, it seems to me, be accounted for fairly simply if one drops deterministic, either/or notions of human predilection. No particular social institutions are "more natural" than any others. Such institutions arise from the interaction of natural tendencies, like mate competition and parental investment, with particular historical and ecological circumstances. Plural mating, as a basic tendency in males driven by sexually competitive urges, may or may not translate into polygynous or monogamous marriage as a social institution. It will depend on the circumstances. Anthropologists and demographers have labored long to pin down some exact correlations here, but there is still no real certainty. Early ideas that polygyny was associated with the intensity of female contribution to economic productivity, for example, don't seem to hold up. It appears just as likely that it is practiced for the production of larger numbers of male children in economies where women do not contribute heavily to production.[29] But these are empirical matters that will one day be settled. The important thing to note here is that we should not be led into the trap of claiming greater "naturalness" for one or other social institutions, but should see these as outcomes, not determinants.

These "naturalistic" arguments are dangerous if not handled properly. We already have a situation in our own culture where monogamy is imposed because it is held to be more "natural" to the "Northern and Western races." We do not want to move to the situation where monogamy can be imposed on the supposedly scientific grounds that it is more natural to the species. Even if it were (and there is good reason to doubt this), this would not constitute an argument in favor of imposing it. We have cited the ubiquity of polygyny here, not to establish its "naturalness" but to counter the various pseudohistorical and ethnographic arguments in the *Reynolds* and *Cleveland* cases—for example, the crucial equation of polygyny with despotism and promiscuity. Any legislation based on this supposed "naturalness" must always be dubious when it comes to institutions. Institutions such as monogamous marriage, as we have seen, are the outcome of particular historical circumstances, and obviously need considerable legal buttressing to be made to work.

This is the point. If they were "natural" they would work without any such buttressing. As Tiger and Fox observed in 1971, no legislation is needed to force teenagers to have sex and engage in courtship, or to make women have babies and suckle and nurture them, or to force young men into acts of competitive daring or married men into the commission of adultery.[30] On the contrary, much legislative effort is needed to control these "natural" proclivities. Natural proclivities, if we decide they are worthwhile, can be left to themselves. To enforce monogamy because it is "natural" involves us in a ridiculous contradiction.

What is natural, in fact, is sexual and parental behavior per se, and the pursuit of those proximately motivated ends that promote reproductive success: sex, parenthood, resource acquisition, security, etc.[31] These can take many institutional forms, depending on environmental circumstances. Legal institutions tend to grow up after the fact of successful adaptive strategies, and to confirm these. Thus, if polygyny works, then it becomes legalized; so with monogamy. But there is this difference: polygynous societies, by their very nature, allow the option of monogamy (and the majority of males at least, at any one time, will be living monogamously), but societies with legal monogamy deny the polygynous option. This has often meant—given the imbalance in the sex ratios, the higher male infant mortality, the shorter life span of males, the loss of males in wartime, etc.—that many women were left without husbands and had to be killed at birth, remain single, become prostitutes, or be siphoned off into celibate religious orders. Polygynous systems have the decided advantage that they can promise, as did the Mormons, a home and family for every woman. In this sense, we could argue that polygyny as an institution is better able to take care of these basic needs than is monogamy.

But we do not need to push that argument to make the basic point: the only "natural" elements here—that could act as as basis for Jefferson's "natural rights" to be embedded in the Constitution—are the needs of individuals. They are the needs we have listed above for sex, security, resources, and reproductive success (i.e., utilizing the resources to bring the offspring to viability). The best legal, institutionalized form for satisfying these needs cannot be predetermined, and there may be many such possible forms in any one society, particularly if it is large and heterogeneous. The only sensible legal strategy, then, is to *leave the institutional options open*. We should constitute legal codes in such a way that flexibility and change are possible, while making sure that both retributive and distributive justice attend to the provision of the basic needs. Apart from anything else, this approach should give the lie to those who argue that biological theory leads to behavioral determinism. Quite the opposite is true here: it leads us to argue for deliberate indeterminacy at the institutional level, even though it accepts the deterministic inevitability of the pursuit of basic needs by individuals.

There is evidence that common law is moving, albeit clumsily, as is its wont, in this direction, and that legislation will no doubt follow in the wake of these crucial court decisions. (Freedom, as Tennyson put it in *In Memoriam*, slowly broadens down, from precedent to precedent.) The development of "no fault" divorce, for example, has changed the face of marriage and made serial polygyny, once the privilege of the rich, a virtual commonplace, and certainly an option open to anyone. Similarly, the notorious California decision in *Marvin v. Marvin* (18 Cal. 3d. 660, 1976) opens up staggering possibilities of "quasi marriage." But it is important to recognize what *Marvin* was and what it was not. The award to the female partner of actor Lee Marvin was not in fact a kind of alimony, despite the coinage of "palimony" by the press at the time. It was in effect simply an extension of contract law. What the court said was that it would not use the fact of cohabitation to debar the plaintiff from the benefits of the consequences of contract. Hence, all doctrines regarding fiduciary relationships would be applied. Previously, the fact of cohabitation would have prevented this. What *Marvin* did not do was extend all the consequences of marriage to the arrangement. Marriage and divorce laws did not apply.[32] But, by recognizing the right of long-standing mistresses to a fiduciary interest, even in the absence of any legal contract, the California court gave quasi-marital status to such unions. Since they are not legal marriages (even if they have some similar consequences), any person—man or woman—could, technically, be involved in several at the same time. This would be de facto and, in its consequences, de jure polygamy—using the word in its strict sense to include both polygyny and polyandry.

I mention polyandry deliberately since a case in Oregon involving a woman and two men living in a ménage à trois has raised just this issue. In *Bauder v. Bauder and Hart* (44 Or, App. 443, 1980), the Appellate Court actually turned down Mr. Hart's claim to an interest in Mr. Bauder's house, but this was on a technicality. The court accepted the lower court's determination that had Mr. Hart followed the correct procedure in staking claim to a share in the Bauder house, then his claim would have been valid:

> If it were shown that husband and wife promised unmarried person who lived with them a one third interest in their property if he deposited a specified sum in joint account and that he did so in reliance on that promise, but interest was not so conveyed, a constructive trust could arise in unmarried person's favor.

The "unmarried person" in this case (Mr. Hart) had fathered a child by Mrs. Bauder. But again, as with *Marvin*, neither this nor the cohabitation was allowed by the court to interfere with the fiduciary interest—the "constructive trust"—that Mr. Hart could have established in his favor. The appeals court ruled that he had not established such an interest and that he had received in "bed and board and the joys of parenthood" a fair return for what he had put into the relationship. But the principle that a woman could live with two men (or conversely that a man could live with two women) in a domestic, sexual, and coparental relationship, and that the parties could establish, with the support of the law, a joint fiduciary interest, gives pause for thought. It certainly suggests that, while the courts will obviously give a privileged position to legal monogamous marriage, they are willing to countenance other quasi-marital relationships, including plural unions. At least they will not use the fact of such a plural union to refuse the parties the normal privileges of the law of confidential arrangements.

Some recent Utah cases concerned with the issue of the rights of Mormon polygynysts to adopt children have shown an increasing tolerance of polygyny. All of these have involved modifications of the notorious *State ex rel. Black* decision (3 Utah 2nd 315, 1955). This followed the famous "Short Creek Raid" in which Arizona law enforcement officers in 1953 attacked a fundamentalist community straddling the Arizona-Utah state line and arrested all 350 inhabitants—men, women, and children. Mr. Black had his parental rights terminated by a juvenile court and sued to get them back. Quoting liberally from *Reynolds*, the Utah Supreme Court threw out his appeal, stating that there could be "no compromise with evil" (that is, polygyny). This decision established that the practice of polygyny alone was sufficient to deny parental rights. Recent courts have been less sure of this moralistic stand, probably under the pressure of increasing demands by other "minorities," such as homosexuals, with regard to adoption. In two recent cases the Utah Supreme Court has held that when it comes to the termination of parental rights, or their assumption (as with adoption), the practice of polygamy (polygyny) in and of itself cannot be sufficient grounds for denial. They arrive at this by the same route as we shall see the New Jersey courts using in the "Baby M" trials —the doctrine of "the best interests of the child." In determining custody, this should be the only standard, and hence lower courts had erred in not reviewing all the circumstances bearing on the child's best interest, and in singling out the polygyny of the parents as the only relevant issue (see *Sanderson v. Tryon*, 739 P. 2nd

623, Utah 1987: *In re. Adoption of W.A.T.*, 808 P. 2nd 1083, Utah 1991 - plurality opinion).[33]

If these cases are allowed to stand as precedents, then it is hard to see how the treatment of Mr. Potter can be upheld by the courts. His only crime was that he actually went through a form of marriage ceremony with his "pals" and declared them to be his "wives" openly before the world. In other words, he was being punished for being honest. Surely Mr. Jefferson would not have approved.

2

The Case of the Reluctant Genetrix

*A judge aims at preventing a party from insisting upon his full legal rights, when it
would be unjust to allow him to enforce them.*

— Lord Denning
The Disciplines of Law

The Stern-Whitehead Contract:
Thou Shalt Not Form Bonds

In March of 1986 a baby girl was born to Mary Beth Whitehead, a
housewife of Brick Township, New Jersey. It was her third child—she
already had a girl (Tuesday) and a boy (Ryan); she called it Sara
Elizabeth. Mr. Whitehead, however—at that point employed as a
garbage collector—was not Sara's father. The baby had been
conceived and born as a result of a contractual agreement between the
Whiteheads and William and Elizabeth Stern, a biochemist and
physician respectively, of Tenafly, New Jersey, whereby Mrs.
Whitehead was artificially inseminated by Mr. Stern's sperm. The
contract had been drawn up on 6 February 1985 by a lawyer, Noel
Keane, of The Infertility Center of New York, a private organization
concerned with bringing together infertile couples and potential
surrogate mothers. The Center's fee for this service was $7,500.

53

The motives of the parties seemed fairly clear at the time. Mrs. Stern, while not infertile, was unable to bear children for medical reasons—just what these were became important later. (It is also important to note at the outset that Mrs. Whitehead was not told that Mrs. Stern was not infertile; she *believed* her to be so.) Mr. Stern had lost all his family in the Holocaust and desperately wanted to have a child of his own blood as a psychological replacement for the lost kin. Mrs. Whitehead saw an advertisement for the clinic and, considering her family's marginal economic conditions and the relative ease and pleasure with which she had already twice given birth, felt capable of performing as a surrogate mother. She was to receive $10,000 for her services, and all expenses would be paid by the Sterns. The parties met, Bill and Betsy liked Mary Beth, and she felt well disposed to them. Richard Whitehead at first was dubious but eventually agreed. The contract—the "Surrogate Parenting Agreement"—was there and then signed and sealed.

Let us pause here to consider this all-important contract. It was not the first that Noel Keane had drawn up. Indeed, he was a pioneer (if that is the right word) in the surrogate mother business and had written extensively about his experiences (Keane and Breo 1981). Right up front, the contract states, in clause 2, that "the sole purpose of this Agreement is to enable William Stern and his infertile wife to have a child which is biologically related to William Stern." (Mrs. Stern was not infertile, but no matter.) In the next clause it puts the whole issue on the line. I quote in full:

> MARY BETH WHITEHEAD, Surrogate, represents that she is capable of conceiving children. MARY BETH WHITEHEAD understands and agrees that in the best interests of the child, she will not form or attempt to form a parent-child relationship with any child or children she may conceive, carry to term and give birth to, pursuant to the provisions of this Agreement, and shall freely surrender custody to WILLIAM STERN, Natural Father, immediately upon birth of the child; and terminate all parental rights to said child pursuant to this agreement.

So, before any of the details are given—even before any mention of the artificial insemination—the contract insists that the natural mother, who must "conceive, carry to term and give birth to" the child, should not "form a parent-child relationship" with it. Clearly this must refer to the postbirth situation since, we must immediately ask, how can the mother *not* form such a relationship with the child to whom she has been so intimately attached for nine months? And if, as there is much evidence to show, the most fundamental moment of this parent-fetus bonding process occurs at parturition itself, then short of bypassing the actual birth process, how can the mother voluntarily refuse to form such a bond? The contract, however, not only assumes she can but makes this the most fundamental of its conditions. It is as if the designer (Keane) knew in advance that the most difficult part of such an agreement was not the numerous medical details but the prohibition of a natural process: that it was *this* that was most likely to derail the proceedings and therefore had to be got out of the way first.

The next provision extracts Richard Whitehead's agreement to the same conditions and to the artificial insemination; and to "rebut the presumption of paternity of any offspring conceived and born pursuant to aforementioned agreement." This is because the law, in the absence of proof to the contrary, assumes any children born to a wife to be the natural children of her husband. (This goes back to Roman law. "Pater est quem nuptiae demonstrant": the legal father of a child is he who can show marriage to the mother.) The third provision of this clause enjoins on Mrs. Whitehead the obligation to cooperate in medical examinations, to carry the baby to term, to surrender all parental rights, etc.

The next clause concerns the payment of fees and expenses, and an agreement to test paternity. If Stern is found not to be the father, then the deal is, understandably, off, and the Whiteheads must reimburse the Sterns for all expenses incurred.

Clause 5 asks the Whiteheads to "understand and assume all risks, including the risk of death, which are incidental to conception, pregnancy and childbirth, including, but not limited to, postpartum complications."

Clause 6 demands "psychiatric evaluations" of the Whiteheads, and permits a release of these to the Infertility Center or the Sterns. The evaluation was indeed made, and the psychiatrist, Joan Einwohner, concluded thus:

> It is the examiner's impression that Ms. Whitehead is sincere in her plan to become a surrogate mother and that she has thought extensively about the plan. However, I do have some concern about her tendency to deny feelings and think it would be important to explore with her in somewhat more depth whether she will be able to relinquish the child in the end.

The explorations in more depth never took place, and this evaluation was never communicated to the Sterns by the Center.

The issue of miscarriage was then addressed. If the miscarriage occurred before the fifth month, there would be no compensation for the mother; if after the fifth month, she would receive $1,000 for her "services." Physical examinations and the possibility of no pregnancy were then dealt with. Then, in Clause 13 came the matter of abortion:

> MARY BETH WHITEHEAD, Surrogate, agrees that she will not abort the child once conceived except, if in the professional medical opinion of the inseminating physician, such action is necessary for the physical health of MARY BETH WHITEHEAD or the child has been determined by said physician to be physiologically abnormal. MARY BETH WHITEHEAD further agrees, upon the request off said physician to undergo amniocentesis or similar tests to detect genetic and congenital defects. In the event that said test reveals that the fetus is genetically or congenitally abnormal, MARY BETH WHITEHEAD, Surrogate, agrees to abort the fetus upon demand of WILLIAM STERN, Natural Father, in which case the fee paid to the Surrogate will be in accordance with paragraph 10. If MARY BETH WHITEHEAD refuses to abort the fetus upon demand of WILLIAM STERN, his obligations as stated in this agreement shall cease forthwith, except as to obligations of paternity imposed by statute.

Thus, it is clear that the "contract" was not for a child as such but for a genetically and physiologically perfect child. Anything less could lead to a demand for abortion, and if this was refused, then the surrogate was stuck with the defective infant, no fee, and no expenses. The "natural father" would be in the clear. Granted, the next clause does admit that some such defects cannot be detected in advance, and if these occur then Stern "assumes the legal responsibility" for any such child. However, this wording is remarkably vague compared with the harsh specificity of the conditions imposed on the mother. Does "legal responsibility" extend to permanent custody or refer only to acknowledgement of paternity and child support?

In Clause 15, "the Surrogate" agrees not to "smoke cigarettes, drink alcoholic beverages, use illegal drugs or take nonprescription medications," etc. And, in the final clause, Richard Whitehead agrees to execute a "refusal of consent" form. In this, Richard expressly refuses his consent to the artificial insemination while agreeing to all the other clauses. This might seem to clash with clause 3, provision 2, but is necessary in this case so that Richard cannot be "declared or considered to be the legal father of the child conceived thereby." This stems from the "presumption of paternity" doctrine already mentioned, and from Keane's experiences with the Michigan courts which we shall consider later.

I have spelled out the conditions of the contract for several reasons. They become, naturally, central to discussions of the contractual issue in this case. Without knowing precisely what was in the contract it would be hard to have any such discussion. But, for the wider issues to be addressed later, it is also important to know just what was demanded of the "the Surrogate" in this instance. It is amazing how much passionate discussion was later undertaken by parties who had never read the contract and had no idea what the specific provisions were. Also, as we have already seen by simply spelling it out, the contract was a document loaded in favor of the "natural father" from the start—as one might expect since he was paying the fees. With a stroke of the pen, and the payment of a hefty sum of money, he appeared to gain control of "the surrogate" to the extent of being able to enforce insemination, amniocentesis, regulation of habits, prevention of the formation of parent-child bonds, and even, at his behest, abortion if the child was not perfect. Very few of those who insisted that "a contract was a contract" and that Whitehead was bound to submit to its clauses, knew what the exact contents of the contract were.

Finally, it is interesting to see, in a society governed by the premise of contracts entered into knowingly by individual contractors, exactly what some people think is reasonable to write into a commercial transaction. I do not have any in front of me, but I imagine that artificial insemination contracts regarding horses or cattle must be written up in some such fashion, although horses might not be required to abstain from smoking. But this was a contract, for a monetary consideration, concerning the conception, gestation, birth, and custody of a human being, in which a natural mother was asked to agree not to develop any maternal feelings and to turn over her child unconditionally to the sperm donor who had paid for this privilege.

But when Sara was born on 27 March, the arrangement fell apart. Mrs. Whitehead did not want to surrender the baby. She describes in *A Mother's Story* (1989) how she was flooded with feelings of guilt over surrendering Sara, as well as guilt over disappointing the Sterns. But it came to her with overpowering strength that she was selling her baby "like a slave." She couldn't do it. The bond was simply too strong. She was allowed to take the baby home, but the Stern's insisted on their rights and eventually, with grief and desperation, Mrs. Whitehead gave up the child. The Sterns immediately named it Melissa and started the adoption process. Mrs. Whitehead refused to go through with the adoption and would not accept the $10,000. She was in such a distraught state that the Sterns agreed to let her have the child "for a few days" (30 March). When she again refused to relinquish the baby, the Sterns, armed with a lawyer (Gary Skoloff), adoption papers, and the agreement, successfully applied for a court order to claim Sara/Melissa.

Their claim was heard by Superior Court Judge Harvey Sorkow on 5 May. By this time, Mrs. Whitehead had been breast-feeding Sara for forty days. She was not represented at the hearings and the judge never interviewed her. He depended solely on the testimony of the Sterns' lawyer. The judge apparently had no qualms about the legitimacy of the contract and issued an ex parte order giving the Sterns sole custody. The grounds were that Mary Beth Whitehead had shown "mental instability" in her refusal to honor the contract, and that she might "flee" with the baby. That she had, of course, the constitutional right to travel anywhere in the United States, was not considered. She was in effect put under house arrest.

A bizarre scenario followed, almost Kafkaesque in its details, many of which cannot be given here since it is not the drama that concerns us but the legal issues. In summary, on 5 May, immediately after obtaining the order, the Sterns alerted the local police in Brick Township and descended on the Whitehead home with their court order. They produced the order which demanded the surrender of one "Melissa Elizabeth Stern." They were momentarily stalled when the Whiteheads claimed no such baby existed and showed a legal birth certificate for "Sara Elizabeth Whitehead." While the local cops puzzled over this discrepancy, Sara was passed through a back window to Rick (Mr. Whitehead), who indeed "fled" with her to Florida to Mary Beth's parents, Mr. and Mrs. Messer. Mrs. Whitehead, once the disappearing trick was discovered, was handcuffed and arrested by the police, who later released her since they could not find any actual basis for arrest. Once released, she too fled to Florida to join her husband and the baby, and she resumed breast-feeding.

They stayed successfully in hiding, making fifteen moves over a period of almost three months, during which time Mrs. Whitehead repeatedly called Bill Stern to try to persuade him to stop the hunt and let her keep the baby, promising joint custody if he agreed. He refused to agree, taped the conversations on the advice of his lawyer (including Mary Beth's threats of suicide), and hired private detectives to find the Whiteheads. Judge Sorkow had frozen the Whiteheads' bank account, the bank was about to foreclose on their mortgage, and they were out of funds. A judge in Florida issued an order, based on Sorkow's ex parte order, for repossession of the child. Later, when faced with all the facts, he rescinded the order, but by then it was too late.

The Sterns waited until Mrs. Whitehead was in the hospital being treated for an infection, then sent in armed private detectives and local police to the grandparental home. The grandmother (Mrs. Messer) was manhandled and thrown to the ground. Ten-year-old Tuesday screamed and tried to beat them off with a hairbrush. The baby was pulled from her crib, taken back to the police station, and handed over to the Sterns, who took her back to New Jersey. The baby had been breast-feeding for 123 days at this point, and the judge ordered her weaned by the police. The Whiteheads returned to New Jersey, but were not allowed to see her for more than five weeks, when the judge allowed twice-weekly visits of one hour in a supervised facility with armed guards present. Mrs. Whitehead was specifically prohibited from breast-feeding her baby; her children were not allowed to see their sister. The Whiteheads by this time had a lawyer (on a *pro bono* basis—they had no money) and they sued for custody. Suits, countersuits, motions, appeals and petitions followed, until at last the trial date, before the same judge whose order had set in motion this bizarre train of events, was set for 5 January 1987 in the New Jersey Superior Court—Family Division, in Hackensack.

The Legal Issues:
When Is a Parent Not a Parent?

The story so far is weird enough, but the layman may be excused for wondering why the courts could not quickly and easily decide to whom the baby belonged. This is, however, the whole point. The baby was conceived and born under circumstances for which no exact legal precedent existed. Nor was there any state or federal legislation which entirely covered the case. It was not unequivocally a simple custody matter, nor was it just an issue of legal adoption, nor was it a blatant case of "baby selling." States have laws covering these cases, but the surrogate mother case was, to say the least, murky. No statute or precedent seemed to cover it clearly. Hence the intense general, legal, and media interest in the "Baby M" trial, as it had now become known.

Whose baby was she, this little child now reduced to a legal initial, "A Pseudonym for an Actual Person," as the court documents had it? Did she "belong" to the mother who bore her, and hence the mother's legal husband? Or did she "belong" to the genetic father who had a "contract" for her? Public opinion, according to the *Bergen Record* and *Newsweek,* who were among the many media running polls, was 70 percent in favor of the view that if "she signed a contract, she should hand over the baby." The minority (less than 20 percent) felt "a baby can't be taken from its natural mother, contract or no contract." The law had no immediate answer.

The response of the overwhelming public majority is interesting. The sanctity of contracts was elevated over the sanctity of motherhood. And indeed, the law by and large *does* encourage contracts and holds the keeping of them to be a "good thing." But the public was misled in thinking that if a "contract" or "agreement" is signed, then that is that: the conditions must be met. The real issue is that, while any contract may be drawn up, the courts may or may not decide to honor it in the event of its breach. They may very well decide that the contract was not legal in the first place, since there are some things that we may not bind contractually, no matter what the public may think. But even if they decide it is legal, the issue then becomes: what kind of restitution will they order to the injured party? In the case in question, Mary Beth Whitehead (and Richard) may well have been in breach of the contract, but the question remained would the courts order "specific performance" of the contract—that is, the handing over of the child to the injured parties (the Sterns)—or would they decide that a monetary penalty (damages) and reimbursement of costs to the injured party would suffice?

Traditionally, and contrary to public opinion, courts have been reluctant to order specific performance. And this reluctance has been particularly strong in what are called "personal service" contracts: typically, contracts of employment. They have been reluctant because to enforce such a contract is tantamount to enforcing "servitude." If someone breaks a contract of employment—by leaving a job before the specified time, for example—then a court will certainly award damages to the employer, but it will rarely insist that the term of service be completed since this would interfere with what is seen as a basic constitutional right to freedom of movement: employees are not serfs. Similarly with the contract of marriage: if one partner breaches this contract, then damages may be awarded to the other, but the court will never insist that the partner in breach of the contract be forced to continue in the marriage (Temple 1984). People who hold the "a deal is a deal" principle rarely seem to invoke this when it comes to their own divorces.

New Jersey follows this general rule of not enforcing specific performance of personal service contracts. Specific performance is a remedy which is granted "only when the usual legal remedy of damages is inadequate" (see *First National State Bank of New Jersey v. Commonwealth Federal Savings and Loan Assn.*, 610 F. 2d 164 171, 3rd Cir. 1979). In fact, the standard as applied in New Jersey is particularly exacting compared to other states: specific performance may be granted *only* if money damages "would not be a just and reasonable substitute for or representative of that subject matter in the hands of the party who is entitled to its benefit" (*Fleisher v. James Drug Stores Inc.*, 1 N. J. 138, 146, 62 A 2d. 383, 387, 1948). An influential study in the *Yale Law Journal* concluded that specific performance should be denied if the disappointed party will be "fully compensated if he receives the additional amount necessary to purchase the substitute plus the costs of making a second transaction" (Schwartz 1979).

New Jersey has further insisted that specific performance should not be granted when it is either contrary to the public interest or would require the court to act inequitably. In *Edelman v. Edelman* (124 N. J. Super. 198, 200, 305 A 2d 804, 806, 1973), the New Jersey Supreme Court ruled that specific performance should be denied if it violated basic principles of human dignity or would be "harsh and oppressive" to one of the parties. Thus, with contracts to bear children and renounce parental rights, courts should be unwilling to enforce compliance when the parties are unwilling to comply. Suppose, after signing a "surrogate parenting" contract, a woman decides she does not wish to be inseminated? Should the court force her to be inseminated against her will? Similarly, it is beyond imagining that a court would enforce either the abortion clauses of the contract, or refuse, in the light of *Roe v. Wade* (410 U. S. 113, 1973), to allow a "surrogate" to abort in the first trimester if she so chooses. We might ask at this early stage whether the same principle might not apply to the forcible removing of an infant shortly after birth from the arms of a desperate nursing mother who wishes to keep her baby despite an earlier promise to give it up.

But for the moment we are simply trying to establish that there is no simple "a deal is a deal" doctrine as far as the law is concerned, and that in this the law is a lot wiser than the public, whose thinking is little above the level of a lynch mob. But then, that is one reason we have the law in the first place: to protect us against our own worst instincts (or perhaps, more exactly, our own worst social and historical constructs).

Back to the details of specific performance. A lot turns on the "uniqueness" of the object of the transaction. If I have a contract with you to buy a specific Picasso, and you don't deliver, then the court may well order specific performance: you must render up *that* Picasso; any old Picasso of the same value will not do. On the other hand, if the contract is for a specific '77 Chevy, then the court would be reluctant to insist that you hand over a *specific* 1977 Chevy since, in the legal mind, a market exists where an adequate substitute can be bought. This being the case, the court would more likely order that you give me the price of same 1977 Chevy and any costs and expenses involved in obtaining another. And note here that the precedents are clear: "subjective harm" is not the issue. That you desperately wanted that specific Chevy (sentimental value perhaps) is not at issue. You can get an adequate substitute.

Of course, we can argue as to how far the doctrine of uniqueness and adequate substitutes applies to a child, but that must wait. For the moment it is enough to establish that performance of a contract is by no means automatic, and that the doctrines announced above might well be argued to suggest that a sperm-donor father has an available supply of surrogate mothers from which to choose, just like 1977 Chevies. The substitute will still produce his child. As the great expert on contract law Corbin (1960) states, the onus is on the party seeking specific performance to prove that "a substantial equivalent for all practical purposes" is not readily obtainable from others in exchange for a monetary payment.

It is remarkable how many people, presented with this argument during the Baby M trials, responded that it was "repugnant" to discuss a child in this manner—as the subject of a "monetary" agreement. These were often the same people who had seen nothing wrong with the contract in the first place and had insisted passionately that it be upheld! But I am only trying to establish that many considerations go into the decision of whether or not to enforce a contract, and that "specific performance" is one of them. Note that this assumes that the contract will indeed be found valid, which itself is open to many questions, as we shall see. But we should already be thinking, as good behavioral scientists, what kind of evidence might be relevant to a decision on specific performance.

Equally, we have to consider the issue of "informed consent." Just because a contract has been signed does not mean it is enforceable if, for example, one of the parties was under duress at the time of its signing, or if relevant information was withheld from any of the parties, or if there exists any reason that rendered one of the parties not in a position to give "informed consent" to the document. Thus, if you have a gun to my head when I sign, or if I am legally insane, for example, then even though my signature is on the contract the court will declare it void. In light of the necessity of informed consent, even if we regard the contract as valid in establishing parental rights for Mr. Stern, can we hold it as valid in *extinguishing* the parental rights of Mary Beth Whitehead? Can a woman in fact ever give "informed consent" to a promise to relinquish the child of her body? When it comes to giving up a child for adoption, for example, every state, with the exception of Wyoming, holds that *consent to adoption prior to birth is invalid unless ratified after birth*. It was this point that I was trying to make at the meeting of infertile couples, and for which I was soundly booed. But it is the law of forty-nine states, including New Jersey, where in 1986 an appeals court ruled that under the public policy of the state a mere private contract cannot renounce parental rights; rather, consent must be withdrawn prior to formal adoption. (See *A. L. v. P. A.*, 13 Fam. L. Rep. 1104 [BNA], N. J. App. Div., 11 November 1986.)

The question then is open: should a surrogate mother have fewer rights in this matter than the mother of a baby put up for adoption? There *is*, it might be argued, a genetic father with rights in the child. This is not disputed. In the case of adoption there is a genetic father also, but he is rarely ever consulted. The issue is, as we have said, whether or not an "agreement" is sufficient to extinguish the mother's parental rights. It would appear not; but this is what the court was to hold. So we must ask what evidence would be relevant to the issue of informed consent. And we must not lose sight of the overriding consideration of the "best interests of the child"—fondly known in legal circles as "BIC." BIC arises only, of course, if the issue of custody is reached—that is, if the courts decide that parental rights exist in both father and mother. This would require a "fitness" hearing in which the court would try to determine which of the parents was most fitted to have custody, probably allowing visitation rights by the other parent, much as in a divorce case. As we shall see, this decision was reached in the Baby M case but without any such fitness hearing—a point which became important in the appeal.

More to the point, perhaps, in countering the "a deal is a deal" mentality is the issue of what contracts can be legally written. All states and the federal government have statutes which specifically rule out certain things as subjects of contracts. Thus, prostitution, slavery, and baby selling are prohibited in all states. And, while a contract, for example, to provide sexual services or to sell a baby, may be written and signed, if a party defaults and is sued, the suit will get nowhere and the plaintiffs might even be open to criminal prosecution. The court would declare the contract "void as contrary to public policy" and not a contract at all. This applies also to areas where there are no statutes; for example, courts will not uphold gambling contracts.

In the various surrogate mother cases around the country that had cropped up before the Baby M case, the specific issue of a mother's refusing to give up her child had not arisen, so the Baby M issue was to be a decisive one. But, in anticipation of more such cases, and in response to other issues in surrogate mothering being brought to court, many states had given relevant judgements and advanced legal opinions through their attorneys general. Many have proposed legislation to meet the contingencies, one of the most popular being that surrogate mothering offends against state "baby selling" statutes.

Is this a fair analogy? Is surrogate mothering baby selling? Legal opinion has largely said "yes." The attorney general of Kentucky, for example, was of the opinion that surrogate mothering violated the baby selling laws of that state, and so he opposed the application of a surrogate mother and her husband to terminate their rights to the child and transfer them to the biological father (*In re Baby Girl,* 9 Fam. L. Rep [BNA] 2348, Jefferson City, Ky. Cir. Ct. 1983). A child born in wedlock was the legal child of the marriage, according to Kentucky law—a doctrine we have encountered earlier; what is more, termination of parental rights in Kentucky was only allowed, by statute, if a child was to be placed with an approved adoption agency. There was no such placement in this case.

Another Kentucky court however took a very different view (*Kentucky v. Surrogate Parenting Associates,* 10 Fam. L. Rep. [BNA] 1105, Franklin City Cir. Ct. 1983). It held that surrogate arrangements are very different from adoption arrangements. Kentucky did indeed have strong laws against selling children, but, asked the court, "how can a natural father be characterized as either adopting or buying his own baby?" He pays not for the child per se, but for the *services* of the surrogate in carrying and bearing the child. Since he cannot be buying his own child, the arrangement did not offend against the baby selling laws. Not so, said the attorney general, because the father's *wife* could be held to be adopting the child and hence paying for it. (The question of homosexual couples was, mercifully, not raised.) But, countered the court, single men could enter into these contracts, in which case there would be no adoption! The Kentucky Court of Appeals, reviewing this case, disagreed scornfully:

> Thus, contrary to the lower court's view, to hypothesize the existence of unmarried, potent males seeking to bear offspring through contractually arranged insemination of an unrelated, unknown surrogate seems more speculative and in the nature of fanciful conjecture than for us to recognize and accept the existence and involvement of an infertile wife. (*Kentucky ex rel. Armstrong v. Surrogate Parenting Associates, Inc.,* 11 Fam. L. Rep. [BNA] 1359 Ky., Ct. App., 1985)

So much for hypothetical unmarried males! What is more, interestingly, Kentucky courts considered the "infertile wife" a sine qua non of the surrogate agreement. Her adoption of the child is the whole point, they said. This then was an adoption procedure; money had changed hands; the action *did* contravene Kentucky laws.

I do not want to pursue the even more bizarre chain of events in the Michigan courts where, as the law now stands, a woman can only legally be a surrogate mother as long as her husband refuses her permission to be one! (See the summary in Katz 1986.) I only cite these mind-boggling outcomes to illustrate the total uncertainty about the legality of such contracts and the disarray in which the law has found itself. Are these indeed "baby selling" contracts? Are they covered by "adoption statutes?" Can a natural father be held to be buying his own child? And what rights does he have over that child if the mother refuses to relinquish it?

Thus, any such contract first has to get over the hurdle of whether or not it is in the first place "void as contrary to public policy," and if it makes it past that test, then the issue of "specific performance" is still moot. But there is yet another hurdle. Such a contract may not be offensive to any specific state ordinances and yet still be void if it infringes one or other of the parties' constitutional rights. We saw in the Mormon case that such constitutional rights were paramount. What relevant constitutional issues might the surrogate mother cases raise? This has been much discussed but boils down essentially to three issues: the constitutional guarantee against slavery (Thirteenth Amendment and Anti-Peonage Act); the "right to privacy" deduced from the Fifth Amendment and applied, for example, to a woman's right to abortion in the famous *Roe v. Wade* case; and the equally derivative "right to procreate" with its corollary "right to marry" that again we saw in the Mormon case and which had been defined in such landmarks as *Skinner v. Oklahoma* (316 U. S. 535, 541, 1942), which forbade the sterilization of criminals. The "privacy" issue had also been addressed by the Supreme Court in *Griswold v. Connecticut* (381 U. S. 479, 485, 1965) and in *Rochin v. California* (342 U. S. 165, 1952), where it was held that no contract should be allowed which "violated basic concepts of human dignity." We have already addressed this issue, for example, in questioning whether there could be specific performance of the abortion or insemination clauses of the Stern-Whitehead contract. Also, the "right to procreate" is ambiguous insofar as it does not specify whether this right extends automatically to custody rights over the results of its exercise. The Baby M case was to test just how far a right to procreate went. Balanced against this is the mother's "right to the companionship of her children." And we could go on.

The fact is that often these basic constitutional rights (or basic rights derived from the Constitution) seem to be obscure or in conflict. They only become definitive through court rulings in specific cases that illustrate their application. And these rulings can appear to conflict in turn. Much ingenious ink is spilled by eager students in law journal "notes" in attempts to reconcile, or find implicit doctrines to reconcile, the varying interpretations of the Constitution (see, e.g., *Harvard Law Review* 1986 at 1936). For our purposes it is enough to note that a contract and its enforcement have to face the constitutional hurdles mentioned. Some commentaries, for example, have insisted that the child is not being enslaved since it it is being given up to its father, and that therefore the thirteenth amendment is not infringed. But this overlooks the issue of whether the contract effectively "enslaves" the mother with its provisions for abortion on demand of the father and essentially forcible insemination, etc. The whole issue is muddied by the fact that family relationships have always been treated by all courts as special cases: thus, children are, according to some ultraliberal critics, effectively enslaved to their parents with the acquiescence of the courts, and marriage contracts are treated differently from ordinary commercial contracts.

One of the interesting aspects of the surrogate parenting issue is precisely this blurring of what have traditionally been separate areas: family relationships and contractual commercial relationships. The writers of surrogate parenting contracts seem to want to have it both ways: they want the contracts upheld as commercial documents, and at the same time they want constitutional protections for the privileged "parental" (i.e., noncommercial) status of the "father." We shall see in a later section how the law is generally being thrown into confusion by the so-called "new reproductive techniques" which make possible the sale of reproductive material and its transfer to alien wombs. It raises the prospect of the prophecies of Huxley's *Brave New World* coming to fruition (if that is the right metaphor), with children being born in "breeding bottles" and bypassing the womb entirely.

I wrote in 1967, in *Kinship and Marriage,* that kinship would be with us as long as motherhood was, and until, as in Huxley, bottles had replaced mothers. (The otherwise impeccable French translators rendered "bottles" as *biberons,* which means "feeding bottles," thus confusing a generation of Gallic readers.) Well, the time has now come when this and more is possible, which, in addition to the specifics of the human drama in New Jersey, was what I believe made the Baby M case so intensely interesting to the world. We were not just deciding the fate of one baby, but getting close to redefining the nature of the family and even the individual in a world of Lockean contractual relations gone mad.

The Scientific Position:
Ethology of the Mother-Child Bond

Now that we have looked at the contract and the legal and constitutional issues it raises, we must look at the scientific evidence that might bear on these. Since we are dealing with something so basic to an anthropological ethology as the mother-child bond—the basic bond by definition of all mammalian society—the nature of the approach is readily dictated to us. We must start at the beginning, literally, with the evolution of the bond and the physiology of it; that is, the evolutionary legacy. If we can establish some hard facts about the nature of this bond, then any legal definitions and decisions will have to take them into account. And where there is conflict over the facts, we have to take that honestly into account as well, since it is our duty to inform the law of such uncertainty lest it be misled by the confidence of "experts."

This is of course one of several possible approaches. Others might stress more the social psychology of interaction, or the Freudian interpretation of personality development, or the nature of our cultural constructions of such categories as "parent" or "mother" or "family," etc. But I am obviously making a case here not just for the interjection of the "facts" of behavioral science, but for a particular version of the facts rooted in the approach of evolutionary biology. I feel I can do this here in a way I could not, for example, in the case of Mormon polygamy. In that case we were dealing with a specific legal judgement that made certain claims, and our aim was to test those claims and not others. This limited us to historical and ethnographic data, and only peripherally could we deal with perhaps the more basic issue of whether polygamy is more natural and appropriate to us as a species than monogamy; an issue about which evolutionary biology has indeed a lot to say. In this case, however, the issue is open. We are not addressing (until after the trial) a specific judgement, but several general issues like specific performance, informed consent, the right to procreate, the best interest of the child, the rights of the natural birth mother, the effects of disrupting nursing relationships, etc. This gives us a much broader basis on which to work and allows us to introduce evidence of a kind precluded in the former case. In effect, we (and, in using the editorial "we," I am not so subtly inviting the reader to join in my version of the effort) are saying to the courts: here are certain facts about the relationships between family members that are relevant to all the issues raised in this case, and we ask you to take them into consideration before rendering a verdict.

As it happens, I was unable to bring these facts before the Superior Court Judge, since he put a stop on further amicus curiae briefs before one had been prepared. But, with the help of the Gruter Institute, Professor Elliott and I were able to get the brief to the New Jersey Supreme Court when it heard the appeal, and to make our points more specific with respect to the actual judgement. The following was the scientific basis for that brief.

One small point on terminology before we launch into the saga. Roman law, and anthropology in following it, made the useful distinction between the "genitor" as the physical father of the child and the "pater" as the social father, i.e., the husband of the child's mother. It follows that a distinction exists, in theory, between the "genetrix," who is the physical mother of the child, and the "mater," who is its social mother, i.e., the wife of its legal father. Usually, of course, the latter two categories would be assumed to coincide— except in cases of adoption, for example, where "genetrix" and "mater" would be different people. For the sake of neatness and economy then, I will sometimes use the Roman distinction to avoid ambiguities like "surrogate mother" or "natural father" or "real mother," etc., and to avoid equally such appellations as "uterine hostesses" or "rented wombs," charming as they may be in their way. We are therefore concerned with the Case of the Reluctant Genetrix, and so, without further ado, let us leap into the evolutionary story.

1. Evolutionary Background

As Earl W. Count (1973) points out, evolution of the "lactation complex" dominates mammalian phylogenetic development. This complex reaches its highest point of development in certain families of the Eutheria, which includes the females and young of our own species, *Homo sapiens sapiens*. The whole point of the "mammalian revolution," in evolutionary terms, was the suckling of live-born young by the females. This was made possible by the development of an existing system of sweat glands (the sebum-hair-sweat histomorphology) that extends down to the premammalian monotremes (echidna and duck-billed platypus). The conversion of part of this sweat gland system to a mammary gland system resulted in milk ducts distributed over the whole chest area. In the human female, however, these were concentrated into highly specialized breasts, making the female of *Homo sapiens*, in a sense, not less but more specialized as a mammal than her animal cousins.

Along with conversion of the sweat glands went the even more remarkable evolution of the mammal's whole facial area—jaws, lips, tongue, cheeks, etc.—into a "suctorial apparatus" (Count's term). The face became a sucking device. The most far-reaching aspect of this is also the least visible: the reptilian cranial nerve system was almost totally changed to subserve the sucking functions. As Count argues, the parallel evolution of the two systems (mammary and suctorial) and their fusion into one functional complex is a remarkable evolutionary phenomenon. Almost all the facial apparatus peculiar to mammals is devoted to sucking; further functions that are useful in adult life, like communication (the mimetic muscles and skin of the face—see Ekman et al. 1972) and kissing (the muscular lips) are secondary and derivative. The same may be said of the female breasts, whose adult function of sexual signalling is not only derivative but may well be linked directly in its effects to the primary oral function.

The result is a mother-offspring mutualism, or symbiosis, which reaches its most intensive development in the higher mammals and in particular in *Homo*. Because of the fetal nature of the human infant and the long period of postpartum development, the symbiosis is more marked, and the disruption of it is more destructive than in lower mammals (although our closest relatives, the chimpanzees, share much of this complex, and the long-range effects of maternal deprivation, as we shall see, are obvious in higher primates generally). To use Count's graphic words, the effects of the lactation complex "reverberate into adulthood." In some sense then, as has been observed, rather than becoming less mammalian than other mammals in the course of our distinctive evolution, we have become more so: we have exaggerated to their extreme these basic features of the mammalian mother-child symbiosis. A consequence of this is that the pregnant female of our species is physiologically, emotionally, and behaviorally prepared for a long period of child rearing. Had she not been so prepared in the course of evolution, we would not be here to discuss the matter. A basic element of that necessary preparation is the establishment of a foundation for bonding between the infant and the mother.

2. Physiology of Pregnancy and Bonding

Mother-child symbiosis begins at conception and continues at least until weaning and the independent motility of the child—probably beyond. Birth is simply an incident—albeit a crucially important one—in this continuous process. The early physiological relationship between mother and fetus is mediated by the placenta, which plays a much more important part than was once assigned to it. Until the fetus has developed its own system of hormone production, the placenta is responsible for generating necessary hormonal products. It does not do this by synthesizing hormones from start to finish (as does the thyroid, for example). Rather, chemical precursors ("part hormones") are transmitted to the infant via the maternal blood system, and in the placenta the precursors are transformed into steroid and polypeptide hormones which then exert effects on both mother and infant. At least thirty-eight hormones are affected. (See Tulchinsky and Ryan, *Maternal-Fetal Endocrinology*, 1980, for the most authoritative discussion.)

The most comprehensive physiological changes, then, involve placental synthesis of steroid and polypeptide hormones and their effects on pancreas, pituitary, thyroid, and adrenal function (a far from complete list). Many if not most physiological systems in the mother are affected. And one must note that there is a synchronous quality to this interaction between mother and developing fetus. The changes differ in quantity and quality from mother to mother, and hence the "experience" of each mother and child is unique to the pair. The profound psychological changes in the mother (to be discussed later) during and immediately after pregnancy, are in part mediated by these physiological changes and clearly affect her bonding with the fetus. The synchrony then can be viewed as a case of special characteristics of the placental hormones affecting the mother and fetus in similar ways, thus increasing the "physiological-emotional" bond between them. Every mother knows that she and the baby have been through this remarkable experience *together*; science can now tell us what the experience of "togetherness" is in some detail. The interruption of this ongoing "feedback" relation—by premature birth or cesarean section for example—can result in severe harm to the infant; the lungs, kidneys, and myelin sheaths being especially vulnerable. Equally, after birth, the baby, still close to a fetal state, can suffer long-lasting harm from a disruption of the ongoing process.

All mammalian females (including human mothers) go through a cycle of long-term hormonal changes during pregnancy—a cycle mediated by the hypothalamus. Early in pregnancy there is a gradual rise in the level of estradiol and progesterone, and a sharp drop in these just before delivery (related, perhaps, to the "postpartum depression" or "baby blues" syndrome). Following delivery there is a rise in the level of prolactin. Nursing causes prolactin and oxytocin to rise, thus suppressing estradiol and progesterone. This in turn causes the normal menstrual cycle to resume. These wide-ranging hormonal changes cause corresponding mood shifts in the mother from extreme feelings of well-being initially, to deep fears and uncertainties about pregnancy, to elation at birth, to possible postpartum depression (Blum 1980). The nipple stimulation effects of suckling include feelings of sexual pleasure in the mother as a result of oxytocin production. This feature has been avoided or ignored by scientists until recently, but it clearly can have a profound effect on mother-infant bonding. The effect is often masked by the rigid feeding schedules imposed on mothers, but is well recognized in those who feed on demand (Campbell and Peterson 1953; Newton 1973; Rossi 1977).

At the very least then, we can say that the symbiotic interaction of mother and fetus causes profound synchronous changes in both, and that the mother's whole psychophysical system undergoes a tremendous upheaval that not only results in the birth of the baby but prepares her for a continuing relationship with the still-fetal infant. The symbiosis, as we have insisted, does not begin at birth; it simply moves at birth into a different phase, where the mother's warmth, smell, texture, voice, and breast milk continue the work of the placenta, the umbilical cord, and the amniotic fluid. The unnatural circumstances created by modern medicine and hygiene may mask this, but they cannot eradicate it. There are 128 million years of mammalian history demanding to be recognized here.

None of this means that a woman other than the natural birth mother (genetrix) cannot raise the child. She can and often does. We shall discuss the implications of this later. (Before the advent of safe bottle feeding she would at least have to have been lactating.) We can say, however, that it is clear that the intended nurturer of the child is the natural mother, since she has undergone the necessary preparation and has the milk.

3. The Mother-Child Unit

At this point it must be stressed that while we continue to treat the triad of mother-father-infant as three separate persons, for many purposes is is more satisfactory to treat the mother-child dyad as a unity. In the small groups in which we evolved (thirty to forty people for 99 percent of our hominid existence), it is unlikely that a woman other than the genetrix would have been lactating and available at the right time. Mother and child were therefore locked together in an absolute dependency, there being no substitute for the mother's milk.

This goes deep into mammalian evolution. By definition the *basic* mammalian unit is the mother and suckling infant. In many mammals, a male (or males) is not attached to this unit, and it subsists independently. In species like our own, where the mothers and young need protection and provisioning, males are usually added, but in a highly variable manner. The constant is the mother-child unit, and the variable is the added male or males. Mammalian species and human societies run through the whole series of combinations from no males added through consanguineous males added, to mother's mate or mates added, to several mother-child units plus one male, etc. But the addition of males is contingent on ecological conditions; the mother-child unit is biologically fundamental. We must keep in mind that 128 million years of mammalian, 72 million years of primate, and 5 million years of hominid evolution are behind the mother-child symbiosis (Fox 1967 and 1973). The implications of this for examining the relative strengths of bonding between birth mother (genetrix) and infant, father (genitor) and infant, and adoptive mother/father and infant are obvious. Especially under circumstances where safe bottle feeding is impossible, the genetrix has a clear advantage for obvious reasons. Where bottle feeding can substitute, an adoptive mother can suffice, but we should consider whether she should be preferred to a genetrix, other things being equal. The genitor may or may not be involved in the bonding process. If he is not, his only claim is a purely genetic one, which, while not negligible to him, is irrelevant to the welfare of the genetrix and the child.

It would be well at this point to say a few words about the definition of "bonding." This is a loosely used term, and even the most authoritative ethology texts do not define it closely. (For excellent discussions of the bonding process see Lorenz 1970 and Eibl-Eibesfeldt 1970.) One reason for this is that it covers a wide variety of phenomena which defy precise definition. It is something more easily recognized than defined. As a rough approximation, I will offer the following:

> Bonding is the intense emotional attachment between two organisms resulting from the totality of their psycho-physical interactions.

One sees bonds forming between parents and children, between siblings, between males and females (courtship bonds, mating bonds, coparental bonds—see Tiger and Fox 1971, chap. 3), between males (Tiger 1969), between females, between friends, between teachers and pupils, leaders and followers, heroes and hero worshipers, people and pets, and so on. Of all these, however, the bond between mother and child is the most basic. While it certainly took an act of impregnation to bring this relationship about, this act was not necessarily itself the result of a bond, and in many mammals there is little or no bonding between genitor and genetrix. While other bonds are variable, the bond between mother and child is absolute, and as a consequence the quality of this bond affects all future bonds ("reverberates into adulthood"). Thus, the early classic "deprivation experiments" established that primates suffering from maternal deprivation were impaired in their adult abilities to perform sexually and maternally (Harlow 1959 and 1961; Harlow and Harlow 1965; Hansen 1966; Seay et al. 1964).

The profundity of a bond can be estimated by the pathological results for the partners attendant on its disruption. Here, unquestionably, the mother-child bond is paramount. It is worth noting that while the bond is reciprocal, most attention by scientists has been paid to the child's attachment to the mother. Indeed "attachment behavior" has become the standard technical term for the child's emotional imperative. Here, however, we must pay equal attention to the mother's "attachment" to the child, and to their mutuality. Hence, the less well-defined but more inclusive term "bonding" is appropriate.

4. Bonding with the Embryo and at Parturition

The emotional bonding of the mother and child starts before birth. This bonding will eventually become essential to the healthy emotional development of the child as much as the mother's milk (in preformula days) is essential to its physical development. The evolutionary function of the preparturition bonding is presumably to prevent the mother from rejecting the infant at birth. We know that in lower animals this "birth-bonding" is precarious, and that, for example, in many ungulates, if the mother does not smell and lick the infant immediately, she will later treat it as a stranger (Rheingold 1963). The function of the bond here is presumably to ensure that the mother raises her own offspring and is not promiscuous with her maternal investment in genes not her own. The human mother, on the other hand, "knows" her own child, and while, as we shall see, olfactory and other clues may well be important in bonding, they are not necessary to recognition. One of the most important cues in mother-infant bonding is that of voice. This goes along with the eventual learning of language by the human infant and the intensity of affect generated by verbal cues. It is not surprising therefore that students of neonate behavior have noted a marked preference for the mother's voice in the newborn (DeCasper and Fifer 1980). The best summary is by Jacques Mehler (Mehler and Fox 1985, 13-14):

> Infants are known to track, distinguish, and recognize the voice of the mother from that of another woman. Miles and Melhuish (1974) showed this by using a non-nutritive sucking procedure. In a similar experiment, Mehler et al. (1978) showed that infants respond differently to their mother's voice than to that of another infant's mother. All their previously mentioned experiments tested infants who

were over a month old. In a more recent experiment, DeCasper and Fifer (1980) showed that even twelve-hour old infants change their sucking rates to reinforce themselves with the voice of their biological mothers. This observation can be interpreted by invoking two possible mechanisms: Either very rapid bonding with the mother after birth, or effective transmission of the mother's voice in utero. For the later mechanism to operate, infants must have the capacity of perceiving their mother's voice in utero, at least during part of gestation. The physiological evidence shows that the receptors are ready to allow infants to perceive sounds during the last few months of gestation (Yakovlev and Lecours 1967). Querleau and Renard (1981) implanted pregnant mothers with hydrophones and recorded all auditory phenomena reaching the infant. The reported results confirm that the mother's voice can be heard fairly free of distortions under such conditions.

I have quoted Mehler at length since he gives such a carefully balanced consideration to the two possibilities: rapid imprinting of the mother's voice at birth and in utero transmission. Since the auditory apparatus is in place in the fetus, and since the mother's voice can be heard in utero for the last few months of pregnancy, parsimony demands that we accept, at least provisionally, the hypothesis of in utero transmission rather than invoking an unexplained imprinting mechanism of almost impossible rapidity (twelve hours). The author has heard the recordings referred to in the quotation and can vouchsafe their remarkable clarity. (Music also can be clearly heard. Beethoven's fifth came through with startling sonority.) Insofar as caretakers other than the mother are in constant contact with the fetus, it could be that their voices are learned in utero. This is not clear, but the mother has unquestioned priority in this respect because of her total contact, and it may well be that the voice echoing in the chest cavity has a priority in the sound environment of the fetus.

Many of the other aspects of the mother-embryo bonding are as open to commonsense observation and the common experience of mothers as to scientific observation. One of the better discussions is in Klaus and Kennel's *Parent-Infant Bonding* (1982), if only because they do not lose site of wide individual differences in response of mothers to the fetus and the possible causes of these. Significantly, mothers who had themselves been the objects of parental neglect or of disturbed parental behavior were least likely to be positive about the fetus (ibid., 11, citing Hall et al. 1980). While there is variation in women's perceptions of the "fetus as individual," at thirty-six weeks 92 percent of the women questioned felt the fetus to be a "real person." In addition to a strong emotional response to the quickening, there was also a growing set of anxieties about the health and normality of the child. Brazelton (1973), examining first-time mothers in psychoanalytic interviews, discovered anxiety that was "of almost pathological proportions." So loaded and distorted was the material, he comments, that "one felt an ominous direction for making a prediction" about the woman's potential as a mother. This was not, however, borne out by the mother's behavior after birth, which was unexceptionable. He concludes that one can view "the shakeup in pregnancy as readying the circuits for new attachments.... A kind of shock treatment for reorganization to her new role ... freeing her circuits for a kind of sensitivity to the infant and his individual requirements which might not have been easily or otherwise available from her earlier adjustment." Brazelton's view is especially authoritative since his research has been central to the issue of the "normal" development of the child. His view therefore of the anxiety traumas of pregnancy as a kind of necessary "priming mechanism" for the mother is essential to understanding the emotional depth of the bonding between mother and fetus. Far from being "abnormal," they are necessary.

It is with parturition that we turn to the better-known processes of mother-child bonding that have been intensively studied over the past three decades. Again, Klaus and Kennell (ibid., 71) have given the best summary of immediate bonding effects during the first hours and days of life, and these are illustrated in the diagram below.

**Mother-to-Infant and Infant-to-Mother Interactions that Can Occur
Simultaneously in the First Days of Life
(Adapted from Klauss and Kennel 1982)**

MOTHER TO INFANT	INFANT TO MOTHER	
1. Touch		
2. Eye to Eye	Eye to eye	1.
3. High-pitched voice	Cry	2.
4. Entrainment	Oxytocin	3.
5. Time giver	Prolactin	4.
6. T + B lymphocytes Macrophages	Odor	5.
7. Bacterial flora	Entrainment	6.
8. Odor		
9. Heat		

Studies leading to these findings were largely prompted by the question of whether or not mother and infant should be separated at birth for reasons of "hygiene." As a result of Klaus and Kennel's work, this practice is now largely discontinued and the baby given to the mother immediately. The pathologies for the infant have been well described, but as important are the depressive effects on the mother which can impair her maternal effectiveness severely (Brown and Harris 1978). A few comments are necessary on the specific items in the diagram that are not self-explanatory:

Mother to infant: 4. Entrainment. The work of Condon and Sander (1974) has revealed that newborns move in time with the structure of adult speech. From the moment of birth, the neonate is "in synch with" its mother's voice and bodily movements. Frame by frame analysis shows the extraordinary "choreographed" nature of this synchronization which increases with mutual interaction.

5. Time giver: Birth upsets the baby's bodily rhythms. The mother's constant and regular attention after birth re-establishes these rhythms which, it is important to note, have been established in the fetus by close association with the mother's own bodily rhythms.

6 and 7. T+B lymphocytes, macrophages, and bacterial flora: These represent the bacteriological and immunological "gifts" that the mother renders to the infant through milk and contact. As to odor, it is significant that at five days breast-feeding infants can distinguish the mother's breast pad from those of other mothers.

Baby to mother: 3. Oxytocin: Nipple stimulation from the baby releases oxytocin in the mother, which in turn hastens uterine contractions and reduces bleeding. (An as yet unpublished study by Dr. Thomas Insel of the National Institute of Mental Health finds that oxytocin directly promotes bonding between both male and female adult voles, and between mother voles and their young.)

4. Prolactin: Also stimulated by sucking, it initially serves to increase milk production but also seems to have bonding functions. When it is provoked in adoptive mothers for example, it seems to produce strong feelings of attachment to the otherwise strange infant. (Prolactin in birds has the same effect on parent-infant bonding.) Klaus and Kennell conclude that:

> Keeping the mother and baby together soon after birth is likely to initiate and enhance the operation of known sensory, hormonal, physiological, immunological and behavioral mechanisms that probably attach the parent to the infant..... We hypothesize that a cascade of interactions between the mother and baby occurs during this period, locking them together and ensuring the further development of attachment. (Ibid., 70-1)

5. Continuing Bonding and Bond Disruptions

At this point we must recognize that most studies of bond disruption, except for those few studies dealing with postpartum depression (Hamburg et. al. 1968), have concentrated on the effects on the baby of the loss of the mother. Our concern, however, is largely with the effects on the mother of the loss of the child. This is for the following reason: while there is considerable evidence of the closeness of bonding between the natural mother and her child, and while there will be some disturbance for the child if not left with the natural mother, there is no hard evidence that, if it is put immediately (and this is important) into a loving and caring environment with substitute parents there will be any long-term harm done to the child. Babies are very adaptable, and while evolution (if we might anthropomorphize) "expects" that the natural mother will be the "environment" of the child and so prepares both for this, the baby can adapt to other parents in the absence of its own. It will have to learn, for example, a new voice with which to entrain, but it can readily do this. Also, if nutrition is good and medical care available, as in modern societies, then the child is not so dependent on the immunological protection of the mother's milk, etc. Thus, once past the immediate neonatal condition, the child can bond with an adoptive mother without too much loss.

Thus, if a baby is taken from its natural mother at birth and given to competent adopters, it need not suffer too much harm. We cannot be definite about this, and clearly initially the situation will not be ideal for the infant since it will be deprived of "ready-made" bonding mechanisms and will probably have to be bottle fed. But adopted neonates do become healthy normal adults, so clearly the deficits can be made up. What we must look for then is (a) the harm done to the natural mother, and (b) the crucial question of timing.

Let us take the second question first since it will be relevant to the issue of when the infant should be separated from the birth mother—the genetrix. This is relatively easy to answer since the work of the ethologically influenced child psychologists, and in particular John Bowlby, suggests a fairly straightforward answer: do it immediately or not at all. The reasoning behind this is that the major bonding processes between mother and child occur progressively during the first two years of life, and numerous studies have shown that even small disruptions of the mother-infant bond in this period can have long-lasting pathological effects. But this works two ways: it could be an argument for the "best interests of the child"; but it could also be an argument for the "best interests of the mother," who is after all a human person with a deep interest in the matter.

To understand this we have in a way to invert the findings on childhood deprivation. Insofar as deprivation of the primary caretaker adversely affects the child, what is its effect on the mother? We shall look specifically at grief later, but for the moment let us consider this fact: if the loss is so devastating to the child, then the other "end" of the loss suffers a similar deprivation. If the child is "geared" to benefit from the bonding relationship to the mother, the mother has to be equally "geared" to the provision of this relationship. In losing the child she suffers a complete "let-down" of this system whose origins we have seen in the pregnancy and immediate postpartum situations.

Now, obviously there will be a wide variation in the response to such deprivation, but that does not matter since we are concerned with only those mothers whose prepartum bonding with the child was so intense that they do not want to give the child up after its birth. Let us ask the question this way: what is it that the mother is "geared up" to provide that can provoke such a sense of loss? Most of this is summed up and synthesized in John Bowlby's three-volume masterpiece *Attachment and Loss*, particularly in the first volume, *Attachment* (1969). Summarizing his own work and that of other researchers such as Spitz, Ainsworth, Ambrose, The Harlows, Mason, etc., he analyzes the following complexes of behavior that act as "attachment" mechanisms between mother and infant:

- visual-postural orientation (for the precocity of this development see Amiel-Tison 1985)
- rooting to the breast and sucking
- crying and stopping of crying
- smiling (an early response to generalized "face forms" later becoming specific to caretakers)
- non-cry vocalization (including mutual "babbling")
- grasping and reaching
- separation anxiety
- approach and following
- greeting
- climbing and exploring
- burying of face
- use of mother for base of exploration
- flight to the mother
- clinging

(This useful list is adapted from Konner 1982 [p. 304], where an excellent summary of Bowlby's work can be found.)

The first six items characterize the first six months of life; the rest develop in the second half of the first year. The emphasis on the first half of the year is on mechanisms involving communication through the distal receptors—smiling, crying, vocalizations, vision, posture, etc. With the development of locomotion in the second six months, it is primarily the proximity-maintaining mechanisms that come into play. Neither drive nor learning theories explain the "unfolding" of this behavioral process. Bowlby views this ethologically: during the long process of hominid evolution, the relatively helpless infant was subject to great danger if it was away from or neglected by its primary caretakers. Hence, selection would favor the development of any systems that maintained and strengthened the mother-child bond in this early period. This goes beyond the need for food or even simply protection, which is already the case in lower primates, as the Harlow experiments have shown (Harlow 1959, 1961, 1974; Harlow and Harlow 1965). Indeed, the development of a "healthy" adult personality seems predicated on successful completion of this early period of attachment.

The second thrust of research—recorded in Bowlby's second two volumes, *Separation* (1973) and *Loss* (1980)—has been on the effects of the disruption of this bond on the mental and physical well-being of the infant and its growth. The results are too well known to need much rehearsing here. The work of Hinde and his colleagues (see, e.g.,

Hinde and Spencer-Booth 1971) has shown that in monkeys even small amounts of deprivation can have far-reaching results, and Bowlby's own work has demonstrated beyond doubt that removal of the mother for long periods can have irreversible effects on human children. There have been modifications, such as Margaret Mead's criticism that in many societies there are numerous mother figures and not just one, but the overall findings have not been challenged seriously. My own observations (Fox 1960) of pathological grief in a society typical of those in which there are many caretakers in a maternal extended family showed that nevertheless there was an extreme attachment to the actual mother and severe pathologies involved in the bond disruption. (However, these were handled very well by the ceremonial healing systems—systems that we lack totally.) Various experiments have shown that partial recovery is possible if the infant is given other attachment figures, and species differences have been found, but the main finding stays firm. Let us try to summarize it here.

The infant is not a tabula rasa but rather is guided by a genetic program that "unfolds" in predictable sequence and "seeks" an object or objects in the world to which it can bond. Initially—during its original period of extreme helplessness—this will almost always be the biological mother. The very exigencies of the "lactation complex," which, as we have seen, is the root biological complex of all mammals and in particular our own species, demand this. (Safe bottle feeding is relatively recent, and even if it works it does not cancel out the already established system.) If a wet nurse or lactating adoptive mother is substituted, then a small initial deficit can be overcome and the baby will attach to this nurturant figure. (Once this new bonding is established, there are always drastic consequences for the infant if *it* is broken.) The younger the infant, the better the adjustment it seems to make. But even this is not clear, since the work of Hinde suggests that even quite short separations early on can reverberate into later life. While various degrees of rehabilitation are possible given other attachments, there is serious evidence that some permanent damage is likely in the emotional system of the growing youngster as a result of any traumatic separation.

We must never forget that Bowlby did not begin his work out of disinterested scientific curiosity but out of a desire to examine the very real suffering of institutionalized youngsters whose bodily and nutritional needs were being met by sympathetic caretakers yet who showed alarming symptoms of "autism" and other severe behavioral disorders (Bowlby 1951). As a result of Bowlby's work, legal systems in many countries have interpreted the "best interest of the child" as leaving it with the natural mother unless she is proved insane or incompetent, whatever other considerations may apply. As a rule of thumb this is not perhaps bad, but, as always, individual cases have to be treated on their merits.

Since we can take this as established, how does it help us with our questions? On the question of timing, the answer seems to be that if one is taking a child from a natural mother one should probably do it at birth rather than wait for bonding processes to establish themselves over and above the mother-fetus bonding already in place. But what of the effect on the mother? We shall examine grief in the next section; here we are concerned with the other side of the coin that had been examined by the researchers. Let us put it like this: if the infant is not a tabula rasa in this active "seeking" process of bonding, neither is the mother. She is the vital other half of the interlocking stimulation program that is the attachment process. She has, as we have seen, been physiologically and emotionally prepared during pregnancy for this role and is primed or geared to carry it on. In our culture we probably deemphasize a lot of the interaction that evolution "intended." The work of Blurton Jones, for example, on the role of milk and feeding in species that carry their young as opposed to hiding them shows that the former, which includes ourselves, feed more or less continuously (Blurton Jones 1972 and 1985). The work of Konner and Worthman (1980) on !Kung San Bushmen shows that among these hunters living in conditions like those of our early ancestors, youngsters are fed up to four times an hour and weaning is very late—three to four years.

Evolution has prepared the mother as much as the child for a continuous, intimate bonding relationship. Whatever the little organism demands, the mother is there, ready to supply; and before the advent of pediatricians, and certainly before Dr. Spock (whose advice is often quite at variance with these findings), mothers handled this interaction with a sureness that did not come from experience any more than the child's demands came from experience. And if the disruption of these processes can be so devastating for the child, then why should we suppose that they should be any less devastating for the mother? One does not even need science to answer: ask any mother who has lost a child.

To anticipate a conclusion then: if we are to ask a birth mother to give up a child when she does not wish to, we should show good cause why the bonding process already nine months old and geared to continue throughout infancy should be interfered with. Whatever the legal or genetic situation, the first biological rights in the child belong indisputably to the birth mother.

6. Grief Over the Loss of a Child

First we should establish that grief is real and measurable. Hofer (1972) has shown that the excretions of parents grieving for the death of a child are chemically different from those of parents not so grieving. The psychoendocrine system changes during periods of intense grief. Even without such direct and hard evidence of bodily changes, no one who has grieved such a loss or has been close to someone who has can fail to know the intensity of the emotion and its systematic effect on the whole organism. This is not purely a human emotion. Lorenz in his early work (1970) described the reactions of lower animals to the loss of an infant or companion where grief-like symptoms were exhibited. Suomi (1975) demonstrated clear-cut depressive behavior in adult monkeys separated from their families (see also Young et al. 1973 for species variation). And who could ever forget Jane Goodall's (1971) narrative of the chimpanzee mother, Flo, and her reaction to the death of her six-month-old infant Flame, and later of her son Flint's extreme grief reaction to her own death? He moped and whimpered for days before giving up any effort to stay alive. An autopsy revealed no organic cause of death. The pioneering work started by Hamburg (1974) and his colleagues on grief and coping has now blossomed into a full industry of grief therapy.

The only real material we can turn to on the grief of the surrogate mother who must lose a child she wishes to keep is that pertaining to mothers who must give up a child for adoption when they wish not to. Sorosky et al. (1978) have done the most complete U.S. study to date (see also Rynearson 1982 and Deykin et al. 1984). In interviewing mothers who had given up their babies ten to thirty years previously, they found that 50 percent said they continued to have feelings of loss, pain, and mourning over the child they had relinquished. Thirty-seven percent said they even remembered the child's birthday and "did something special" to celebrate the day. Thirty-one percent experienced feelings of comfort and satisfaction with the decision, but as we have maintained there will always be a range of variation in the intensity of bonding. However, 82 percent continued to wonder how the child was growing up and whether it was happy, and 82 percent also wished for a reunion. Thus, only a tiny minority of birth parents seemed not to care, and at least half were still suffering grief symptoms. It is impossible to reproduce here the heartbreaking poignancy of the letters the authors quote, but they make clear that in many of these cases the grief was as extreme and traumatic as that suffered by parents who had lost children through death—and this up to thirty years after the loss.

In extreme cases of such grief the "learned helplessness" syndrome can set in. First discovered by Seligman and Maier (1976) in dogs, in its human manifestation it can be described as a feeling of complete hopelessness in coping with the emotional stress of a situation, resulting in physical breakdown. Gastric ulceration and depleted brain levels of norepinephrine are common symptoms (Weiss et al. 1976). Parents of children dying of leukemia had abnormally high levels of 17-hydroxicortico-steroid, a major urinary metabolite of cortisol, suggesting that they were under prolonged measurable psychosomatic stress (see Hamburg 1974; Freedman et al. 1963).

One could go on quoting more such evidence, but it all points to the conclusion we started with: measurable, physical, debilitating, and psychologically and somatically crippling grief can be the outcome of the loss of a child, however that loss is accomplished. To give up a child and never see it again is to have it die from the perspective of the parent. There will be individual differences, but clearly where the attachment to the child is extreme so will be the grief. If a mother is so attached that she is unwilling to part with the child, and is willing to fight to keep it, then we should ask ourselves whether we are willing to face the consequences of extreme grief pathology in the mother in order to satisfy the demands of a surrogate or adoption contract.

7. Can the Well-Being of the Baby Be Held Constant?

Since the "Best Interests of the Child" will often be a factor in surrogate mother cases, we must briefly reopen the question of the potential harm to the baby of adopting it at birth or later. There have been several European studies which, while primarily directed towards problems of behavior genetics, throw some light on this. They are concerned with the impact of adoption on the expression of heritable traits of an antisocial nature. They show two things: that girls are less vulnerable than boys, and that *multiple adoption* ("multiplacement") increases the probability that undesirable traits will occur (see, e.g., Cloninger et al. 1982).

On the long-term effects of "maternal deprivation" and on the long-term effects of infant traumas generally, there is still much dispute. What is not disputed is that the "Harlow effect" holds good: total maternal deprivation has long-term disastrous results. The "Hinde effect" also seems certain: periods of maternal deprivation alternating with maternal care are disruptive and have long-term effects. What is less certain is the long-term effect of inefficient or unloving care (leading to Bowlby's "anxious attachment"), or even substantial abuse. We have seen that we should add "multiplacement" as a factor with long-term effects, although these are mild and only concern heritable traits.

A school of thought represented prominently by Kagan (1981; Kagan et al. 1980), Bateson (1976), Dunn (1976), and Sameroff (1978) has repeatedly demonstrated that developmental maturation will enable children to "recoup" from all but the most devastatingly adverse circumstances. Chisholm (1983), who holds to this view in his studies of Navajo infancy, states it as follows:

> Thus, in spite of the fact that attachment theory so strongly suggests that mutually insensitive and unresponsive mother-infant interaction can constitute a significant developmental perturbation, and in spite of so many studies showing at least short-term effects, we must still reckon with the troublesome facts that anxious attachment does not always produce clear later effects, that the entire significance of early experience for later behavior is being questioned, and that the infant, who influences the behavior of others, may at the same time influence the direction of his or her own development. (P. 35)

It may then be that "anxious attachment" which results from less-than-optimal mother-infant interaction, can be readily compensated for by the emotional equivalent of a "growth spurt" following physical deprivation.

There has been more serious questioning recently of the whole "bonding hypothesis"—probably a reaction to the excesses of "Bowlbyization" in the courts and hospitals (see Herbert et al. 1982; Lamb and Hwang 1982). Much of this is simply methodological criticism of the early studies, and suggests a more serious retesting rather than an abandonment of the hypothesis. In the same way that early Bowlbyites were perhaps too ready to see permanent and irretrievable damage from a disruption of the bond, these later critics are too ready to see zero results. The truth obviously lies somewhere in between, with a more ethologically sensitive approach to the totality of the mother-infant experience rather than a purely experimental "confirmation versus disconfirmation" approach being the appropriate research response (see an excellent summary in Daly and Wilson 1987).

The evidence is obviously not all in yet, but we can repeat our provisional conclusion: that unless the baby is severely deprived of maternal care or is subject to multiple placements, then there is no conclusive evidence of ill effect from adoption at birth or later. To this extent we can stay with our assumption that the "harm" to the baby need only be minimal; that to the genitor it will be variable but small; while the genetrix (birth mother) remains the most vulnerable by far of the "triad."

8. The Role of the Father

Here we shall assume that the father/pater is the genitor, so that there is no doubt about his genetic investment in the child. The question is, given his 50 percent genetic claim on the baby, is this outweighed by the mother's massive metabolic-emotional investment in the child through pregnancy, childbirth, and bonding? A careful distinction has to be made here between the bonding process that takes place between mother and fetus, and mother and infant, and the feelings a potential father might have for his child. The father's feelings may be strong, as may those of other parties with a genetic investment in the child—grandparents and siblings, for example. But these are essentially subjective, "one-way" feelings affecting only the interested parties. Certainly a father who is with the mother throughout her pregnancy, assists at birth, and afterwards cares for and feeds the baby, will develop a strong emotional bond, as Klaus and Kennel (1982, 57-62, 87-88) testify. But this is not comparable to the "objective" status of the mother-child bond developed in pregnancy and immediately after birth. The simple fact that none of the other parties, including the genitor, has actually carried the child and gone through the physiological changes described in the previous sections means that any serious bonding between them and the child is based on social interaction at a much later date (Mackey 1979; Mackey and Day 1979). This type of bonding cannot compare with the physiological bond forged between baby and mother. Her metabolic investment is massive: his is negligible.

Moreover, where the father has not been involved with the pregnant mother, the birth and the early postnatal experience—as will be the case with sperm donors and fathers who are parties to a surrogate contract—the bond is even later in forming. It does not reach the degree of "mutualism" that exists in the mother-child symbiosis until later in the child's life; that is, only later in the child's life does the father-child bond reach a point where its disruption can also have serious consequences for the infant.

Thus, for the genitor, until the bonding process has taken place, another child with one-half his genetic endowment is, as the law says, "a substantial equivalent for practical purposes." A substitute child is readily obtainable from another surrogate since the overwhelming majority of surrogates voluntarily comply with their agreement to turn over the baby after birth. Neither the delay involved, nor the fact that the father has contributed a sperm from his limitless supply of sperm, is sufficient to outweigh the claim of the genetrix to the child of her body. For the mother there is no effective substitute for *this particular child*. Its loss to her is effectively its death, with all the potentially grievous consequences we have previously summarized. There is no way in which having another child can make up for this loss. (Perhaps we should remind ourselves that there will be variation in the degree of intensity in the mother-child bonding. But we are here concerned with cases where the bonding is obviously intense, as evidenced by the mother's refusal to give up her child despite her earlier agreement to do so. There will also be variation in the intensity of the genitor's feelings towards his child, although in surrogate cases we can expect them to be strong since he has gone to all this trouble and expense to obtain a child. But we must also note that in general the track record of fathers—given the desertions, defaults on child support [80 percent] and abuse cases—is weak compared with that of mothers.)

For the genitor who is not locked into this bond there will be serious disappointment, but since no bond has formed, it will be easier for him to adjust and make up for his "loss" by fathering another infant. He can only have bonded in imagination, not in physical reality, with "his" child. And while hurt to the imagination is not to be underestimated, again it cannot be even remotely compared with the hurt in reality to the mother. The genitor deserves sympathy in this case; but does he deserve exclusive custody of the child over the protests of the genetrix?

The Court's Decision:
Parens Patriae Super

I shall not dwell in detail on the Baby M trial, since it rapidly became a media circus with the world press corps and all the major television channels in noisy attendance. For three weeks it was the favorite national soap opera, and all the details were lovingly exhibited day by day, while the weekend papers opened their op-ed pages to the pundits who pronounced for and against, and very occasionally wrote a perspicacious piece of commentary. The details are now known to the world. And in any case, it is not so much the trial per se as the judge's decision that concerns us here. To what extent did the judge take into consideration the facts we have deemed, in the foregoing sections, to be crucial to the case? And to what extent did his judgement reflect these?

For a start, the judge managed to rule out a great deal of testimony that might have been relevant, and to include a great deal that was not. He refused to hear a number of "experts" who were speaking "hypothetically" and without direct reference to the parties in the case. Thus, a number of low-level and in some cases grossly incompetent "experts" were allowed to testify because they had interviewed the Whiteheads and/or the Sterns, while people we have had occasion to consult at length, like the authors of *Parent-Infant Bonding,* were barred. Evidence about the long-term harm to mothers, for example, was not allowed on these grounds, because, it seems, the purported harm to *this* mother had yet to occur and was therefore "hypothetical." On the other hand, the Stern's were allowed to call as a witness the "celebrity" psychiatrist Dr. Lee Salk, who had not interviewed any of the parties either, but had read all the transcripts of the interviews and "made an assessment" on the basis of these. He was paid $5,000 for his trouble, which almost backfired when he concluded that Mrs. Whitehead was "not a surrogate mother but a surrogate uterus." The careful case against her, which Skoloff had been building up, showing her to be "manipulative, impulsive and exploitative" (the judge's words) among other things, suffered a momentary setback as a mild surge of public outrage greeted Salk's casual inhumanity. It was the first time the hard face of popular opinion allowed itself to wince slightly at the predicament of Mrs. Whitehead.

But too much damage had already been done. The judge was, after all, protecting his own actions, and the way to do this appeared to be to paint such a terrible picture of Mrs. Whitehead as a person and mother that no one would be able to fault him for denying her her parental rights, rights of which he had effectively deprived her from the beginning and without any trial. A guardian ad litem—Lorraine Abrahams—had been appointed to represent Baby M. This meant that a further set of "experts" could be called to testify, without breaking rank, against Mrs. Whitehead. Their testimony was supposed to be "independent," and the guardian swore to this in court, but in fact the experts had met for a total of more than twenty-four hours with the guardian, before and during the trial, and were obviously working in tandem. Together with the experts called by the Sterns, they hammered away at Mary Beth's character. The quality of some of the testimony can be judged from the profound observations of Dr. Marshall Schechter, professor emeritus of child psychiatry at the University of Pennsylvania, who, along with the other "experts" received $12,000 for his trouble. (All of Mrs. Whitehead's witnesses appeared without fee. She had nothing to pay them with.) I can do no better than quote the great humorist Russell Baker in the *New York Times*:

> Dr. Schechter ... has firm ideas about the right and wrong way to play patty-cake. The wrong way, he testified at the Baby M custody trial in Hackensack, New Jersey, is to say "hooray" when the kid claps her hands together. The right way?

When the baby claps, the grown up should imitate the action and clap back while saying patty-cake..... As an expert witness he urged the judge to end Mrs. Whitehead's parental rights in order to "protect the child." He didn't like Mrs. Whitehead's having four stuffed pandas for the baby to play with either. In the play department, Dr. Schechter is a kitchen-ware man. "Pots, pans and spoons would have been more suitable than pandas," he testified. Now if the courts heed the experts, she could end up without even the right to see the baby.

That other great black humorist of the modern condition, Franz Kafka, could scarcely have invented a better scene out of his bleak imagination than the Superior Court in Hackensack presented to us at the expense of New Jersey taxpayers. Even well-meaning attempts to help Mary Beth went ludicrously wrong. One of her character witnesses was her neighbor, Sue Hergenhan. While the Whitehead's were in Florida, Hergenhan had written a letter to the judge purporting to come from Mrs. Whitehead. Presented with the letter in court, Mrs. Whitehead denied having seen it. Hergenhan was recalled to the stand and sobbed a confession. The judge practically had apoplexy and accused "somebody" of "playing fast and loose with the court." Hergenhan's otherwise moving testimony was rendered worthless.

Somewhere in all this the contract issue got lost. The judge initially had ordered two trials: one on the contract, one on custody. The appeals court ordered that there must be only one trial, so the judge ordered, with almost theological finesse, that it should be one trial but in two parts. The first part was heard in a matter of hours, with each counsel putting the case for and against the legitimacy of the contract. The judge barred any "expert" testimony on the contractual issue. He did not need it, he said. What is more, he was not going to get "mired in inquiries dealing with ethics, morality and theology." This meant that the first part of the trial was going to be very brief indeed. As the judge and Skoloff wanted, it moved quickly into the custody phase, which in turn became a battle over the character of Mrs. Whitehead.

Skoloff was a custody lawyer, and before the trial he had announced that his tactic was indeed to turn this into a custody battle which he "knew how to win." How to win was, first of all, to delay the trial as long as possible with numerous requests for "more time." The longer Baby M was with the Sterns, the less likely was any court to order her return "in the best interests of the child." This tactic worked perfectly, with the connivance of the judge and the guardian, and it took an order of the Supreme Court of New Jersey to get the trial started on 5 January. Further delaying tactics were introduced by the judge's ruling that details of Mrs. Stern's purported infertility should not be made public to protect her privacy. Three newspapers sued to have the information made available. The judge also ruled that Mrs. Whitehead should not have the information made available to her, and, what is more, she should not be present at any part of the trial when these matters were discussed. As a portent of things to come, both the appellate and supreme courts overruled him on both issues.

The next tactic was to present a picture of the Sterns as an upright, middle-class, well-educated, professional couple who could give an excellent home to the baby, as against the working-class (although the term was never used), impoverished, shiftless, unreliable Whiteheads, who could not. In particular, the calm, serious, and capable Mrs. Stern was to be contrasted with the feckless, manipulative, dishonest, overprotective, and undereducated Mrs. Whitehead. Harold Cassidy, the Whitehead's *pro bono* lawyer, refused to meet Skoloff on his own terms. He would not indulge in "expert" mud-slinging against the Sterns but rather tried to build a good picture of Mrs. Whitehead's character as a wife, mother, and neighbor, with his experts countering as best they could the accusations of the Sterns' (and the guardian's) highly-paid witnesses. While the testimony of these experts might appear absurd to us, looking at it from a distance, we must remember that it constituted the body of "expert testimony" on which the court had to draw in reaching a conclusion. Even if the judge had been truly impartial, which he clearly wasn't, he could not, in his judgement, go beyond the testimony presented. He could perhaps look for inconsistencies and the like, but basically he could not do anything but treat all experts as equal, patty-cakes and all. In the end, he would have to decide between the "strength" of the opposing testimonies; it was not his business to challenge the actual findings. Anti-panda and pro-pots-and-pans testimony would go into the hopper along with narcissistic, schizoid, and polar personality, as well as the rest of the catalogue of vices, delinquencies, and inadequacies of Mrs. Whitehead. These were, of course, "rebutted," but, as we have seen, the judge was predisposed to believe anything about Mrs. Whitehead that would retrospectively justify his original actions, and Cassidy refused to press anything so savage against the Sterns as Skoloff was willing to do against the Whiteheads. The result was a foregone conclusion, and it is to that result we must now turn.

Judge Harvey Sorkow, having reserved eighteen seats in the small courtroom for his family, relatives, and friends, rendered his judgement on 31 March 1987 after a three-month trial of unprecedented media attention and worldwide publicity. He set the tone from the start (all quotations are taken from the full text in the *New Jersey Law Journal* 119, 653-665, 16 April 1987):

> The primary issue to be determined by this litigation is what are the best interests of a child until now called "Baby M." All other concerns raised by counsel constitute commentary.

This attitude was to determine the whole judgement. Most of the legal issues we discussed at length earlier were dismissed by Judge Sorkow as "non-issues." One might remark that the trial should have been about whose child the baby was. But the judge would have none of that. As Skoloff had wanted, the trial became a custody battle and the judgement a custody judgement. There can be no equitable justice for the adult parties in the case, said the judge, and in any case it wasn't his place to find it: "The court will seek to achieve justice for the child." It will do this on the basis of the doctrine of *parens patriae*—roughly, "the country as parent"—which the judge, or rather his clerks, traced back to the Greeks and up through English Chancery Law and Equity Courts to the merging of their powers and the establishment of the rights of the Superior Court, Chancery Division, Family Part, by the New Jersey Constitution of 1947.

One must remember that Sorkow was essentially a family court judge, not a contract lawyer or a constitutional expert. He saw his business therefore as the subordination of any other consideration to "the best interests of the child," this being the traditional matter of family court disputes. His rude dismissal of contract and constitutional issues as "mere commentary" reflect this stance.

> All should listen again to the plea of the infant as voiced so poignantly by several of the professional witnesses, statements with which this court agrees to such an extent that it will use its total authority if required to accomplish these ends.

Thus dominated by the notion of *parens patriae*, and clearly of the opinion from the start that the Whiteheads were unsuitable parents (had they not defied a specific order issued from his own bench?)

while the Sterns were exemplary, he proceeded to validate the contract, terminate Mrs. Whitehead's parental rights, order the adoption by Mrs. Stern of Baby M, and grant sole custody to the Sterns with no rights of visitation to the Whiteheads. Everything was premised on the "best interests of the child." For example, we have discussed the issue of "specific performance." The judge took this into account, but ruled:

> This court holds that whether there will be specific performance ... depends on whether doing so is in the child's best interest.... We find by clear and convincing evidence, indeed by a measure of evidence reaching beyond reasonable doubt, that Melissa's best interest will be served by being placed in her father's sole custody.

So much for specific performance.

On the contract itself, the judge leaned heavily on the fact that there was no New Jersey Statute as such covering surrogacy. Laws against baby selling did not apply, he said, because the baby had not been "sold" to her natural father, who only paid for the surrogate's "services." (She was indeed a rented uterus.) Adoption statutes did not apply, he said, because Mr. Stern did not need to adopt his own child, and, cunningly he argued, adoption by Mrs. Stern was not mentioned in the contract. Failing any statutes to govern the case, he argued, the contract should be treated as an ordinary commercial contract, regardless of the peculiar nature of its conditions. Thus, when it came to the issue of Mrs. Whitehead's parental rights, the judge refused to accept that statutory tests, as in adoption cases, applied. (There is a presumption, in law, that the biological mother is the "fit" parent unless a hearing specifically finds her to be unfit, that is, engaged in active, harmful behavior with regard to the child. Mrs. Whitehead was not entitled to such a presumption, said the judge, because in the contract she had agreed not to be a "mother." So presumptions about motherhood could not apply to her.)

He dismissed the argument that there had been fraud in the contract. True, the facts about Mrs. Stern's medical condition had not been made known to the Whiteheads; neither had the psychiatrist's report on Mrs. Whitehead's potential unwillingness to give up the baby. But (a) the term "infertile" could be held to cover conditions that render it dangerous to have a child, and (b) such information was the responsibility of the clinic as agent, and the Sterns were not responsible for their agent's actions. Since the Whiteheads had chosen to litigate against the agent and not the Sterns in this matter, they had de facto connived in this conclusion themselves, the judge concluded. In other words, there may have been fraud, but, technically at least, the Sterns were not guilty of it. And since all that really mattered was "who would be the best parents," this let the Sterns off the hook.

Constitutional matters got equally short shrift, although the judge had to tread a bit of tightrope here. While the best interests of the child should dominate all other concerns *once the child was conceived* he argued, it was indeed an invasion of privacy and thus unconstitutional to enforce any of the clauses *up to the time of conception* (insemination, for example). Even after, it was clearly unconstitutional to enforce the abortion clause. (Having defined a new rule of law, the judge boasted, a quick exception—abortion—must be noted.) But all the other clauses, including the all-important termination of parental rights clause, must be "specifically performed."

> The sole legal concepts that control are *parens patriae* and the best interests of the child. To wait for birth, to plan, pray and dream of the joy it will bring and then be told that the child will not come home, that a new set of rules applies and to ask a court to approve such a result deeply offends the conscience of this court.

Nothing, note, is said about the destructive effects on the mother who may wish to keep the child of her body. In fact, this is dismissed as another "non-issue." She can just go back to where she was, he says. She didn't really want any other children of her own anyway; her husband had had a vasectomy to this end. Therefore, it was in no way harsh or inequitable to enforce specific performance here. (The "right to procreate" issue again is interpreted entirely in favor of the father.) In fact, any state interference with this right of the father to specific performance of such a contract would itself be unconstitutional. Above all, the interest of the child is what is to be protected (again):

> Premised on the historic equitable principle of *parens patriae*, this court invokes the maxim of treating done that which ought to have been done and this court ... orders specific performance of the surrogate parenting agreement.

The essential provisions of the judge's ruling read as follows:

1. The surrogate parenting agreement of 6 February 1985 will be specifically enforced.

2. The prior order of the court giving temporary custody to Mr. Stern is herewith made permanent. Prior orders of visitation are vacated.
3. The parental rights of the defendant Mary Beth Whitehead are terminated.
4. Mr. Stern is formally adjudged the father of Melissa Stern.
5. The New Jersey Department of Health [is] directed to amend all records of birth to reflect the paternity and name of the child to be Melissa Stern.
6. The defendants must refrain from interfering with the parental and custodial rights of the plaintiff (Stern).

I have not gone at length into the judge's summaries of the "expert" testimony and the other reasons that led him to conclude that Baby M's best interests would be served by granting sole custody to the Sterns. This is partly because the one-sided and prejudiced nature of these comments can only be judged by a careful comparison of the trial transcripts to see how deliberately the judge picked on all the testimony that would be most damaging to Mrs. Whitehead's character and her role as a potential mother. It is also because I want to comment on this in the next section, and because the New Jersey Supreme Court addressed it directly in the final judgement, which we shall examine later on. Here we must pause to examine some of the wider social issues raised by the case.

Class and Contract vs. Motherhood: A Very American Dilemma

One of the most quoted generalizations in social science is that the history of society has been a history of the change from social relations based on *status* to those based on *contract*. This originated in 1861 with Sir Henry Maine, in his famous *Ancient Law,* a book which can be said to have launched the modern school of British anthropology with its strong emphasis on law, rules, and the language of jurisprudence in conceptualizing "primitive" societies. Maine was concerned, like his great contemporaries Morgan in the United States, Durkheim in France, and Tönnies in Germany (as well as Marx and Engels), with the vast change from "primitive" forms of organization based largely on kinship, to those of modern society where the realm of kinship had shrunk and relations between the state and the individual had come to dominate. Maine was not so much concerned with the "why" of this, as Marx and Engels were, but with the "how."

And the how in this case was the gradual rise to dominance of an idea: the idea of contract and the contracting individual.

In other words, it was not simply that the "rule of law" as such, or the power of the state as such, came to dominate, but that the rule of *contract law*, backed by the power of the state, eventually usurped all others in importance. Crucial to this development was the displacement of the family as the basic legal unit, and its replacement by the individual contractor.

> The movement of the progressive societies has been uniform in one respect. Through all its course it has been distinguished by the gradual dissolution of family dependency, and the growth of individual obligation in its place. The Individual is steadily substituted for the Family, as the unit of which civil laws take account. (Ibid., 149. The capitals are Maine's.)

The ties between "man and man" that constitute status were at first those that men were born into and could not change, or could change only with great difficulty. The prototype of these ties was family relationships. However, if society was to "progress" then some other basis had to be invented by clever jurists to replace the ancient, biological, and sacred ties of family relationships and all relations based on the model of blood relationship. This new and brilliant idea was worked out by the Roman jurisconsults, who took the primitive notions of promise, obligation, pact, and convention, and from them developed the doctrines of stipulation, verbal contract, consensual contract and ultimately real contract to form not only a body of law but a new way of thinking about man, society, morals, and even the gods.

> I know nothing more wonderful than the variety of sciences to which Roman law, Roman Contract-law more particularly, has contributed modes of thought, courses of reasoning, and a technical language. Of the subjects which have whetted the intellectual appetite of the moderns, there is scarcely one, except Physics, which has not been filtered through Roman jurisprudence.... Politics, Moral Philosophy, and even Theology, found in Roman law not only a vehicle of expression, but a nidus in which some of their profoundest inquiries were nourished into maturity. (Ibid., pp. 301-2)

Thus, for Maine, the essence of change in "progressive" societies was an intellectual revolution spearheaded by jurists.

Marx and Engels, of course, would have regarded this intellectualizing as mere "superstructure" rationalizing the changes in relations of social classes to the means of production. With the rise of merchant classes and the beginnings of "mercantile capitalism," there had to be a shift in thinking. But even so, Maine has a point: whatever the ultimate reasons, the language of "Roman Contract-law" virtually became the language of the "moral sciences," and in so doing became the dominant way of thinking about social and moral issues. And insistently to the fore throughout this developing thinking was the diminution of kinship and expansion of the role of individuals—individuals bound each to each by contract and not by blood or sacred obligation.

> Nor is it difficult to see what is the tie between man and man which replaces by degrees those forms of reciprocity in rights and duties which have their origin in the Family. It is Contract. Starting, as from one terminus of history, from a condition of society in which all the relations of Persons are summed up in the relations of Family, we seem to have steadily moved towards a phase of social order in which these relations arise from the free agreement of Individuals. (Ibid., 149)

There are exceptions: children under years of discretion, orphans under guardianship, the adjudged lunatic, are governed by the "Law of Persons" (as opposed to the "Law of Contract"—to use Maine's terms). But why? Because "they do not possess the faculty of forming a judgement on their own interests; in other words, that they are wanting in the first essential of an engagement by Contract." This crucial condition—of the ability to "form a judgement on their own interests"—becomes the linchpin of the modern persona.

Maine looks for a formula to express the "progressive" movement of society. Thus, for example, the Hindoos are not a "progressive" society because, although they have elaborate laws (particularly the laws of Manu) they do not have a developed Law of Contract—only a Law of Persons, i.e., a Law of Status. He expresses the formula in his famous phrase as follows:

> If we then employ Status, agreeably with the usage of the best writers, to signify these personal conditions only, and avoid applying the term to such conditions as are the immediate result of agreement, we may say that the movement of the progressive societies has hitherto been a movement *from Status to Contract*. (Maine 1861. 150-1. Maine's italics.)

Maine acknowledges that this has not necessarily been a smooth transition from social relationships based on status to those based on contract. Feudalism was a major backsliding into status, but once started, the movement inexorably snowballed because, Maine argues, this was the way we came to *think* about our social relationships and hence more and more insistently to act on them. Also, the growth of the territorially organized national state—again a product of Roman influence—especially among the previously nomadic northern tribes, led to an emphasis on the individual and his relationship to this state, conceived ultimately as a contractual relationship. Thus, the development of political theory, when emancipated from its religious base by the inevitably secularizing effects of the Reformation, moved inexorably into a theory of a social contract whereby men, in their own self-interest, made a compact with each other and/or with a sovereign to govern themselves (Hobbes, Locke, Rousseau). It was as if the only way we could *see* each other was as a body of individuals bound by agreements freely entered into "on their own interests," i.e., in their own self-interests.

The United States of America was the first modern nation to form itself consciously on this model. It dissolved the old contract with the king, with its overtones of a relationship of status, and substituted a society based on a contract drawn up freely among its members—if not exactly by referendum then by a meeting of representatives of the individuals being bound together by the compact (the model being the original "Mayflower Compact," not the royal charters). The individuals in the states would "contract" together to form their own constitutions, and then the states would come together to form their own contract to make up the United States. Of course, there was inbuilt from the start a glaring contradiction due to the existence of slavery. Slavery was firmly based on status, and slaves were dependents like children, unable to meet the "basic standards" of individuals who could form contracts. Indeed, treated as they were as property, they were the *subject* of contracts, and many constitutional issues in the early nineteenth century turned on this issue. But as Maine was writing, in 1861, a massive civil war was being fought to rid the contractual body politic of this anachronistic remnant of the old familial rule of status and the law of persons. The Civil War (just underway as Maine published his book) can in this light be seen as the last great stand of status versus contract, and status was the decided loser. When we look at this with the benefit of hindsight, an air of inevitability hangs over it. There was no way the anachronism could persist in a commercial society where contract was king. This is why an aristocracy was also unthinkable, to say nothing of the theocratic, polygynous communalism of the Mormons. The only emperor is, as Wallace Stevens puts it so elegantly, the emperor of ice cream.

In his magisterial survey, *A History of American Law*, Lawrence Friedman (1985) bears out Maine's contention. Indeed, he quotes Maine's formula with approval as summing up the nineteenth-century state of affairs (p. 532). But note that he sees the nineteenth century as the time when the great leap was made, rather than as a gradual movement over time:

> The 19th century was the golden age of the law of contract. As late as Blackstone [1769], contract occupied only a tiny corner of the temple of common law. Blackstone devoted a whole volume to land law, but a few pages at most to informal, freely negotiated bargains. In the 19th century, both in England and America, contract law made up for lost time. This was a natural development. The law of contract was a body of law well suited to a market economy. It was the general branch of law that made and applied rules for arm's-length bargains, in a free, impersonal market. The decay of feudalism and the rise of a capitalist economy made the law of contract possible; in the age of Adam Smith it became indispensable. (Friedman 1985, 275)

Note that Friedman fails to mention what Maine had so laboriously demonstrated: that Roman Law had itself elaborated the law of contract to a very fine degree and that this infused all our later thinking. But Friedman and Maine are not really in disagreement. While our general thinking may have been profoundly influenced, the law itself, paradoxically, took a step backwards under feudalism, as Maine himself observes. Thus, the nineteenth century did not have to invent contract law; it had to rediscover and reapply the Roman law of contract. Friedman continues:

> After 1800, the domain of contract steadily expanded; it greedily swallowed up other parts of the law.... The amazing expansion of the contract clause [14th Amendment] also illustrates the voracious appetite of the concept of contract. The constitution forbade states from impairing the obligation of a contract. But what was a contract? The Supreme Court gave broad and unexpected answers. A legislative land grant, a college charter, even a legislative exemption from tax: all were included in the concept. (Ibid., p. 276)

Friedman's sober prose here explodes into a kind of astonished wonderment at the "voracious appetite" of contract and its "swallowing up" of most areas of law. It is perhaps his own metaphors that drive him to the following interesting insight:

> In part, these cases used the concept of contract as a metaphor. The state was duty bound to support a broad, free market; to do so, business had to be able to rely on the stability of arrangements legally made, at least in the short and middle run. The contract clause guaranteed precisely that kind of stability, or tried to. The root notion of the growing law of contract was basically the same. Freely made bargains would be honored and, if necessary, enforced. There would be no *ex post facto* tampering with bargains, for whatever reason. (Ibid., p. 276)

In other words, even if all bargains were strictly speaking not contracts, they would be treated as such since this was the root metaphor for agreements freely entered into by individuals (or by corporations treated as individuals, although Friedman does not say this). Of course, there were progressive modifications, and even the survival of some old ones, like the 1677 Statute of Frauds (since contracts must not be fraudulent and had, for example, to be in writing as proof of the parties' agreement, etc.). Also, doctrines were gradually evolved to decide on responsibility for damages in the event of breach. But the gist of Friedman's summary of nineteenth-century law in America is simple: contract is king. "Progressive societies" such as the one in the United States "organized social relations through free voluntary agreement; individuals pursuing their own ends, made their own 'law,' perfected their own arrangements." This was the way it was and still is, in theory and popular opinion.

This little excursion into ancient history and modern law has not been undertaken for its own sake but to understand better the nature of the reaction to Mary Beth's breach of contract. She was not only challenging the Sterns, she was challenging, if Maine and Friedman are right, the very basis of our civilization. In insisting on the rights of status—which is to say motherhood—over contract, she was threatening, in the popular mind, the very thing on which our nation, and the "progressive" civilization of which it is a part, is premised: the inviolability of contract. If she had merely been a challenger to some truly commercial agreement on the basis of, say, nonperformance, she would never have created any animosity. "Let the buyer beware," the public would have said; "there's a sucker born every minute"; and other gems of popular wisdom. But what she was in effect saying was that there were *some* relationships between individuals (mothers and children in this case) that you can't write contracts about. These are, to use the words of a popular book on the issue, sacred bonds. This is a return to the language of status, and a crushing rebuke to the principle on which we operate our social and moral lives: namely, a deal is a deal.

Many in the minority that supported her—and we are here talking of knee-jerk (i.e., genuine, honest, and spontaneous) reactions, not those of the sapient sutlers of the law—were indeed conscious of their anachronistic position. A large number of them were Roman Catholics to whom the "sacred" values of the Holy Family took precedence over the secular principle of contract. The Whiteheads themselves were working-class Catholics, while of the Sterns, he was Jewish (nonorthodox), she was Presbyterian, and they vowed together to bring up Melissa as a Unitarian! No one seemed to see this as ludicrous (even hilarious) at the time, even the Unitarians, who were quite pleased by the publicity. But there was here a definite clash between the Protestant-Jewish mercantile mentality and that of the Catholic familists. Many of the amicus briefs offered in support of Whitehead were from Catholic organizations. The Vatican, toward the end of the trial, came out and roundly condemned the whole business of surrogate parenting, although it is doubtful that this did Mary Beth any good in the eyes of the court. Her lawyer was an ex-seminarian.

Most commentary at the time politely refused to deal with this issue, as is the American way. We are embarrassed to deal with obvious religious or racial clashes of this kind, and tend, as with social class, to pretend that the issues are simple intellectual or moral ones on which "each individual" may make his own judgement free from such distasteful undertones.

But we are not free from them. We are the heirs to a longstanding battle between state and kinship, between contract and status, between family and individual, between secular-Protestant and sacred-Catholic, that has been decided in favor of the state-contract-secular-individual wing and from which, according to the overwhelming majority of us, there is no going back to the dark ages of status. Might as well tell most Americans that we should abase ourselves once again before the king of England, or reintroduce slavery. As far as we are concerned, *that* issue has been settled. And if we do not see an immediate connection between Mary Beth's defiant stand in favor of the absolute rights of motherhood on the one hand, and slavery, monarchy, and the rights of individuals to order freely their own affairs on the other, then we *sense* this connection in our spontaneous rejection of her claim, and in our insistence that if there is any sanctity it applies to contracts and not to motherhood.

Of course there is tension. Americans are supposed to be passionately devoted to Mother and Apple Pie. Motherhood does indeed have a sacred status, in theory, that far outweighs fatherhood, for example. Mother's Day is unquestionably the senior festival, its paternal counterpart having been largely invented by the greeting card companies. Foreigners are alternately amused and appalled by our excessive devotion to our mothers, and college footballers always greet the television cameras with "Hi Mom!" I have never, in more than thirty years, heard "Hi Dad!" "Momism" has indeed been the target of attacks either considered (Geoffrey Gorer) or vicious (Philip Wylie). So we are torn. But it is then very interesting to see, when the chips are down, that the Momism is essentially superficial and sentimental—a kind of lip service to the atavistic goddess of status—while the vast majority of us—female and male, black and white—plump for contract over motherhood when the issue is joined.

I stress this because it is not self-evident that it should be so: why should not 90 percent of respondents have agreed that "a baby should never be taken from its natural mother?" Because the great American public really knows, in its heart, what is truly the vulnerable principle on which civilization and security and all that is good and beautiful rests: Contract: A Deal Is A Deal. The collective wisdom is, indeed, as we say to excess these days, awesome.

We have mentioned the unmentionable in passing: religion and social class. But these too go the heart of the matter, for the kind of classes that we have today have a religious origin and persistence, and the triumph of contract was a religious triumph of a kind. But it is almost impossible to discuss these things objectively in a society that has declared religion *as such* to be "a good thing" regardless of the profound differences between religions, denominations, and sects, and that is, in its own collective self-image, either classless or entirely middle-class.

Secularism and the triumph of contract go hand in hand. The reign of contract is an end product of the process Max Weber called "rational-legal." This ultimately triumphed over the "traditional" mode of governing social relationships. Though cast in political terms rather than those of jurisprudence, Weber's distinction closely parallels Maine's. "Traditional" societies were essentially those based on status, and in the general march of social progress they gave way to those based on "rational-legal" ties, of which the most important is that of contract. But Weber (1930) saw this as having happened only once in the world's history: in Western Europe after the Protestant Reformation. Much as Maine saw the whole of Western thought as infected with the Roman idea of contract, Weber saw our society become irrevocably committed to the "Protestant Ethic," even when this became secularized, as in science and humanistic ethics. It demanded the banishment of magic from religion, necromancy from science, status from law, and feudalism from the polity. It was the enthronement of the opposite of these, summed up in the phrase "rational-legal." And it is significant that Weber thought it not enough simply to stress the progress towards "rationalism" but to stress the overwhelming importance of the "legal" component.

The "bearers" of this rational-legal culture were the Protestant merchants, the bourgeoisie, the capitalists. Their devotion to the "calling" of work, their devout reinvestment of capital, their need for a disciplined work force and above all for a rational legal structure in which individual contracts would be honored, were what created and continue to sustain our modern capitalist world. All capitalist countries—Protestant, Catholic, Jewish, Confucian, tolerant, or religiously indifferent—have come to share, in varying degrees, the same secularized version of the Protestant Ethic in their worlds of science, law, politics, business, and even education. (The inability of Muslim countries to do so wholeheartedly is one of their greatest problems in joining the modern world [see Gellner 1981].) Marx and Engels would not disagree that the Protestant bourgeoisie were the "carriers" of this great revolution; where they would disagree is in the motive force behind it. For them the motive was not religious, as it was for Weber; the religious overtones were rationalizations of the change in control over the means of production that was a dialectical product of the contradictions of feudalism. But for our purposes we do not have to decide this debate. What is at issue here is tying up the devotion to contract with that other pillar of our market society: the dominance of the Protestant ethic of the dominant middle class.

When Phyllis Chesler, speaking up for Mary Beth Whitehead, declared with stunning honesty, "The entire Catholic working class of America is on trial here," the reaction was embarrassment and dismissal (see Chesler 1988). My informal sample of several hundred middle-class, liberal, well-heeled, well-intentioned, well-educated informants (i.e., the people I live and work among) was almost uniformly outraged. "It has nothing to do with class," my informants reacted. "It has to do with the best interests of the child. The Sterns can obviously give her the better home and the better chance in life. I mean, just *look* at the Whiteheads." And so on. It should be noted that my informants were actively involved in saving whales, baby seals, wetlands, and the environment generally, were keen to house the homeless (but not too close to home), feed the hungry, and even adopt third-world orphans. Their liberal humanitarian qualifications were impeccable. But for Mrs. Whitehead they seemed to hold a special place of disgust in their hearts. I tried, occasionally, to make some argument like, "On these premisses we should take all the children at present in "unsuitable" working-class homes and put them quickly into middle-class homes where they would have better chances in life...." But I was told that this was not a "class" issue; it was purely personal. The Sterns were—and anyone but a prejudiced fool could see this— simply the "better" parents. They were, after all, people like us, and not like those dreadful Whiteheads. "Would you," one of the informants asked me triumphantly, "want your children reared by these people?" My reply was that I certainly wouldn't want them reared by the vindictive Sterns, with their syncretistic and cynical indifference to religious meanings, their notion that they could buy whatever it was they wanted, hire armed thugs to enforce their wishes, and pay big fees to experts to justify their excesses. This met with little sympathy from the informants, who saw the Sterns, quite rightly, as "people like themselves."

There was certainly an amount of discomfort among the informants over the obvious point that even if "class" was not involved, money certainly was. Only the rich could afford the services of surrogates; the Betsy Sterns of this world were highly unlikely to be hiring themselves out as rented wombs for $10,000. And the possible future scenarios were disturbing, with pictures of black and third-world poor mothers enrolling in large numbers as surrogates for the American rich. But the informants were adamant even here. What we were talking about could not be, by definition, a "class" issue since America had no class issue. The so-called working class consisted of people who, with enough application and education, could become middle-class and hence suitable parents. They were conceived of, insofar as they were thought of at all except as recipients of occasional charity, as in a kind of transitional state of social illness that could be cured with the right social medicine. Once this utopia was achieved, then we would be back to contracts between equals, and none of this nonsense about class would be relevant. (This was never so precisely articulated. I am trying to summarize what seemed to be an implicit ideology.)

Several commentators in the press, again to the acute embarrassment of my informants, said loud and clear that the issue was indeed about money and class. Ellen Goodman, for example, in her syndicated column, said that the "M" in "Baby M" stood for money.

As this test case on surrogate mothering shifts focus from contracts to custody, from the conflicting rights of parents to the best interests of the child, there is barely even a veiled message about the role money may play in its outcome. People are behaving and testifying as if class—a dirty word in the American language—or socio-economic background, if you prefer, is irrelevant.

The lawyers do not bring in economists to describe the difference between the Whiteheads and the Sterns. That would be too crass. They bring in psychologists.

Nobody suggests in court that the wife of a garbage collector and the husband of a pediatrician are not equal under the law. Nobody states overtly their ability as providers. But it is money that determined Baby M's birth, and money that may well decide her custody.

In the beginning, both the Whiteheads and the Sterns chose to believe that Mary Beth wanted to carry this child for altruistic reasons. I don't dispute that belief. But in real life the wealthy don't become surrogates and the poor do not buy surrogates and the hired matchmakers do not work for love.

Psychologist Lee Salk may have been too crude in his testimony when he said that Mary Beth signed on to be a "surrogate uterus" not a surrogate mother. But the financial arrangement is telling: She would be fully paid by the customer only if she delivered his product, finished the job. (As quoted in Chesler 1988)

The judge would hear none of this. Such talk made him indignant. In his lengthy defense of surrogacy he took up the argument that:

an elite upper economic group of people will use the lower economic group of women to "make their babies." This argument is insensitive and offensive to the intense drive to procreate naturally and when that is impossible, to use what lawful means as possible to gain a child. This intense desire to propagate the species is fundamental. It is within the soul of all men and women regardless of economic status.

It is difficult to see just what the judge is getting at here. The "intense desire to propagate" may well be in the souls of us all, but it is not within the *means* of poor infertile couples however strong it may be. "Lawful means"—such as adoption, surrogacy, etc.—are not open to the poor. So how does the invocation of this universal desire answer the charge that the rich will inevitably exploit the poor on this matter? It doesn't, of course, but is simply a way of dismissing the class and money issue once again with an airy wave of the metaphysical hand.

The only real precedent for the Baby M case came in English common law. In March 1987 Sir John Arnold, in the High Court of Justice—Family Division, dealt with a parallel case in which a Mrs. P., a poor mother on welfare, had contracted with Mr. B. as a surrogate mother. She bore twins, and then, like Mary Beth Whitehead, felt unable to go through with the arrangement. Sir John found nothing wrong with the arrangement per se, but, as with Judge Sorkow, decided the custody issue (brought by the County Council of Staffordshire) on the "best interests of the child" doctrine. He considered all the evidence that the children would be better off with the middle-class B family—much the same kind of evidence presented in favor of the Sterns and concluded that these factors were "weighty." However:

I do not think, having given my very best effort to the evaluation of the case dispassionately on both sides they ought to be taken to outweigh the advantages to these children of preserving the link with the mother to whom they are bonded and who has, as is amply testified, exercised over them a satisfactory level of maternal care and accordingly it is, I think, the duty of the court to award the care and control of these babies to their mother.

Perhaps Sir John, like most British people, was more at ease with the idea of a class hierarchy than are Americans. He saw it as part of the order of nature that there should be a working class, that it recruits

its members by birth, that so long as a working-class mother—even one on welfare and lacking regular support from a husband—is a caring and loving mother, she has a right to her child, and that the countervailing economic, social, and intellectual advantages of the father's situation are not of more weight than is the mother's love for the babies. So simple. And it took him only fourteen pages of typescript to reach this conclusion.

However, in the convoluted Baby M case, what the court and counsel for the Sterns had to do to meet this challenge was present the class issues as though they were in effect *personal merits and defects* of the parties. Thus, the Sterns' impeccable middle-class behavior was the result of their sterling personal qualities, while the Whiteheads' "low-class" behavior was the outcome of their individual personality profiles. As Ellen Goodman so astutely notes, economists and other social scientists were not called upon to testify as to the *cultural* content of the behavior (and certainly it would never even have occurred to the Whiteheads' lawyers to pull in anthropologists as such). This would have spoiled completely the implicit agreement among all concerned that what we had here was a classic contractual situation between four equal, consenting adults acting "on their own interests." So, for example, the long catalogue of complaints against Mary Beth was always presented to show how she was behaving in some personally defective way. No one ever asked to what extent her relationship with her children (possessive, smothering, overidentifying, etc.) was in fact typical of working-class mothering. The informants were less inhibited: several let drop that the buying of four large, stuffed pandas was "typical" of "that type of person." It was typically irresponsible working-class behavior, in other words: a failure by the Whiteheads to adapt their spending habits to their limited means, or to buy constructive educational toys approved by Mensa.

But when confronted with this as a "class" issue, the informants backed off immediately and went along with the court's line that these were failures of individual judgement. "Not all working-class people are like that," they would reply, with noticeable lack of conviction. When asked how many working-class people they were intimate with—as opposed to *stereotypes* of working-class people—in order to make such a judgement, they could generally only come up with the casual acquaintance of a garage mechanic or, occasionally, of a white cleaning lady. For the most part they just wanted to be rid of the subject.

The judge had no hesitation in describing the different "backgrounds" of the two parties. Here are the Whiteheads:

> Mrs. Whitehead decided to leave high school in mid-tenth grade at the age of 15 1/2 against the advice of her parents. While in school she held a part-time job primarily as a hand in a pizza shop. She began working at her brother's delicatessen where she met Richard Whitehead. The Whiteheads were married on December 3 1973. Mrs. Whitehead was 16 years old. Mr. Whitehead was 24 years old.

Richard, it was then noted, had come from a broken home, served thirteen months in Vietnam as a Specialist 4th Class, and had been honorably discharged. He and Mary Beth had the two children (1974 and 1976) and then Richard had his vasectomy. The judge continues:

> From the date of the marriage in 1973, until moving in 1981 to the home in which they now live in Brick township, the Whiteheads resided in many places. Indeed, from the date of their marriage through 1981, the Whiteheads moved at least 12 times, frequently living in the homes of other family members.

> In or about 1978, the Whiteheads separated during which time Mrs. Whitehead received public assistance. The Monmouth County Welfare Board sued Mr. Whitehead to recover payments made to Mrs. Whitehead....

> The Whiteheads filed bankruptcy in or about 1983. The bankruptcy petition, made under oath, failed to disclose an interest the Whitehead's had in real estate and to list ownership of an automobile....

> There are two mortgages on the Whitehead's residence.... When this suit started both mortgages were in default and indeed foreclosure actions had begun on both of them.....

> Mr. Whitehead ... has had 7 different jobs in the last 13 years. There has also been at least one period of unemployment during which time Mr. Whitehead collected unemployment compensation.

> Throughout the marriage and continuing to the present time, Mr. Whitehead has been an alcohol abuser.

Various details then followed, including driving offences, Richard's refusal to stick with his AA meetings, and his confessing to a couple of two-week binges. Mary Beth is castigated for referring to this as "his problem" and is accused of "minimizing the effect by saying that Mr. Whitehead is not a violent or abusive drunk." Shame on her. She also preferred her own judgement about Ryan's needs to those of "school professionals." This despite the fact, the judge notes sternly, that 90 percent of parents accept the recommendations of child study teams.

I have quoted this stuff at some length—and then by no means all of it—because the judge dwelt so lovingly on it. To him it was obviously a picture of two immature, irresponsible, and totally unfit individuals. To many of those who live close to the working class, it is a fairly typical picture of a family on the economic margins struggling to survive. Much was made of Mary Beth's short-term employment as a go-go dancer, which occurred when Richard was unemployed and they badly needed more money to put food on the table. Of all things that shocked the informants, particularly the women, this one got them the most. A go-go dancer! The high school dropout Whiteheads lived with relatives and lied about their assets to try to preserve what pitifully few they had, while Richard sought some relief in alcohol, which, unlike the relief sought by the middle classes, tended to be public and noticed by the fuzz a few times. They separated and came together again. They tried desperately to buy into the American dream of their own house but couldn't keep up the payments. It all sounds depressingly familiar.

Contrast this with the Sterns, biochemist and pediatrician and able to shell out $30,000 on the surrogate contract and many times that on the lawsuit. Here is the judge's approbatory summary:

> Mr. and Mrs. Stern testify that they moved to their present home because of its easy New York commute and thinking ahead to have a family, Mr. Stern said that the town has a good school system. The Stern home is located near parks, the library, and is a short walk to the shopping area. The Sterns are economically able to provide for Baby M. Mrs. Stern is a pediatrician on staff at the Albert Einstein Medical School. Her earnings will supplement the family economy. She will not work full time because she is aware of the infant's needs that will require her presence. The Sterns espouse different religions but plan to participate in a Unitarian or non-denominational religion with the child. They plan to enroll Baby M in a nursery school at about age three not for learning purposes but for socialization. As she grows up, opportunity for music lessons and athletics will be made available. With the strong emphasis on education already exhibited by the Sterns, it is understood when they say that it is expected that Baby M will attend college.

Further comment should be unnecessary. The picture is clear enough. The contrast between Mary Beth as part-time go-go dancer and Betsy Stern taking lucky little Melissa shopping at Bloomingdale's (she testified to this—I'm not making it up) was just too much. The shiftless working class are not fit to raise their own children. But, and this has been the point, very few people wanted to see this in class terms. This "socioeconomic" material was dwelt on by the judge as proof of the vast difference in "personality" between the stable Sterns and the unstable Whiteheads. The success of the Sterns, as the true Protestant Ethic proclaims, was evidence of their superior worth in the eyes of God. That the Whiteheads were a not untypical marginal, working-class family, no worse and no better than many others, that Mary Beth's "individual" behavior in particular was typical of a mother socialized in such a milieu, and that Richard was no different from millions of working-class fathers was ignored. That the Sterns represented classic traits of the new "information class," a subdevelopment of the Protestant bourgeois success ethic, was likewise ignored. The class/money factor was blatant but denied. That the Stern's greater resources, greater knowledge, and greater ability to manipulate the legal system stacked the deck entirely in their favor was denied. The parties were all equal individual contractors. Any other assumptions both for the court and the informants were too uncomfortable to contemplate.

Others have commented on the class factor (see the March/April 1988 issue of *Society*, for example, and the brilliant and caustic discussion in DeMott 1990), but few seem to have seen it in the light of the historically- and ideologically-related factor of contractual individualism. But, as we have seen, Mary Beth struck at the heart of our basic value system, with her insistence on the supremacy of the dark collective values of status, and her unashamed espousal of working-class values of motherhood and wifehood. What the informants, the judge, Skoloff, the Sterns, and millions like them heard her say was:

"I do not have to keep my word in a contract where I am asked to repudiate my child for money; some things cannot be bought despite promises and written agreements. What is more, I have the right to be whatever kind of mother I want, including a typical working-class

Catholic mother, if that is what I am, with all its faults and deficiencies in the eyes of the middle class."

We middle-class children of contract, individualism, and the idea of a totally middle-class America (when the wrinkles are ironed out) couldn't stand it. If contracts don't always count, and if uppity poor white trash can make *their* "sacred" values count for more than the sanctity of contract, then what price progress and the American way? "These people," the judge (speaking for the informants generally) decided, had to be put back firmly in their place. And he might have got wholly away with it. Lord knows there was, from the initial three-minute standing ovation given the Sterns by the press corps to the rhapsodic exultations in the media itself, a chorus of relieved agreement. But one thing told against him: like the rest of that chorus, he didn't really know the law. Or rather, he knew a little law, which is a dangerous thing. For he so clearly twisted it to benefit his own prejudices that the New Jersey Supreme Court took only a fraction of the space he had used in his judgement in order to overturn him on all but one crucial and tragic point.

Before we get to that let me offer a word to my social science colleagues who will be a large part of my readership and were heavily represented in the informants. We are in fact unable to operate on our own "cultural relativity" assumptions when the "other" is not a distant native but is as close to us as our own working class. We can only tolerate this class, in our emotions if not in our books, as a kind of social sickness to be cured, eventually. The massive educational enterprise in which we are all engaged is in fact designed as such a cure. Get the children of the working class to college and we will make them whole. What Mary Beth did was to force us to accept our own snobbery, the worst accusation that can be levelled at a liberal egalitarian social scientist. She forced us to acknowledge that there is a working-class culture and that, on our own relativistic premises it has as much right to exist within its own scheme of values as our own; that it has a right to rear its children into that scheme of values; and that this is just as valid as the middle-class scheme that we espouse.

Someone comfortable with the idea of distinct social classes, like Sir John Anderson, does not even see a problem here. But we cannot admit to this. Snobbery prevents us, and then we hate ourselves for our snobbery and hate Mary Beth for making us hate ourselves—that is, those of us who recognize what is happening. But the majority of my sensitive, liberal, culturally relative, social science colleagues never even rose above the snobbery. If Mary Beth had been Samoan or even just black, they would have supported her right to her distinctive culture. But she was from the working class, and the Sterns were obviously better parents, and that was that. If Mary Beth had been a *black* working-class woman, we would have been ashamed—even found it impossible—to tell her that she was an "unfit parent" simply for behaving like a black working-class mother. That would have been "racist" and we would have been suitably morally indignant. Had we expressed such an opinion, politically correct vigilante groups would have hounded us on our campuses. But Mary Beth did not have that luxury. She had no protective coloring. Her faults, dear informants, were not in her class but in herself.

And even those of the informants who saw the logic of this position and accepted its reasoning were bothered by an even worse realization: they still spontaneously, in their hearts, believed the Sterns *were* the better parents. It is hard for good American liberal humanitarians to discover that they are genuine, honest snobs. And they are not inclined to thank the messenger who brings this bad news. A go-go dancer stands no chance against a pediatrician. It was the Richard Whiteheads who fought the Vietnam War (albeit in a fourth-class capacity), not the Bill Sterns. But this did the Whiteheads no good with the informants either. We do not need to elaborate.

The Appeal Decision:
Enlightenment in Trenton

We have seen that Judge Sorkow dismissed as "non-issues" most of the concerns expressed here, both legal and ethological. The contract was not in dispute as a contract and was legal because no legislation actually forbade surrogate contracts as such. Informed consent was a "non-issue" since all the people involved were freely consenting adults: no one had been coerced. Specific performance was to be granted since the father "owned" his child, and therefore only the child's "best interest" was the determining factor in deciding specific performance. The feelings of the mother, the siblings, and the grandparents were equally "non-issues." The right of the genetrix to a "grace period" was a non-issue since this was something granted to mothers giving up children to adoption, which was not the case here. The sanctity of contract again was in the fore when Judge Sorkow declared: "Would [counsel] have all contracts in limbo until the result of the intended agreement is available ...?" That agreements to give up the child of one's body are different, and must be different, from ordinary commercial contracts was thus dismissed as another "non-issue." The potential harm to parties other than the child, especially the genetrix herself, was put on the non-issue list, but the potential disappointment to the "joy and expectation" of the genitor and his wife were given much weight. On the constitutional issues, the "right to procreate" was widely interpreted to reinforce the genitor's right to custody, while most of the objections to surrogacy stemming from the Bill of Rights were again non-issued out of consideration.

Together with some colleagues in the Gruter Institute for Law and Behavioral Research, I had considered these issues, and eventually I and Donald Elliott, from the Yale Law School, wrote an amicus curiae brief and submitted it to the Supreme Court. The brief contained only some of the material we have looked at here, if only because (naturally) the group was unable to agree on the custody issue.(I only realized later that the minority (one male, one female), which was pro-Whitehead, consisted of immigrants, foreigners if you like, who were perhaps better able to take a disinterested, if not wholly dispassionate, view of the American class system.) The amicus brief stressed two points: that a prebirth contract should not be effective in renouncing parental rights, and that specific performance was an inappropriate remedy in this instance and should be denied. It might be thought that this last would have decided the custody issue automatically in favor of the Whiteheads, but not so. Specific performance may indeed be denied, but this affects only parental rights: it means that Mrs. Whitehead's parental rights cannot be terminated—that the child does not automatically "belong" to the genitor exclusively. It does not say what will happen in the issue of custody, which is a separate issue and should be decided, as in an adoption case, by a "fitness hearing" specifically devoted to the relative merits of the contending parties to be custodial parents. No such specific hearing was ever held in this case. The judge decided the issue of "fitness" on the basis of what he had heard at the trial. There was no real enquiry, for example, into the fitness of the Sterns to be parents.

The New Jersey Supreme Court handed down its verdict on the appeal from the Superior Court decision (217 N. J. Super. 313, 1987) on 3 February 1988 in an opinion written by Chief Justice Wilenz, with all six other justices concurring. This unanimous (7-0) decision:

1. Found the contract to be invalid and contrary to New Jersey law and public policy;
2. Found the ex parte order giving temporary custody to the Sterns to have been invalid;
3. Voided the adoption of Baby M by Mrs. Stern;
4. Restored Mrs. Whitehead's parental rights;
5. Affirmed the order giving custody of Baby M to Mr. Stern; and,
6. Remanded to the lower court—but with a different judge—the question of the nature and extent of Mrs. Whitehead's future visitation rights.

(It should be noted that Mrs. Whitehead had in the interim divorced and remarried, but the court retained her name as it had been during the trial to avoid confusion.)

It is clear that the Supreme Court agreed entirely with our brief regarding the contract, contra the opinion of the Superior Court Judge. The brief's emphasis was different for the simple reason that at least half of it rested on the assumption that the contract might be found valid, and was concerned to argue that even so it should not be enforced. The court, however, invalidated the contract largely on the basis of its incompatibility with New Jersey law, so the question of its enforceability did not arise. But in arriving at this decision, and in particular in deciding the issues of the ex parte order giving the Sterns temporary custody, of the termination of Mrs. Whitehead's parental rights, of the issue of informed consent, and of the balancing of harm to the parties, the justices reflected many of the brief's findings and arguments.

On the validity of surrogacy contracts the court was firm in its rejection, which we must note at some length since we had not anticipated such a decisive and eloquent turndown:

We invalidate the surrogacy contract because it conflicts with the law and public policy of this State.... [W]e find the payment of money to a "surrogate" mother illegal, perhaps criminal, and potentially degrading to women.... [W]e void both the termination of the surrogate mother's parental rights and the adoption of the child by the wife/stepparent. We thus restore the "surrogate" as the mother of the child.

The court determined that the illegality of the contract stemmed from its use of money to procure an adoption through private placement.

> Its use of money for this purpose—and we have no doubt whatsoever that the money is being paid to obtain an adoption and not, as the Sterns argue, for the personal services of Mary Beth Whitehead—is illegal and perhaps criminal.

In addition, the court argued, the contract was in fact "coercive." The mother had agreed "irrevocably" to surrender the child to the adoptive couple prior even to conception. She had agreed also, and illegally, to surrender her parental rights. The court turned the "best interests of the child" argument—used by the lower court entirely to boost the Sterns' case—completely around. The contract itself, they said, totally ignored the "best interests of the child."

> In this case a termination of parental rights was obtained not by proving the statutory prerequisites but by claiming the benefit of contractual provisions..... The contract's basic premise, that the natural parents can decide in advance of birth which one is to have custody of the child, bears no relationship to the settled law that the child's best interests shall determine custody.

In other words, the contract had preempted the right to decide custody "in the best interest of the child," which can only lie in the power of the courts. It was not the child's interests that the contract sought to protect, but the genitor's. The rights of the child were never considered. Indeed, "the surrogacy contract guarantees permanent separation of the child from one of its natural parents," thus running contrary to public policy in the state, said the Supreme Court. "The surrogacy contract violates the policy of this State that the rights of natural parents are equal concerning their child, the father's right no greater than the mother's.... The whole purpose of the surrogacy contract was to give the father the exclusive right to the child by destroying the rights of the mother...." But, above all, the judges reserved their severest condemnation for the issue mentioned above: the failure of the contract to give any regard for the best interests of the child. "There is not the slightest suggestion that any enquiry will be made at any time to determine the fitness of the Sterns as custodial parents, of Mrs. Stern as an adoptive parent, their superiority to Mrs. Whitehead, or the effects on the child of not living with its natural mother." They conclude severely: "This is the sale of a child, or, at the very least, the sale of a mother's right to her child, the only mitigating factor being that one of the purchasers is the father." So the father here is "buying his own child" the court said; he is paying money to obtain exclusive rights to it. He can't do that under the law. The contract is invalid from beginning to end.

On the issue of "informed consent," the judges found that no potential surrogate could be said to be fully "informed" in advance of pregnancy and birth:

> Under the contract, the natural mother is irrevocably committed before she knows the strength of her bond with her child. She never makes a totally voluntary, informed decision, for quite clearly any decision prior to the baby's birth is, in the most important sense, uninformed, and any decision after that ... is less than voluntary.

The justices also recognized the potential harm to the mother that we stressed:

> The long-term effects of surrogacy contracts are not known, but feared—the impact on the child who learns she was bought ... the impact on the natural mother as the full weight of her isolation is felt along with the full reality of the sale of her body and her child.

As regards the father's "right to procreate," they insisted that it was "no more than that." The right had been fulfilled by the artificial insemination and did not extend to the right to custody, for example. This latter right had to be independently established (as in this case the judges felt it had been).

On a further crucial point, the court echoed our words quite closely. In voiding the ex parte order it argued as follows:

> When father and mother are separated and disagree, at birth, on custody, only in an extreme, truly rare, case should the child be taken from its mother *pendente lite*, i.e., only in the most unusual case should the child be taken from the mother before the dispute is finally determined by the court on its merits. The probable bond between mother and child, and the child's need, not just the mother's, to strengthen that bond, along with the likelihood, in most cases, of a significantly lesser, if any, bond with the father—all counsel against temporary custody in the father.

It should also be noted that the court went out of its way to repudiate the "too harsh" judgement of Mrs. Whitehead's character:

> It seems to us that given her predicament, Mrs. Whitehead was rather harshly judged—both by the lower court and by some of the experts. She was guilty of a

breach of contract, and indeed she did break a very important promise, but we think it is expecting something well beyond normal human capabilities to suggest that this mother should have parted with her newly born infant without a struggle. Other than survival, what stronger force is there? We do not know of, and cannot conceive of, any other case where a perfectly fit mother was expected to surrender her newly born infant, perhaps forever, and was then told she was a bad mother because she did not. We know of no authority suggesting that the moral quality of her act in those circumstances should be judged by referring to a contract made before she became pregnant. We do not find it clear that her efforts to keep her infant, when measured against the Sterns' efforts to take her away, make one, rather than the other, the wrongdoer. The Sterns suffered, but so did she. And if we go beyond suffering to an evaluation of the human stakes involved in the struggle, how much weight should be given to her nine months of pregnancy, the labor of childbirth, the risk to her life, compared to the payment of money, the anticipation of a child and the donation of sperm?

The court even faced up to the class issue:

We have a further concern regarding the trial court's emphasis on the Sterns' interest in Melissa's education as compared to the Whiteheads'. That this difference is a legitimate factor to be considered we have no doubt. But it should not be overlooked that a best-interests test is designed to create not a new member of the intelligentsia but rather a well-integrated person who might reasonably be expected to be happy with life. "Best interests" does not contain within it any idealized lifestyle; the question boils down to a judgement, consisting of many factors, about the likely future happiness of a human being. Stability, love, family happiness, and, ultimately, support of independence—all rank much higher in predicting future happiness than the likelihood of a college education.

One might have been forgiven at this point for expecting a resounding decision in Mrs. Whitehead's favor. But in the end the court ducked this one. While Mary Beth might provide love, she might not provide stability or the possibility of autonomy. The experts were against her; her own witnesses were divided; and, above all, "most convincingly, the three experts chosen by the court-appointed guardian ad litem of Baby M, each clearly free of all bias and interest, unanimously and persuasively recommended custody in the Sterns." This is the only place where this otherwise extraordinarily well-argued and sane judgement falls into absurdity. But it was clear that the judges, for all their good sense and sound argument, could not, like the informants or the rest of their class, find it in their hearts to deprive little Melissa (as she now was) of her trips to Bloomingdale's. Having dumped the major expert—Judge Sorkow—without ceremony, they fell back on the other "experts" to save them from the consequences of their own logic and enable them to deliver Baby M to the Sterns in her own "best interest."

At the same time, they fully restored Mrs. Whitehead's parental rights and hence her rights to visitation. She is the "legal mother," they said, adding somewhat ironically that she should not be "punished one iota because of the [illegal and possibly criminal] surrogacy contract." This was of course only with respect to visitation; she had already been punished more than an iota by the whole process: the illegal and criminal contract had caused the issuance of the original ex parte order by an ignorant judge, which led to Baby M's being kept in the primary custody of the Sterns for a year and a half, which in turn became a major argument for leaving her there so as not to disturb her settled situation. However, the visitation matter was sent back to another lower court, and although Skoloff and the Sterns continued to fight, and to abuse the now remarried and pregnant Mary Beth (to the point where they had to be rebuked by the judge, who told them that it was not visitation rights that were now at issue but rather the limits on those rights), generous visitation rights were eventually granted, including summer visits of the child with its mother.

The New Reproductive Techniques: Offspring without Sex

That's it for Baby M. We have seen the uses and the limits of an anthropological ethology in trying to be helpful with the settlement of a difficult law case. Our brief really ends here. But we have to recognize that "surrogate parenting" is only one of several New Reproductive Technologies (NRT's), and all of them raise some similar issues. So-called in vitro fertilization, where sperm and egg are brought together in a petrie dish and the resulting fertilized egg implanted in the womb of, say, an infertile woman, has raised hopes for "curing" infertility ever since the technique was perfected in Oldham, England, in 1978. But the egg of an infertile woman, together with her husband's sperm, can also be implanted by simple artificial insemination techniques into a surrogate mother who has been paid for this purpose. This raises an interesting conundrum, since the surrogate in this case does not contribute any genetic material to the child she bears. Yet she is still the genetrix in our sense, and the in utero bonding and bonding at birth will still take place. How would her claim to a resulting child stand up in court? There could be no issue of breach of adoption laws since the wife of the sperm donor—the equivalent of Betsy Stern—would also be the genetic mother of the child. How should the claim of the totally genetic parents here stack up against any resistance by the genetically unrelated "surrogate? Does the contribution of a bit of the male donor's limitless supply of sperm, and the flushing out of a few ova from the female donor's fallopian tubes, match up to nine months of gestation and the risks of childbearing and childbirth? Is the surrogate in this case going to feel the child is any the less "her's" because she did not contribute the egg?

Even more bizarre scenarios can be considered (see Hollinger 1985 and Robertson 1986 for the legal tangles that might ensue). Take the case of an infertile husband with a wife who is fertile but cannot, for some reason, give birth. Her flushed-out ovum could be combined with sperm from a donor and implanted in a surrogate. Here we would have *four* people involved: a genetic mother married to a prospectively social father plus a genetic father (probably unknown) and an actual genetrix, or birth mother. One can run around the possibilities, with the most bizarre being sperm and eggs from unknown donors being externally fertilized and then implanted in a surrogate who surrenders the eventual child for adoption to two other (possibly infertile) social parents: five people, none of whom had sex with any of the others. In the case of frozen sperm, a child could be that of a dead man; and with frozen embryos a child could be born to long-dead parents. With frozen sperm and ova from dead parents combined, children could technically be orphans at the moment of conception. It will only take a breakthrough in incubator technology to bypass the surrogate mother altogether and produce offspring not only without sex but without mothers either; then we are truly in Huxleyland. For the moment, however, the "rented womb" is still needed and hence will run into all the problems discussed in this chapter, should the genetrix lay claim to the child.

Several countries have now introduced legislation to control or outlaw surrogate parenting, so injurious do they seem to accepted notions of love, marriage, family, and the "normality" of parent-child relationships. As early as 1984, the famous "Warnock Report" (Department of Health and Social Security 1984) in England examined these issues (as well as those of embryo research) for the British Parliament, which later endorsed embryo research but criminalized surrogacy. The issues evoke deep feelings everywhere, and there is no consensus. On the one side, the scientists and doctors, and the increasing number of infertile couples, claim "progress," while the opposition claims everything from "inhumanity" to the gross "unnaturalness" of the whole business, the Catholic Church obviously being a leading voice in this opposition. Feminists seem to be interestingly divided on this issue. Some see it as a case of "freeing" women from the necessity of childbirth to pursue careers and "self-fulfillment"; others see surrogacy as the apotheosis of "sisterhood" and cooperation among women; yet others see it as an attack on woman in her role as mother and a handing over of yet more "patriarchal" control to males—especially the medical profession, which particularly excites feminist indignation (and not without reason) (see Stanworth 1987).

It is scarcely surprising that there should be such passionate debate. This great leap forward in technology—like so many others—leaves us unprepared for what appears like a total redefinition of the family, of marriage, of "lawful procreation," and even of the individual: how much of himself—and in this case certainly herself—does the individual "own" for example? If I may "sell" an ovum to some third party, have I any rights and duties toward the end product of the ovum so disposed of? The same with sperm. If I donate sperm (actually I would be more likely to sell it), do I have paternal obligations to its eventual bawling and gurgling consequences? We simply find these possibilities—the majority of us—too remote from our traditional (and often religiously-backed) notions of family, parenthood, and love for offspring.

But how can we attack or defend such practices as unnatural if we have no established standards for what is "natural" in the first place? And how can we have these if relativism informs all our enquiries and tells us that whatever definitions we come up with will merely be social/cultural constructs? I would agree, for example, with those who say that the nuclear family is not a sacrosanct "natural" entity but simply one kind of institutional possibility. I have been saying so for thirty years or more. But as a student of mammalian behavior I would have to disagree that "motherhood" is a similar construct depending on context for its meaning. As a first approximation I would say that no matter the provenance of the genes, a hard look at the mammals tells us that the genetrix does indeed bond with the child in the womb and at parturition, and hence has a "natural" claim to it. If this hypothesis is true (and since it claims to be science and not just opinion then it is open to being falsified), it at least gives us somewhere to start.

Opponents have said to me that this hypothesis contradicts "sociobiology," which has established that we seek to "maximize our inclusive fitness," i.e., our own genes and their replicas ("genes identical by descent") in others. What then of the "mother" whose offspring bear none of her genes? I would answer that this objection is a poor reading of sociobiology which, while truly stressing *genetic* investment (the legacy of Hamilton 1963) is just as interested in *parental* investment (the legacy of Trivers 1972)—which is what we have been largely concerned with in the Baby M case. In addition, we must face the fact that these genetic outcomes sociobiologists speak of are not proximate motivations—although they are often written about as if they were, thus confusing everyone. No animal, man included, "seeks to maximize inclusive fitness." What we all seek is certain proximate goals which, if achieved, will have the effect of optimizing our reproductive fitness. Thus, we seek sex, shelter, provisioning, territory, dominance, companionship, love, respect, kinship (i.e., bonding with kin), and so on. Of course, we want children, as such, but not to maximize our reproductive fitness; we want them because it's nice to have kids, because heirs are important (Bill Stern's motivation), or with thoughts of care in old age, or because a large family is a sign of status, or dozens of other proximate motives. If we get all these right, we will surely get some genes (or at least some related genes) into the next generation. Of course, the males in our "we" may or may not be proximately concerned with whether or not the genes they promote are in fact their own. This indeed is culturally variable, and does not always vary directly with "patriarchy" and "matriarchy" either. (In many patriarchal societies men lay claim to all children borne by their wives, regardless of who the genitor is.) But it does not really matter. Nature works by rule of thumb, not absolute accuracy. If people nurture the children they think are theirs, most of the time they will be, and this is enough to get kin selection working.

It doesn't have to be 100 percent. For most of human evolution anyway, there has been no sure way to determine the paternity of offspring.

But to get back to the issue of proximate versus ultimate motivation. Perhaps we are meant to pursue the maximization of reproductive success, but it is doubtful that we are *motivated* to pursue such maximization as an immediate goal. Those who use birth control, or even homosexuals, for example, are not less enthusiastic about sex. Those not married or seeking children are still concerned passionately with status and resources. And so on. As far as human behavior is concerned, it is these *proximate* mechanisms that matter. All sexually reproducing organisms are programmed to produce them regardless of the consequences in genetic investment. It is only of concern to long-term evolution what the genetic consequences of them are. People are not motivated by long-term genetic consequences. They are motivated by love and lust, pleasure in possession and power, affection and comradeship, and so forth. The genes will largely take care of themselves. Thus, a woman who has gone through gestation and parturition will be "primed," as we have seen, to bond with her child. If the bond takes, then she is not likely to repudiate it simply because she knows the genes in the child are not her own. The child is already eliciting "mothering" responses, as indeed a nonrelated adopted infant will do for the parents who take it into their care. Claims of genetic relatedness then should not take precedence over those involving these powerful proximate—especially bonding—mechanisms.

We thus end up with the same conclusion as in the polygamy case: concentration on institutions, like the nuclear family, is probably misplaced. Other cultures take in their stride the idea that a child may not have a "father," or that children can be born to a dead man. These are not the important things. These cultures still try to satisfy basic needs, such as those on our list of proximate motivations above. The various institutional forms by which they do this can vary widely (they are indeed "cultural constructs"), but they are forms which still must answer the basic individual needs or risk severe cultural dislocation. This is where relativism fails. Cultural constructs, however varied, must be rooted in biological reality or they will surely collapse. Thus, the NRT's will survive or not insofar as they augment or attack these basic realities. We have looked at only one example: if we try to force bonded mothers to give up their children in the name of contract (a cultural construct), we will fail—or at least deserve to fail. But the same principle can be extended to any of the other NRT's. Do they or do they not help or hinder the pursuit of those proximate motivations that are programmed into us by evolution to ensure the production of future generations? Here, comparative enthnography may help us in showing the limits of human tolerance for variation—which are quite wide in fact.

Efforts so far to deal with the issue of NRT's have been largely legislative and restrictive. Surrogacy, for example, simply gets outlawed. We are trying to be philosopher kings again. But as the Baby M case has shown, we often do not know in advance what the problems will be. Thus, a case-by-case approach through the common law may well throw up more workable solutions to actual problems than will grand schemes of legislation aiming to solve hypothetical problems all at once. If I may venture an opinion on the surrogacy issue: I do not think surrogacy should be banned, since it has been proven to work in many cases with quite satisfactory results. I do, however, as is obvious, think that a surrogate mother (a genetrix half related or wholly unrelated to her child) should not be required to give up the baby if she does not wish to. That seems to me the moral of this case. We can deal with the case of the unfrozen embryo, the product of a long-dead billionaire (and his mistress) whose fortune has already been divided among the other heirs, excluding the unstable great-niece in whom the revived embryo was implanted by an unscrupulous lawyer, when it arises. Michael Chrichton is already probably at work on the novel.

But besides being a great novelist, Crichton is also a good scientist, and we should heed his heartcry in the introduction to the frightening *Jurassic Park* (1990) after noting that biotechnology research is carried out, mostly without supervision, in two thousand laboratories in the United States alone where more than five hundred commercial firms spend more than five billion dollars a year on it.

> Suddenly [1976] it seemed as if everyone wanted to become rich. New companies were announced almost weekly, and scientists flocked to exploit genetic research. By 1986, at least 362 scientists, including 64 in the National Academy, sat on the advisory boards of biotech firms. The number of those who held equity positions or consultantships was several times greater.

Crichton compares the older disdainful attitude of "pure" scientists to that of their "applied" colleagues with this new rush to get onto the biotech bandwagon. Share prices of successful firms (or at least firms perceived as successful) could rocket over 1000 percent in a year (my observation, not his). He continues, about the disdainful attitude of pure scientists:

> But that is no longer true. There are very few molecular biologists and very few research institutions without commercial affiliations. The old days are gone. Genetic research continues, at a more furious pace than ever. But it is done in secret, and in haste, and for profit.

Much of the work is thoughtless and frivolous, he claims (genetically engineering paler trout for better visibility in the stream), but above all, "the work is uncontrolled. No one supervises it. No federal laws regulate it. There is no coherent government policy, in America or anywhere else in the world.... But most disturbing is the fact that no watchdogs are found among the scientists themselves. It is remarkable that nearly every scientist in genetics research is also engaged in the commerce of biotechnology. There are no detached observers. Everybody has a stake."

And, one might add, a contract.

PART II

SUCCESSION

Introduction

The Lineal Equation

In looking at the constellation of laws, customs, and usages surrounding kinship, reproduction is the appropriate starting place. Clearly, without it there would be no kinship. We have looked at the fuss and bother caused by our passionate concern with the manner of our reproduction, and with our rights over its products. But anthropologists in particular have been equally or more concerned with what happens afterward: with the problem of continuity in kinship: with what happens to the offspring, and offspring of the offspring. In particular, the British school, from its origins, has been concerned with kinship continuity as a problem with legal dimensions rather than, say, psychological overtones. This follows from the founding ideas of the study of kinship in Britain, which came predominantly from jurists, and from two jurists who disagreed profoundly with each other, thus setting the stage for a major debate about succession which dominated the nineteenth and early twentieth centuries.

John Fergusson McLennan was, as his name suggests, a Scot. He trained as a lawyer and earned his living as a Parliamentary draftsman for Scotland; i.e., his job was to redraft laws passed by Westminster so that they would be consonant with Scottish law. (People are often surprised to find that Scottish and English law are not the same in many important areas, such as marriage, murder, and inheritance.) His real passion, however, was to continue the work of his predecessors in the Scottish enlightenment (Hume, Kames, Fergusson, Millar, Adam Smith, Dugald Stewart, etc.) in looking at the "moral improvement of mankind." To this end, he wanted to know about the "origins and development" of systems of marriage and succession, and the successive stages of their relationship to each other. He started by studying "marriage by capture" and trying to deduce what sort of kinship system such a practice would have produced. Independently of similar thinkers on the continent, he proposed a sequence leading from promiscuity through "motherright" (kinship through females only) to "fatherright" (kinship through males only), with our system of kinship though males and females coming later with the institution of the nuclear family (McLellan 1865; see also 1876). This was also remarkably like the system proposed by the American lawyer L. H. Morgan (1877), which was in turn taken up by Engels and became the cornerstone of the Marxist theory of the origins of the family (Engels 1905; see also Krader 1972). Although Morgan and McLennan argued about details—particularly the importance of kinship terms—they were in basic agreement about the overall universal sequence, and about the importance of looking at the laws, rules, and customs of the tribes concerned. The jurisprudential element was firmly there in both.

The other founding father of the British school was the redoubtable Sir Henry Sumner Maine, Regius Professor of Civil Law and Master of Trinity Hall at Cambridge, and Reader in Roman Law and Jurisprudence at the Inns of Court. My eldest daughter studied philosophy at Trinity Hall, and when I first visited her there I stood reverentially before Maine's portrait for a few moments of pious contemplation. She asked me why I was so impressed by Maine, and in the conversation that followed I developed, under her keen (and sceptical) prompting, my first ideas about Maine's prescient conclusions on the influence of Roman contract law. These conclusions we examined in chapter 2, where I discussed Maine's *Ancient Law* (but see also Maine 1883 and 1884). Of course, the world of social science knew about Maine and his ideas. But in a general reaction away from legalistic evolutionism and functionalism, and towards psychologism, symbolism, structuralism, and postmodernism (to name a few), Maine has been more or less forgotten and relegated to the "history of ideas." But history is the history of ideas, and we neglect the great ones at our intellectual peril. Enough preaching; let us get on with the story.

Maine was not interested in the "universal history of mankind" and hence the tracing of its universal stages of development, since he thought the only developments that mattered had taken place in one special group, the Aryans—or, as we would say, the Indo-Europeans. For these special peoples, from the Hindus in the east to the Celts in the west, the original state had been one of the "patriarchal joint family." This state still existed in parts of Europe and in India in the late nineteenth century, and for several years Maine lived in India as legal member of the Council of India—the Viceroy's ruling cabinet— where he studied the ancient laws and modern practices.

McLennan could not accept Maine's position, since in his logic the Aryans as much as anyone else must have passed through the stage of "matriarchy." The more historically-minded Maine could find no evidence for this. But while they differed over details, what is important is that these two lawyers—together with the American lawyer Morgan—set the legalistic tone for the analysis of non-European kinship systems, and laid out the major differences between the systems of "fatherright" and "motherright"—or, as we would call them today, systems of matrilineal and patrilineal succession.

Our use of these latter terms, while not originated by A. R. Radcliffe-Brown, was clarified and codified by him in an article published in 1935. Written in a legal context and entirely for a legal audience, it appeared in the *Iowa Law Review* (vol. 20, no. 2) while Radcliffe-Brown was at the University of Chicago (see Radcliffe-Brown 1952). Radcliffe-Brown, a Cambridge man like Maine, had picked up on the whole legalistic tone of the debate while ditching almost contemptuously the developmental or social evolutionary concerns of its founders and even of his teacher at Cambridge: W.H.R. Rivers. He spoke of the necessity to distinguish between rights in rem and rights in personam even when dealing with the Kariera aboriginal hordes of Australia. These hordes are "corporations" possessing an "estate" and hence must institute laws of succession to determine inheritance.

There were, for Radcliffe-Brown, only two ways to determine succession if society wishes to avoid damaging conflict between the father's family and the mother's. Succession must go clearly and unequivocally in only one line—the male or the female. It is possible to use both lines if different items are being passed down. Thus, moveable goods could follow one line and immovable the other, for example. (For Radcliffe-Brown, inheritance was a form of succession—to rights over property real and incorporeal.) He also recognized that adherence to the line of succession is rarely absolute, but still argued that a "preponderance" of rights, duties, and property must go in one line or the other. Thus was the term "unilineal" born, and "unilineal descent groups" became an almost obsessive object of study for British anthropologists from then on. Radcliffe-Brown would have nothing to do with speculation on the origins of such systems. We know nothing about that, he insisted. But we could speak of their "sociological origins" or "functions"—their raison d'être, as it were. And this was, as we have seen, to provide clear and nonoverlapping principles of succession, thus avoiding social conflict.

Radcliffe-Brown dismissed as aberrations—or at least as "presenting difficulties" with which he could not deal—all those systems (including our own Anglo-Saxon-derived one) that were not unilineal. This lack has now been made up, and we know that such systems—many more than Radcliffe-Brown imagined, actually—deal with the problem in their own ways, which are quite good at avoiding damaging conflict. But he did focus our attention on the need to take seriously the elegant nature of systems of unilineal succession, and their positive qualities as systems for regulating "rights and duties."

His opening paragraph stressed the need, if we wanted "to understand aright the laws and customs of non-European peoples," to avoid interpreting them in terms of our own legal conceptions. Actually, what he did was to adapt our own legal conceptions to the proper understanding of these peoples. Whether in fact we should regard unilineal descent groups as "corporations" is a moot point, but in dealing with them this way Radcliffe-Brown elevated the discussion of such systems to a respectable level and refused to see them as relics of former stages of development, which is where the social evolutionists had left them.

However, when he said "non-European," he should have said "contemporary non-European," since he himself draws on examples from ancient Greece (the *genos*) and Rome (the *gens*) to illustrate the principles of patrilineal succession. For indeed both these founding societies of the western European tradition had derived from nomadic Indo-European pastoral tribes, which settled in the two peninsulars and developed urban civilizations of a high order. But in many things, and for a long time, they kept to their roots. McLennan had been drawn into his study by remnants of marriage-by-capture among the Romans, and for Maine the patriarchal origins of the Indo-Europeans were often illustrated by reference to archaic Roman law. Indeed, we cannot understand much about the early history of these civilizations without taking account of their origins as tribes practicing unilineal descent and patrilineal descent at that. (Efforts have been made by die-hard martiarchalists to find such a phase in Greek history—they never try it for the Romans—but there is in fact no evidence at all that Greeks were ever matrilineal. This notion depends on the misinterpretation of religious customs [by the otherwise insightful Jane Harrison (1927) in particular] and on such customs as son-in-law succession inferred from legends. The issue is not, however, germane to our present discussion.)

Given that the Indo-European Greeks and Romans were in origin patrilineal in their determination of succession, with what kind of historical problems can this knowledge help us? In the chapter on Antigone, Greek tragedy, and the issue of European individualism, I have tried in a very simple way to show how Radcliffe-Brown's point is absolutely correct if we regard the ancient Greeks as an "alien" society and stop trying to interpret what they meant by "kinship" or "family" in terms of our own later and very different notions. If I am correct, we can only understand the heroine Antigone if we see her as defending a patrilineal ideology of succession, rights, and duties. She is often praised by critics for upholding a "sacred law," but it is rarely observed that the law in question was a patrilineal law, even if it was already archaic at the time of Sophocles' writing (fifth century B. C.).

Also, and here the issue becomes much bigger, our own interpretation of our own "individualism" may be at fault, if we see its beginnings in such events as Sophocles' depiction of Antigone's rebellion. What we are seeing in fact is part of the long battle, as I have phrased it, between "kinship law" and "state law"—a battle of which the Greek tragedians were well aware and which they articulated beautifully. The battle is still going on, and while certainly the individual does do battle with the state, so does the kinship unit.

The individual contractors who are the ideal units of the centralized state—and particularly its industrial version—as Maine announced, are latecomers to the scene. Their emancipation from the kinship unit is not complete, although in advanced industrial nations it is close, and as we saw in the Baby M case, we are still riven with conflict over this evolving issue. There is then perhaps more continuity than appears at first sight between our concerns in the Baby M chapter and those of the Antigone piece. "The war between kinship and the state" *is* alive and well. Also, this chapter is in a long tradition of the love affair between anthropology and the classics, started in the nineteenth century by Sir Richard Burton, Sir James Frazer, Mr. Gladstone, Gilbert Murray, and Jane Harrison, and aided and abetted by the classical archaeologists. It is a fine tradition, even if it appears too "Victorian" for present tastes.

The Antigone chapter draws me into the discussion of the "real meaning" of passages of Sophoclean Greek. This is an area where experts continue to differ, and I am no expert in ancient Greek. I have to draw here on dim memories of wet winter afternoons in an English classroom more than forty years ago where a restless teenage boy, whose mind was wholly on the forthcoming rugby game, had reluctantly to construe his appointed passage from the battered Greek or Latin text du jour. But some things, like riding a bicycle, seem hard to forget. And whatever those old-fashioned English grammar schools did wrong by more enlightened educational standards, they certainly drilled the classics into us. I took a refresher course by working through Chase and Phillips' *A New Introduction to Greek* (1982) and found nothing unfamiliar. In the intervening years I have frequently gone back and read and reread my favorites, among whom Sophocles ranks highest anyway. So, expert or not, I had to take a chance. I was very much encouraged by George Steiner, who rekindled my enthusiasm and who has written by far the best book on Antigone ever penned, yet who admits equally that he is no Greek scholar. Being a good Greek scholar, but not being otherwise well informed (for instance, anthropologically and legally) can in fact be a hindrance, as I hope to show. I do it with trepidation, however, especially as I remember the withering scorn poured on my efforts by the patient but exasperated classics master in that long-ago damp and drowsy classroom. (My greatest joy, recently, was to hear Robert Fagles, our latest and to my mind most original translator of Homer and Sophocles, pronounce my interpretation of the first line of *Antigone* to be "definitive." These are rare and beautiful moments to be treasured.)

But, for better or for worse, what this archaic education did for us was in essence an anthropological sensitization experiment: it took us, via their own languages, into the strange, alien worlds of the ancients, and made them familiar to us literally word by word. And since these cultures were ancestral to us, since we had soaked them up in the process of becoming what we are, what we learned was not just "comparative" but—how can one put it?—culturally genetic. We were actively participating in our cultural patrimony, however unwillingly. No glib courses in "Western Civ." can hope to do the same.

Being trained in the classics had another useful side effect, as Richard Jenkyns points out in his wonderful study of *The Victorians and Ancient Greece* (1980). (One should also not miss his brilliant and beautiful *Three Classical Poets* 1982.) It was in direct continuity with the Victorian scheme of classical education and so helped us to see how the otherwise often baffling Victorians saw the world. "As time separates us from the Victorians," he writes,

> the difficulty of imagining how they thought and felt grows greater. Twenty years ago a fair number of British schools were offering what was in essence a Victorian classical education, with the emphasis on the detailed reading of texts and the composition of prose and verse in both Latin and Greek. Those who were put through this mill fortuitously acquired some understanding of how part of a Victorian gentleman's mind was furnished. Today there can be very few schools that still use the old system, perhaps none.

Alas, yes. Our direct ancestors the Victorians, from whom we are still striving to differentiate ourselves, and our remote but powerful ancestors the Greeks and Romans, are slipping inexorably away from us. History is becoming bunk, or rather acceptable sound bites in glossy text books sanitized of gender-specific language. Perhaps the old system had to go, but personally I mourn the loss. It brought both "the ethnographic other" and our own tribal ancestors very close to us, and revealed the common humanity behind the cultural differences— dazzling as these were. But I digress.

Similarly, the seemingly arcane concern with the nature of the avunculate in the last chapter is not as far removed from our contemporary anxieties as its exotic subject matter suggests. For one thing, it takes us into the heart of the issue of matrilineal succession, thus balancing our concern with the patrilineal version in the case of the Greeks. But because the "special relationship" with the mother's brother is also found in patrilineal and bilateral societies, it raises the issue of the basic or derivative nature of this relationship, and so takes us back to the issue of the basic state of human kinship. And if we discover something "irreducible" in this state, then this irreducible element will be central to any discussion of family law, laws of adoption, laws of succession and inheritance, laws of paternity, etc.

I was drawn to the study of matrilineal kinship through my own experiences among the Cochiti Indians of New Mexico in the late 1950s. Most of my teachers and colleagues had dealt with patrilineal societies in Africa, New Guinea, China, and Australia, and even though I had mastered the mechanics of matrilineal systems, I was still inclined, as they were, to find matrilineal kinship odd. But after the Cochiti (and Navaho and Apache) experience, I was converted to the view that there was great natural logic and even great humanity about such systems, which were, of course, the predominant form of kinship organization in pre-Columbian North America.

In Cochiti, I was adopted into a matrilineal clan (Oak—*hapanyi*), I thought as a simple courtesy, but the proper ceremony was conducted and, I found, was taken very seriously. After the ceremony of adoption, conducted by the women, the oldest man and the oldest woman of the clan addressed me. She said, speaking for the women (I translate rather freely from the Keresan):

> You are now our child, our brother, our *nyenye* [woman's term for mothers' brothers and sisters' sons]. You need not feed us or plaster our houses—our husbands will do that—but you must see to our children, that they learn the old ways and are cunning with the new. That they marry and are good to their children and their old ones, and that they are safe from witches.

He said:

> You are now our *nawa* [reciprocal term between a man and his mother's brothers] and we are your relatives forever. You must care for our old ones and teach the little ones. You must never marry one of your clanswomen but must be guided by us in that. You must look always to the children of your "sisters" to see that they know the right way, and to your "mothers" and *nawa* to know the right way for you. You are *hapanyi*, and the children of your sisters will be *hapanyi* until they

join the *shiwanna* [ancestor spirits] in the clouds and dance with their people [i.e., clanspeople] forever.

From then on I was able to feel what it was like to be a "sister's son" and a "mother's brother" from the inside—as much as any outsider who has no real stake in the society can. And I can report that it was not hard or alien. It was something that in the context seemed wholly natural to me. The younger people were falling away from the "old ways," and their elders thought I might, with my interest in these things, persuade them to return. Well, I wrote a book that documented some of these things for them (Fox 1967)—the best an exile in Europe could do for his clan, for his sisters' sons. But I fear the forces of change have been too much, and one book cannot stem such a tide. It can however put the old ways on record and show how they worked, and in many ways worked better than the alternatives offered by Spanish priests or American television.

I spoke of the "humanity" of such systems. They all differ, of course, but the Cochiti or Navaho versions, for example, have no concept of an illegitimate child. The concept of illegitimacy is something that the Spanish priests and later American missionaries taught them. If a child has a mother, it has a clan, and that is what is important; a social pater can be added later if needed. Also, the division of labor between the father and the mother's brother (the father representing the patrilineal moiety and the mother's brother the matrilineal clan) made for a much healthier "male role model" situation than the imposition of all the elements of this role on the father. It also meant that the mother had two males (or sets of males) to call upon *by right* in meeting her and her children's social, economic, and spiritual needs.

This ability to split the "parental role" between father and brother seemed to me something peculiarly human, and I still think it is. But it is, as we shall see, probably derived from elements that were present in our primate ancestry and which we reworked into a human solution.

Again it was Radcliffe-Brown who set the terms of this debate, with his lecture on the mother's brother in South Africa, as early as 1924. This was not just a seminal paper in kinship studies; it also became a rallying point for those who wished to ditch nineteenth-century evolutionary speculations in favor of a "functional" approach based on the legal notions of "rights and duties." It also depended on a theory of "sentiments" and their extension, which was itself to be influential with later writers like Murdock (1949), who married it to behaviorist psychology and "stimulus generalization." These things are not much debated in anthropology now, where in the never-ending search for novelty we are whoring after ever stranger gods. But they are a way into the current "sociobiological" debate, and a very interesting one, since this approach too has intruded itself into the study of law, as with the work of John Beckstrom (1985) on the very subject of inheritance. The issues raised by Radcliffe-Brown in his notes to the lawyers of Iowa, and his address to the South African Association for the Advancement of Science, are still germane and do not go away because we have decided to move to the greener pastures over the intellectual hill.

Matrilineal succession and the avunculate are not institutions peculiar to a few peculiar "primitive" tribes. They are generated by universal forces that drive all systems of succession including our own, but which have particular expressions under particular circumstances. They are, to use a not very apt analogy, a bit like recessive genes: they are always there in the social-behavioral genome, but they only get expressed under certain favorable circumstances. All societies are "carriers" of these traits, even if they are not expressed, or only feebly expressed. It only takes a slight change of circumstances to bring them out. When it comes to deciding on laws of succession, we do not have too many options. We can leave property, for example, to all our children, or just to our sons, or just to our daughters (this almost never happens); or we can leave it to the children of siblings. In patrilineal societies the children of siblings would be the children of brothers, but the other option—of passing property and status to the children of sisters (most often from mother's brother to sister's son)—occurs in a sufficiently large minority of societies to deserve our ongoing concern.

Radcliffe-Brown insisted that there should be "clarity" in this business of transition, and to him that meant only two real choices: either through the male line or through the female line. We know now that systems of partible inheritance do exist, and that uncontrolled they do have the problems he foresees. We also know that they can be managed so as to limit the fragmentation of inheritances—particularly land.

After my conversion experience with the Cochiti, I had another one with the bilateral (or cognatic) Tory Islanders of North-West Ireland, who ran just such a system and neatly avoided its worst excesses by a rule of usufruct, where rights in land were held but not activated by the totality of heirs (Fox 1978). Even here, as we shall see, a potential avunculate was de facto realized as a result of the system of residence at marriage, in a society avowedly bilateral in its kinship system and ideology. But as Radcliffe-Brown also showed, it was not absent from patrilineal societies, where the privileged relationship between a man and his sister's sons, like a partially expressed social gene, illustrated that this crucial relationship was as much a part of the patrilineal scheme of things as it was of the matrilineal, although different in its expression.

To say more would be to anticipate too much of what is to follow. And the subject is so vast that many conclusions will be drawn by the reader that are not overt in my limited discussion. But I hope these two chapters will show that the step from the familiar to the exotic can be, in anthropological terms, quite short. Nothing human should be alien to anthropology, and the current insistence on the absolute otherness of the other seems to me to be massively misplaced. To borrow from Pogo: We have met the Other, and He is Us.

3

The Virgin and the Godfather: Kinship Law versus State Law in Greek Tragedy and After

Today it is Creon's secretaries who deal with the case of Antigone.

— F. Durrenmatt

Kinship or Individual: Who's against Whom?

In a rhetorical flourish at the end of my preface to the revised edition of *Kinship and Marriage* (1983), I wrote:

> The war between kinship and authority is alive in legend. In story and fantasy kinship struggles against bureaucratic authority, whether of church or state. It undermines, it challenges, it disturbs. The Mafia constantly fascinates because "the family" demands total loyalty and provides total security. When the state fails to protect, people look longingly at the certainty of kinship.

Enough. I wrote a good deal more about the "resilience" and "subversiveness" of kinship, and so on in the same vein. But a point was made to me by several colleagues that struck home. We thought,

141

they said, that the battle, in the occidental world at least, had been between the *individual* and the state or church.

Indeed, the growth and origins of individualism have been a pretty constant theme in social science and historical literature. A recent distinguished contribution from anthropology itself is Dumont's *Essays on Individualism* (1986). In this growth of individualism, it was objected, kinship—in the form of clans or extended families and the like—has been as much an enemy as the state itself. The burgeoning individual has had to throw off the kinship yoke as much as the yoke of the state in order to be fully autonomous—the creature of "contract" as opposed to "status" in Maine's classic distinction we have already explored. Do we not now, I was asked, live in a relatively "kinshipless" society in which the autonomous individual is the recognized unit, to the point where children can sue their parents for inadequate care and education, and a foetus has rights against its mother?

I would answer two things. First: the extreme assertion of individualism seems to me to be a peculiarly Anglo-Saxon affair. It may not, as is commonly held, be a product of late Renaissance humanism, the Protestant Reformation, the philosophy of John Locke, the Industrial Revolution, or any other claimed cause. It may well, as McFarlane (1978) and others have argued, go well back into Anglo-Saxon tribal custom, transferred to Britain and nurtured there with minimal Norman interference. There may never have been strong, relatively independent kinship groups in the Anglo-Saxon (and Jute and Frisian) tribes; the tribe itself may always have been superior, the individual warrior its unit. Tacitus certainly thought so. Families existed (and always have), of course, but strong independent extended families have not. Kinship was not unilineal but classically cognatic in these tribes, and the Sib (Sippe) was an ego-centered group, not a descent group (Fox 1967, chap. 6). Individual ownership of land, for example, goes way back in English history, when it was unknown among the continental peasantry. English laws of inheritance, by effectively disenfranchising younger sons, never allowed the build-up of huge aristocratic clans. The Tudors were among the first European monarchs to tame the noble houses and create a meritocratic bureaucracy. Although the great noble houses of the eighteenth-century Whig Oligarchy might have appeared to constitute a kinship system to counter state power, they were never serious challengers and disappeared in the rampant individualism of the nineteenth century, their younger sons constantly descending into the middle class.

Once the Scottish clans were once and for all defeated at Culloden and broken by the Highland clearances which sped most of the clansmen to Canada, that remnant of the kinship world was doomed (except in Sir Walter Scott-inspired sentiment that had even Queen Victoria and her German consort decked out in "authentic" Highland costume invented by canny cloth manufacturers anxious to cash in). Even so, the Duke of Argyll, as the head of the Clan Campbell, exercised an extreme influence on the English imagination with the thought that he commanded the allegiance of five thousand swordsmen; a fascination much like the one a powerful Mafia chief can exercise today in America. (Those who understood the situation knew it was the command of forty seats in the House of Commons that was his real power. But there were always those claymores ready in the background.)

The second point, then, is that we tend, as a result of our peculiar history, to see the world in terms of the inevitable struggle of individual and state, with the individual, we hope, triumphing against the state (and state church) that is always trying to infringe on his autonomy. Dumont sees this as a gradual secularizing of a religious idea of the individual. But as we have seen, the "idea" may well have been there in Anglo-Saxon institutions well before religious theories caught up with it or secularization (after Calvin) got under way. Locke, then, is our central political philosopher, not so much for any original contribution as for articulating this struggle and expressing the case for the individual. Spencer, Mill, and Marshall continued the intellectual battle against the collectivism of both left (socialists) and right (idealists) (see Parsons 1937 for what is still the best account). We have, of course, never wholly settled the issue, and continue to agonize over the proper balance. It is *the* problem of our current political lives, and our philosophers are obsessed with it. But—and this is the crux of my second point—can we wish this simplified view onto the rest of the world, and is it even so simple in our own world? For, between the individual and the state there always stands at least the family and, for most of the world, much more. However individualistic our legal systems become, for example, they always recognize the family, however defined, as being a peculiar form of social institution within which the usual individualistic rules of contract do not apply in most cases. In other systems than the Anglo-Saxon, the family is accorded a much larger role, even if the struggle I have spoken of is always present.

And there is a paradox here too. It is often put to me that the state in fact does a lot to promote the family rather than to destroy it. This is true. But it does not affect my argument, which is that the state abhors not the family but kinship. In promoting the self-sufficiency of the nuclear family unit, the state is in effect attacking the essence of kinship, which lies in the extension of consanguineal (or pseudoconsanguineal) ties beyond the family into strong and effective kinship groups. To put it another way, from the state's point of view, the highest level of kinship group it likes to see is the nuclear family, which is in fact the lowest level of operative kinship group possible that is compatible with effective reproduction and socialization of the young. To be exact, this could be done by the mother-child unit with the state as provider. But this is not the state's aim, and in fact causes it a great deal of trouble—viz., the welfare system. The state (in reality, as opposed to in utopia) prefers males to act as providers to the mother-child unit and imposes sanctions when this doesn't happen. The reasons are purely economic. But as we have seen, the state usually dislikes intensely the idea of the male supporting several mother-child units, i.e., polygyny. One could ask why the state should be concerned as long as the male can provide for them. But, religious objections aside, the state frowns on the possibility of the growth of large kinship units and actively discourages it by breaking up large inheritances and hysterically pursuing the legal-military destruction of such deviancies as the Mormon experiment. (Islamic countries are a special case since polygyny up to four wives is allowed by the Koran. But, before the fundamentalist revival, the "modernizing" leaders and parliaments of Islamic nations had actively discouraged the practice by law and example. Nevertheless, Islamic societies have still to be ranked among those where the individual acts towards the state essentially through the mediation of his kin group [see Gellner 1981].) The paradox then is that, in promoting the nuclear family, the state (or church) is paring kinship down to its lowest common denominator while appearing to support basic "kinship values."

I would argue that a lot of our intellectual life, from political philosophy to literary criticism, is biased by this late seventeenth-century Anglo-Saxon view of the world as a struggle between the state and the individual. It leads us to fail to see clearly what has been happening in history and the rest of the world as we impose this model upon it. As anthropologists, we should be sceptical of the model in the first place, and open to the possibilities of reinterpreting certain classic examples of this supposed struggle.

The Problem in *Antigone*:
The Virgin's Motives

As always, we should start with the Greeks. I am prompted to do so since so many commentators have taken Greek tragedy as the first example of the literary recognition of the "individual versus the state" struggle. And indeed, the Greek polis was the first real example of a state organization that was not kinship- and tribal-based, so it is plausible that this is where the first evidence of ideological sensitivity to the struggle should emerge. Marx certainly thought so. The great classicist who did so much to introduce anthropological ideas into the study of Greece, E. R. Dodds, waxed passionate on the very issue we are addressing:

> It was a misfortune for the Greeks that the idea of cosmic justice, which represented an advance on the old notion of purely arbitrary divine powers, and provided a sanction for the new civic morality, should have been thus associated with a primitive conception of the family. For it meant that the weight of religious feeling and religious law was thrown against the emergence of a true view of the individual as a person, with personal rights and personal responsibilities. As Glotz showed ... the liberation of the individual from the bonds of clan and family is one of the major achievements of Greek rationalism, and one for which the credit must go to Athenian democracy. But long after that liberation was complete in law, religious minds were still haunted by the ghost of the old solidarity. (Dodds 1951, 34)

It was not only religious minds that were so haunted. But Dodds beautifully expresses the "progressive-individualist" notion that has dominated our thinking on this topic: the individual had to be freed from the "bonds" of kinship and family before becoming a true person who could participate in the "new civic morality," and hence in the eventual struggle against the burgeoning morality that became the "individual versus the state" theme we are pursuing. To Dodds, the persistence of "primitive" kinship values is a hindrance in this progressive struggle.

When looking for the origins of the new individualism, commentators have looked in particular at Sophocles' *Antigone*. This, we are to suppose, displays the prototype of the dawning, individuated, almost existential conscience in its struggle with the dominance of the impersonal law of the polis and with political necessity. Since this play is part of the famous Theban "trilogy," including *Oedipus Tyrannus* and *Oedipus at Colonus*, and since the Oedipus saga has been of much interest to anthropologists in other contexts—evolutionary, structural, and psychoanalytical—it seems a good place to start.

Let us look first then at *Antigone*. I am inspired to do this by reading and rereading George Steiner's remarkable *Antigones* (1984), which was finished in the same year as my previously quoted bold remarks on kinship (i.e., 1983). No discussion of the play can ever be the same after this exhaustive analysis of all the "Antigones" that have followed—some closely, some loosely—Sophocles masterpiece, and all commentaries on them. The basic story, as given in the Argument to the Loeb Classics edition, is as follows:

> Antigone, daughter of Oedipus, the late king of Thebes, in defiance of Creon who rules in his stead, resolves to bury her brother Polynices, slain in his attack on Thebes. She is caught in the act by Creon's watchmen and brought before the king. She justifies her action, asserting that she was bound to obey the eternal laws of right and wrong in spite of any human ordinance. Creon, unrelenting, condemns her to be immured in a rock-hewn chamber. His son, Haemon, to whom Antigone is betrothed, pleads in vain for her life and threatens to die with her. Warned by the seer Teiresias, Creon repents him and hurries to release Antigone from her rocky prison. But he is too late: he finds lying side by side Antigone who has hanged herself and Haemon who has also perished by his own hand. Returning to the palace he sees within the dead body of his queen who on learning of her son's death has stabbed herself to the heart. (Smyth 1926, 311)

The play was first presented c. 440 B.C. and hence was the first of the "Theban Trilogy" (not a trilogy in the strict sense—simply three related plays), but it is the *last* episode of the legend: the culmination of the tragedy of the House of Cadmus and the ultimate fate of the children of the doomed Oedipus and his mother-wife Iocasta. We must return to Oedipus himself, inevitably, for clarification (as we must take a side glance at the equally unfortunate House of Atreus), but for the moment let us look at some of the issues raised by the actions of his children: the daughters Antigone and Ismene and the sons Eteocles and Polynices.

The plot is simple and as outlined above (except for the important information that Eteocles, the loyal brother, was also killed fighting against the rebel Polynices, and Creon buried him with honor). What has excited the huge volume of commentary, adaptations, translations, and imitations from the 1530s on is the drama of the conflict between Antigone and Creon. Commentators and adaptators have sided with one or the other, but overwhelmingly, of course, with Antigone. Hegel, in part two of the *Lectures on the Philosophy of Religion* (II.3.a.), was perhaps the first to give Creon his due, but even he called it a tie with his famous formula that the "tragedy" lay in the fact that they were both right: Creon, acting as a responsible ruler driven by "necessities of state," Antigone as a conscience-driven individual moved by deep family loyalties. In the most famous latter-day interpretation—the latest one of many for the stage—Anouilh has Antigone as an existentialist heroine acting out of individual "commitment," and Creon, again, as the reasonable representative of state authority and the law of the polis. When the play was put on in occupied Paris, both the Resistance and the Germans applauded with equal enthusiasm.

But, while attention has focussed on the Creon-Antigone struggle, no one has seriously challenged the "individual versus the state" interpretation. Of course, a lot of baggage goes along with this. Steiner (1984) lists five antinomies that are "constants of conflict in the condition of man" and with some of which, therefore, every tragedy must deal:

    men vs. women
    age vs. youth
    society vs. individual
    living vs. dead
    men vs. gods

He rephrases these later as masculinity vs. femininity; ageing vs. youth; private autonomy vs. social collectivity; existence vs. mortality;

and human vs. divine. The greatness of *Antigone*, he avers, lies in its being the only tragedy to encompass all these oppositions. (If he were a disciple of Lévi-Strauss he might add that in doing so it "overcomes" the oppositions—or, as they are puzzlingly described, "contradictions"; but Steiner is too canny for such easy overinterpretations.) I think he is right, and this is a pretty good summary of the major themes of all tragedy and of *Antigone* in particular. But I want to call attention to his insistence that it is the "individual" who is at issue in the struggle with "the state"; or "individual autonomy vs. social collectivity." Like many other commentators, Steiner sees Antigone as standing up for "family values," but he sees the "issue" as one of individual assertion of conscience in the face of the demands of "state necessity." As the most authoritative commentator on the text of *Antigone*, Sir Richard Jebb (1902) puts it squarely in his introduction:

> The simplicity of the plot is due to the clearness with which two principles are opposed to each other. *Creon represents the duty of obeying the state's laws; Antigone, the duty of listening to the private conscience.* (xviii, his emphasis)

The early Hegel is interesting in that he does see the situation as an issue of male/state versus female/family. The dead, in Greek theory, pass from the power of the state to that of the familial gods. In this passage, the supreme duty lies with the women of the family to bury their dead, thus ensuring the passage to Hades. But, says Hegel, there are times when the state does not wish to relinquish its rights, even over the corpse. This is the driving energy of the Antigone plot. (See Bradley 1909 for what is still the finest commentary in English on Hegel's meaning.) Creon (the state) wishes, for sound political reasons, to make an example of Polynices, who has committed treason by bringing foreign armies against his native city. He here obeys the "law" that the polis must be preserved at all costs. But Creon chooses to do this by denying burial to Polynices, and thus runs up against a greater and more profound law: that kin must bury their own dead to ensure their passage to the afterlife.

Let us not forget the fate of the Athenian commanders after the brilliantly successful sea battle of Arginusae. Faced with a storm that might destroy their fleet, they took their ships into safe harbor, and in doing so neglected to gather up the bodies of dead Athenian sailors.

They were tried for this impiety and executed. Socrates, who, like Creon, always put prudence before divinity, presided in the council at the time of this trial. He boldly stood against the indignant tide and refused to put the matter to the vote. Later, ironically, he was put to death himself by the same council, on a charge of impiety. At his trial (see Plato's *Apology),* Socrates cites this episode as an example of his unfitness for a political life (and as a further irony insists that he would not have been in office had it not been the turn of his *phratria,* a quasi-kinship group of which more later). But there is no question that here we do have a clash between individual and state; what I am questioning is whether there is really such a clash in Antigone's case.

The case of the admirals at Arginusae should, despite what the famous commentators have said, tell us what Antigone is about; what Sophocles really meant. Naturally, we are here on familiar if dangerous ground. How can we really know what a fifth-century Athenian really meant, or more importantly what his audience understood him to mean? But it is ground that anthropologists have often trodden. We have been trying for a long time now to explain what the myth makers of alien cultures really mean, although we have not settled on a consensus regarding method and interpretation. But here we have some texts and some scraps of history, and this is close to all we ever have, so let us not be daunted.

The Burial of the Dead: She Is Her Brother's Keeper

That it is the kin who must do the burying, and in particular the female kin (symbols of the warrior's "homecoming"—his return to the womb-tomb), has been, as I have said, regarded as part of the "baggage" that helps us interpret the essential "individual versus the state" conflict. After all, Antigone had to have something to oppose the state about, and it had to be something about which she felt deeply. But one gets the impression from many of the commentaries that any issue would have done as long as she felt strongly enough about it. I am going to suggest that the commentators have the cart before the horse, and that burial of kin is the essence of the meaning; Antigone's or Creon's "individuality" is only manifested in the *style* with which they play their conflicting "kinship" and "political" roles. The commentators, in other words, have confused style with substance. Antigone is either an appealing and courageous heroine, or an annoying, pig-headed, religious fanatic, depending on the reader's sympathies. Creon, likewise, is either the embodiment of reason or a vicious sadist (although I feel there was no doubt that Sophocles meant us to understand that Creon was in the wrong, despite Hegel's authoritative opinion to the contrary). But these individual styles are not what is at issue. They provide a kind of dramatic subplot to the main theme.

Thus, Sophocles, brilliantly, from a dramatic point of view, pits Antigone's religious fanaticism against her sister Ismene's pragmaticism: "Yes," says Ismene, " it is terrible, but there isn't a lot we can do about it, so we'd better learn to live with it." Antigone will have none of this: Polynices *must* be buried. Now, here there are interesting individual differences. But the play is not, as a modern play (say, *Long Day's Journey Into Night*) might be, *about* these differences; they give color and point to the plot, but they are not the plot itself. The issue is not Antigone's stubborn devotion to her own point of view; it is her stubborn devotion to *the divine law*. She is not an existentialist heroine before her time, given to some bloody-minded "commitment"; nor is she the supreme individualist challenging the power of the state. Above all, she is not, despite many comparisons of this kind, a sort of Joan of Arc listening to her own private voices, which she considers to have authority over all external voices. Antigone would have thought Joan a complete crackpot and paid her no attention. The truth is the contrary: Antigone is not challenging the state in the name of individual conscience; she is not challenging any law in the name of that conscience; she is upholding a law in the name of religious duty. She is, at least in my reading of Sophocles, the supreme example of the unwaveringly loyal female kinswoman doing her utmost to fulfill her duties to her kin group. If this involves her in a struggle to the death with the political authorities, so be it. She knows she represents a higher law, and after the intervention of Teiresias (the blind, sequentially hermaphrodite prophet who is the major catalyst of *Oedipus Rex* also), Creon admits this, but too late: Antigone, Haemon (his son and her betrothed), and Eurydice (his wife) are all dead.

In death, Antigone is vindicated. But what is vindicated is not her right to her individual conscience, but her adherence to a supraindividual law—almost a law of nature, at least of divine nature. This is why, to Sophocles, she is a heroine and a tragic figure. It never ceases to astonish me that her repeated insistence that she is *not* acting "individually" or "rebelliously," but in strict accordance with divine law, is taken as a manifestation of her instinct- or impulse-driven femaleness—in contrast, of course, to Creon's male "reasonableness." Although such commentators usually mean this as some sort of compliment to Antigone, they should be investigated for sexism! They amply illustrate my point that we are viewing the whole plot through our very particular "individual versus the state" spectacles, and hence are only left with Antigone's stubborn individual style.

But as I keep wearisomely repeating, this is not the issue. Ismene, despite her very different "style," in the end joins in Antigone's protest, not because she is convinced that individuals must assert themselves against the state, but because she is stung by her sister's call to religious duty. She asks Creon to let her share her sister's fate. She doesn't often get much credit for this from the commentators, and Antigone is priggishly nasty to her, while Creon dismisses it as an idle gesture. But it helps to make my point. The "individual" issues for Sophocles are matter for personal conflict and dramatic effect; they are not what the play is about. Thus, the moment when Ismene tearfully asks Creon to bury her alive with Antigone is, for me, a supreme moment of the play. It must have drawn a gasp of relief, admiration, and approval from the seventeen thousand Athenians in the Theater of Dionysus. The other surviving female of the House of Laius had come back to her duty, despite her all-too-understandable individual and womanly fears. The kinship group had closed ranks against the state, and the beleaguered Creon was more than ever on the defensive after this.

The Issue in the Epics:
No State to Speak Of

Although the language of the *Iliad* and the *Odyssey* echoes throughout the Greek tragedies, Antigone's theme could never have arisen in these epics. There could not have been a conflict of individual or kinship versus the state because there was no state; there were only tribal groups and tribal loyalties. People could disobey their tribal rulers, of course, but this was more like a child disobeying a parent than a citizen defying a bureaucracy. Both rulers and followers were expected to keep divine laws.

Antigone belongs to this archaic world, which is why Creon, the embodiment of the polis, couldn't stand her. There could have been no Antigone in the *Iliad*, for there everyone was under the rule of the gods; the state did not stand apart with its secular purposes. Thus, there could have been no Creon either.

Students discover this when made to think about the difference between the two great quarrels: that of Antigone versus Creon, and Achilles versus Agamemnon. The latter is often misinterpreted. Students are often angry with Achilles. While they recognize he had a legitimate personal complaint against Agamemnon, they do not see why he went as far as he did in refusing to fight for "his fellow Greeks." It has to be pointed out that he had no "fellow Greeks" in any nationalistic sense. This notion is ours, and neither the protagonists nor the other Greeks shared it. They knew that the alliance of tribes that sailed for Troy was a loose agglomeration of (often related) tribal chiefs of whom Agamemnon, while more than simply *primus inter pares* was nevertheless no more than, say, the High King of Ireland—an almost ritual leader with limited powers over his territorial "kings." He could summon them to war, but he had no power to keep them there.

The Greeks were not engaged in a "great patriotic war"—a nationalist struggle—but in a raiding expedition on the coast of Asia Minor in which the siege of Troy was one incident: the one that gets related in the *Iliad*. Thus, Achilles was quite within his rights to behave as he did to force his point, even at the expense of "his fellow Greeks." Sir Moses Finley (1979), as usual, puts it succinctly:

> The fact is that such a notion of social obligation is fundamentally non-heroic. It reflects the new element, the community, at the one point at which it was permitted to override everything else, the point of defense against an invader. In the following generations, when the community began to move from the wings to the centre of the Greek stage, the hero quickly died out, for the honor of the hero was purely individual, something he lived and fought for only for its own sake and his own sake. (Family attachment was permissible, but that was because one's kin were indistinguishable from oneself.) The honor of a community was a totally different quality, requiring another order of skills and virtues: in fact, the community could grow only by taming the hero and blunting the free exercise of his prowess, and a domesticated hero was a contradiction in terms. (Pages 116-117)

But this "new community"—the incipient state—did not exist yet in the epics. So, while the Greeks wanted their hero back, and even deplored his refusal of Agamemnon's overtures of peace, they never questioned his right to sail home, as he threatened to do several times. Even Agamemnon conceded that Achilles was right, and pleaded temporary insanity—"Zeus made me do it." Thus, at this tribal stage of Greek society the issue does not arise, as it does not arise in any tribal society, or in any conglomerate of tribes, or even in primitive divine monarchies. Spencer, and Durkheim following him, may have been going a bit far when they said that at this stage of social evolution individuals did not exist, except for chiefs. But one knows what they meant. It is why only the doings of chiefs are reported in the *Iliad*, and why Aristotle was led therefore to think that tragedy could only be about "noble persons." *Death of a Salesman* would have been incomprehensible as a tragic subject, and until the nineteenth-century novel, salesmen and their like were fit subjects only for comedy.

In the epics we *can* have a conflict between individual and society. This is often the essence of them. But "society" is here not understood as "state." (The failure to make this distinction, Dumont points out—following Sir Ernest Barker—vitiates many of the arguments of Locke and Rousseau.) Rather, society is the culture, the way of life, the "proprieties" in Havelock's terms (Havelock 1978). The epic teaches the proprieties by showing the awful consequences of their breach. Thus, in the *Iliad*, it is Agamemnon himself who breaches the proprieties and brings about the disaster. Achilles only breaches them in the sense of over-reacting, both to Agamemnon's insult and later in despoiling Hector's body. But in a sense both of these were "acceptable" behavior in a hero when the "wrath" had come upon him (Redfield 1975; Friedrich 1977). And he mends both offenses: he makes up with Agamemnon and accepts his apology (and unbelievable oath that Briseis is still a virgin), and he restores Hector's body to Priam. Again, we have the assertion of the primacy of proper burial in the hierarchy of proprieties. (For an interesting account of burial as a clue to understanding Greek society and "state," see Morris 1987).

But in no case of the "individual versus society" conflicts do we have a quarrel between individuals and the state. In Creon's case, he does not act as a tribal chieftain with a grievance against a subject, but as the chief executive officer of a constitutional monarchy, answerable, in the end, to the citizens of the polis. He does not act purely for spite or personal gain, but out of necessities of state. The cases are parallel only in that, in the wider context of the "proprieties," it is Creon, like Agamemnon, who is the offender, and Antigone, like Achilles, who is the offended party (and she too "overreacts"). But this is an appeal precisely to those more archaic values of the epic, and the audience would have well understood this. Antigone offended against the perceived necessity of "state interests"; Creon offended against "what was done."[34]

If one does not distinguish between these cases, then much confusion is inevitable. It is one thing to offend sacredly established custom, another to break a municipal ordinance. Creon understood this, and hence the strength of Antigone's appeal, by trying himself to invoke the "gods of the city" or even the "divinity of kingship" (*Zeus Basileus*), almost contemptuously handing over to Antigone what he had hypocritically tried to claim for himself: the "Zeus of blood-kinship" (*Zeus Homaimos*), or the "Zeus of the Family Hearth" (*Zeus Herkeios*). But his appeal was limited. Only one person can be a king, while everyone has a family. And to deny proper burial went even beyond what the divinities of the polis could plausibly demand.

What we must grasp is that at the tribal stage allegiance was personal, familial, based on kinship or pseudokinship. The war between kinship and the state had not begun, because the tribe was, conceptually, a large kinship group, and the "individual" was defined by his kinship status and kin-group membership. There were tribal "assemblies" that all the warriors attended, and these have a superficial look of the polis assembling in the agora to debate. Indeed, the Homeric poets might have read certain practices of the town assembly back into the gatherings of the *Iliad*, and, conversely, these assemblies of equal citizens might well have originated in the old tribal assemblies. But in the *Iliad* the assembled troops were essentially brought in as witnesses to the doings of the chieftains. In an oral culture, as Eric Havelock (1978) points out, decisions could not be written down; they had to be remembered. And for truly important decisions, the collective memory was necessary as a witness. Also, the "sense of the meeting" could be taken, since it was important for the leaders to know how far they could carry the armies with them. But these gatherings were not assemblies of citizens for the purpose of taking votes. As Finley (1979, 110) points out, these assemblies were "passive spectators." "The defense of a right was purely a private matter." He adds that the poet "was composing at a time when the community principle had advanced to a point of some limited public administration of justice. But he was singing of a time when that was not the case, except for the intangible power of public opinion."

By the time in which the poet sets the *Odyssey,* the "limited public administration of justice" had not advanced much, but the idea was taking shape. The polis definitely existed in Ithaca. At the beginning, Telemachus takes his complaints against the suitors to a not very sympathetic assembly in the agora. At the end, when he and Odysseus have dispatched the suitors, their followers go to the agora and justify themselves—not without lively debate and dissension, especially since most of the citizens there were relatives of the suitors. Here a notion of the secular state and secular purposes emerges, and the characters of the *Odyssey,* even down to the lowly swineherd ally of our heroes, are that much more "individual." Odysseus has here been transformed from a tribal "king" to a very powerful nobleman, himself subject to the laws of the political community. At this stage, even a "king" was as often as not a *turannos*—a tyrant. This to the Greeks was not necessarily an evil kind of government (although in its bad form it could turn into that), but one that ultimately drew its legitimacy from the acquiescence of the governed, rather than from right of descent. Oedipus was, we must remember, as the correct title of the play (rather than its Romanization to "Rex" that we regularly use) insists, a *turannos* as far as Thebes was concerned. Had the Thebans recognized him from the start as their true "Rex," he would have been "Basileus." Creon too was a *turannos,* for although he had a shadowy claim by descent to the throne of Thebes, it was only in the "usurper" line. Nevertheless, he was the chief official of a polis and was ultimately answerable to it; he was not a tribal chief or oriental despot. And while one can say with confidence that, by any definition, a "state" existed with the fully developed Greek polis, it can be argued that an equally fully developed idea of the autonomous individual was something that itself came even later—after Plato and Aristotle and with the the development of Hellenistic thought (Dumont 1986). Even so, Socrates' quarrel was clearly that of an individual with the Athenian state, and as such was not like Antigone's with Creon in this crucial aspect: Socrates had no mediating kin group that he represented in his quarrel; he stood alone, and, indeed, like Joan of Arc, listened to his voices—his *daemon.*

To summarize: the "state" in Sophocles' mythical Thebes had a somewhat more advanced form than that of Homer's Ithaca but not as advanced as Athenian democracy. It was not yet at the point where all the free (male) citizens voted, but it was at the point where they assembled and voiced opinions, and where a tyrant could not rule with impunity. But there was a rudimentary "public administration of justice." Creon had laws and police to enforce them, and everyone, including the royal family, was expected to obey them; definitely a step above the self-help system described by Finley for archaic society. Thus, we can speak here of a genuine "individual/family versus the state" issue: there was a state because, in the classical formulation, there was a sovereign who claimed a monopoly of the legitimate use of force.

Problem Passages:
Odd Words and Sorry Poets

We shall return to this theme as well as look at the reality of kinship and political institutions in Athens, but for the moment let us see what the raw text has to offer to support my thesis. A good place to start is the first line. *Totus locus vexatus* was an early despairing commentary, and this is puzzling since Sophocles was not one to waste an opening statement. *Antigone's* performance did not take place in a theater where it was fashionable to arrive ten minutes late. It was performed as part of a religious festival dedicated to the god Dionysus, and seventeen thousand Athenians sat on hard stone benches in the hot sun to watch the comedy and the satyr play as well as the prize-winning tragedy. And *Antigone* was to become the most popular tragedy of them all.

This was a religious occasion, not secular entertainment, and the audience expected a religious message not a humanistic moral. (This should help us in interpreting the "meaning.") So they were silent, even reverent, and totally expectant, when the masked male actor representing Antigone addressed his counterpart playing Ismene.

Would Sophocles have fed the audience an unintelligible line? Of course not—see his other plays. The opening line of *Oedipus Tyrannus* clearly addresses the Thebans as members of the lineage of Cadmus:

'Ω τέκνα, Κάδμου τοῦ πάλαι νέα τροφή,

Children, new raised to Cadmus of old time.

In the opening of *Oedipus at Colonus,* he clearly states his old age, his blindness, and his relationship to Antigone:

Τέκνον τυφλοῦ γέροντος 'Αντιγόνη, τίνας

Child of a blind old man, Antigone ...

Why then the despair of the commentators and the confusion of the translators over the first line of *Antigone*? The line has been translated in wildly different ways; the latest poet-translator, Stephen Spender, simply abandons the attempt and starts without it. Yet the line, which for me does what it is supposed to do and sets the theme of the play, is of great anthropological interest:

῏Ω κοινὸν αὐτάδελφον 'Ισμήνης κάρα,

O koinon autadelphon Ismenes kara

Here is a sample of translations, with the name of translator and the date of translation:

Own sister of my blood, one life with me. (L. Campbell 1896)

Ismene, sister, mine own dear sister. (R. C. Jebb 1900)

Ismene, sister of my blood and heart. (F. Storr 1912)

O sister, Ismene, dear, dear sister Ismene! (E. F. Watling 1947)

Ismene, dear sister. (D. Fitts and R. Fitzgerald 1947)

My sister, my Ismene. (E. Wyckoff 1954)

Come, Ismene, my own dear sister, come! (P. Roche 1958)

My own flesh and blood—dear sister, dear Ismene. (R. Fagles 1984)

(I would have quoted Yeats, but he took it from the French, not the original, so it isn't helpful.)[35]

Obviously, "sister" and "Ismene" can be agreed on, but little else. There is, for example, despite the translators' fondness for it, no possessive pronoun in the line at all. As for Roche's invocation to "come" (twice), even his eloquent plea for poetic feeling and nuance over mere literal accuracy does not justify calling this a "translation." But if we look at it word by word, we see that "translation" is impossible if we mean literal translation, which might look something like this:

O kinsperson, selfsame-sister, Ismene's head.

But even with the first noun we are in trouble, for *koinon* means "kindred person" and, according to Jebb, "refers simply to birth from the same parents." But it is also etymologically related to, for example, *koine*, the "vulgar" or "common" language, and can suggest "commonality," or "communality" as we use its English equivalent in expressions like "a kindred spirit." The second term is "sister" with an intensifier that means "full" or "true"—literally "self" or "same." This is perhaps the least problematical term (except for the proper noun), but what are we to make of "Ismene's head"? Except in the eccentric translation of Hölderlin, the head never appears literally, and everyone takes it as a periphrasis. What exactly it meant to fifth-century Athenians we just don't know. Even Jebb (1902, 49) is driven to find Latin parallels—it "usu. implies respect, affection, or both," he says—and the translators have, with relief, taken this to heart. But of course we often, in Indo-European languages, use body parts as kinship metaphors, speaking, for example, of the "head of a family." Steiner seems to suggest this in his proposed "literal" translation of the line:

O my very own sister's shared, common head of Ismene.

But it seems to me that this both gains and loses at the same time. The intrusive possessive pronoun has shown up again, and there is nothing in the original Greek, grammatically or otherwise, to suggest that the head is common or shared. The probable relation of *koinon* to *kara* is that both may suggest "springing from the same source" (if we can have "godhead" then we can have "kinhead," if you like). Thus, the idiom, which must have meant something forceful to Sophocles' audience, probably reinforced the opening word directly. It is not so much that the head is common, as that Antigone and Ismene share a common "source." Remember that Athena was born from the head of Zeus—a point to which we shall return—so this is not such a far-fetched idea in the Greek context. (And note how Sophocles relentlessly uses kinship words to introduce all three plays: children, child, kinswoman.)

But, we then might ask, why is Antigone saying this? If Ismene is her true (full) sister, then *of course* they are kin and share common descent. She knows this, Ismene knows it, Sophocles knows it, and the audience knows it. But surely this is the point. Sophocles chooses to open the play with a line that trebly stresses their common blood—their relatedness by descent—because this is precisely what the play is *about*. And a failure to see this clearly as *the* theme of the play—not "Antigone as Joan of Arc"—leads often to an unnecessary overinterpretation of the line. Its plain, unadorned statement is its strength. It says: "this play is about kinship, folks, and the bonds that unite those of common blood—particularly siblings." It signals this issue as much as the opening line of *Oedipus Tyrannus* signals the unity and common curse of the people of Thebes as the lineal descendants of Cadmus (with the added irony, surely not lost on the sophisticated Athenian audience, that Oedipus does not believe himself to be of that line and hence not governed by its fate.) With the first line of *Antigone* we are immediately at the center of the action: the sisters, as the last living members of the line of common descent, have all the duties of the women of the line thrust upon them. It is their burden, and they must share it totally and without reservation. Indeed, this is what Antigone goes on to say in detail to Ismene (interestingly, using the Greek dual form, which she drops after Ismene's demurral).[36]

But it is all telegraphed in that first line, which alerts the audience precisely to the meaning of the *agon*—the struggle that is to follow. It is captured quite well in the paraphrase with which Don Taylor opened his BBC TV production of the play in 1987:

Ismene, listen, the same blood flows in both our veins, the blood of Oedipus.

Steiner (1984) and Knox (Fagles and Knox 1984) hover close to seeing this and could be quoted at length for their many mentions of "kinship"—indeed it is inescapable if one looks at the words squarely. But ultimately even these most astute of commentators overinterpret, because still hanging in there is the Joan of Arc syndrome: the idea of Antigone as supreme individualist. For all its strangeness, Hölderlin's marvellous German coinage perhaps comes closest to the essence of the line:

Gemeinsamschwesterliches, o Ismenes Haupt!

"A willed monster" Steiner calls it—and I cannot do it justice. But anthropologists will instantly recognize the *Gemein* as the root of *Gemeinschaft*—a word they are totally familiar with from Tönnies (1887) in its contrast to *Gesellschaft*. Tönnies was stressing the difference between the natural community based on kinship ties with the "association" based on individual contract. (It is Maine's distinction in another guise of course.) Thus, it is the "kinship community of the sisters" that is captured in Hölderlin's word, while Ismene's head is left uninterpreted, which is just as well. (When I presented the word to a bilingual informant—my department chairman, in fact—and asked for his spontaneous response, he answered, "sisterly togetherness.") Goethe and Schiller may have laughed out loud at some of Hölderlin's seeming blunders, but his bold coinage here seems to hit the mark better than Goethe's weak "most sisterly of sisters." If I had to render the "head" into some English equivalent, I would try a first line something like this:

O kinswoman, true sister-in-descent, Ismene.

Now, this is not intended as a mellifluous "literary" translation, nor is it "literal," but it is directed at anthropologists who have their own idioms that others find hard to handle, just as the Athenians had theirs. By insisting on the jargon-word "descent," I should be flagging, for such an audience, an interpretation heavy with meaning, just as Sophocles did for his specialized audience with his in-group jargon-word "head." The subconscious processes will be at work as I continue. So let them ferment while I try to make some sense of the most disputed passage in the play. (In trying to explain the "head" problem to audiences—the fact that although we know the literal meanings of words their idiomatic use may escape us—I ask them to imagine a critic of the future, some two thousand years hence, faced with a few scattered texts from an almost lost civilization, and not having much idea of the context, finding "cool" contrasted with "square"—or "gay" contrasted with "straight." He would be driven into paroxysms of ingenuity in trying to make sense of these distinctions.)

A way into the famous disputed passage is perhaps via Hegel who has been much criticized for his "two rights make a wrong" analysis but who always, to his credit, insisted that the struggle ultimately was between the family and the state—or rather between family values and civic values. But then Hegel too was protesting against the overindividualized interpretation of society. This does not prevent him, however, from falling back into it where Antigone is concerned. Thus, Steiner points to Hegel's distinction between *Kriegstaat* (the "war state") and *Privatrecht* ("private right"), which has to do with "preservation of the family." But one still has the feeling that ultimately this "family" is really a kind of emotional resource for the individual, who is the real point of the struggle. Thus, Steiner summarizing Hegel says: "The division between polis and individual itself reflects the engagement of the Absolute in temporality and in phenomenal contingencies." And so on in the same vein.[37]

The problem here is precisely with "the family." What *is* it? Much that is eloquent about family values is said in the commentaries. Thus, for Hegel and those who follow him, the state only values a man for his actions; the family values him for himself. In this, the relationship of brother and sister is paramount, being a nonerotic valuing-of-another-for-himself relation between man and woman, the two poles of the human dialectic. And so on. Actually, in light of modern genetics, one might quibble with Hegel's contention that because siblings have no reproductive interest in each other they are not "estranged by self-interest." Each has, in fact, an exact, measurable ($r = .25$) inclusive-fitness-maximizing interest in the other. But be that as it may, it does not help us any more than Hegel's "non-reproductive" formula does in understanding the real meaning of "family" or "kinsperson" in *Antigone*.

We are cursed, in a way, in English, in having the dual Latin and Germanic inheritance, since it has given us the two words "family" and "household." Once a language has two words, it will invent a conceptual distinction between them, whether one was there originally or not. (Thus, "cow" becomes the live animal, and "beef" the consumable dead flesh.) Most languages do not make the "family/household" distinction that has led anglophone anthropologists sadly astray. The Roman *familia*, like its Greek counterpart, *oikos*, was not thought of apart from the household, and the latter could include other relatives, servants, and slaves. It is interesting that the *Oxford English Dictionary* still prefers as its primary definition: "Members of a household, parents, children, servants etc." Even etymologically the two words may be related in some proto-Indo-European *fa- or *ha- (Sanskrit dha-), meaning "neighborhood," their derivatives being diminutives of some kind (Partridge 1983). But between the household on the one hand and the *sib* or *Sippe*, the *curia* or *gens*, and the *phratria* or *genneta* on the other, there was no intervening "family" in either Germanic or Graeco-Roman society. (The same is true in Celtic, the only other language/culture of this group with which I am thoroughly familiar.) There were "relatives" of course *(cognati* or *kind* or *muintir)*, but these were not a social group; they were a category, of which the "family" was the coresidential unit.

"House," of course, was often used metaphorically to refer to a noble line, as in "The House of Stuart." But again, this was neither a family nor a household but a lineage. Even if our commentaries were to replace "family values" with "kinship values"—which would be more accurate perhaps—we still have to ask "what kinship values?" The particularistic values that Hegel and his followers describe most certainly apply universally to kinship; but as we all know, who is or is not kin, and even among that wide category, what *kind* of kin (no pun intended) is very variable. The values apply, but to whom? Simply to talk about "family values" in this universalistic fashion will not do, especially when one knows that it is some modern concept of "the family" that the commentator has in mind and that cannot even have existed for the fifth-century Greeks.[38]

Thus, for example, for the Hegelians, Steiner states that "in death, the husband, son or brother, passes from the domain of the polis back to that of the family" (1984, 34). These males become the "familial" responsibility of "woman," and where the task falls upon the sister it "takes on the highest degree of holiness." Well, this may be true in a world where "absolutes engage in temporality" and the like, but was it true for the Greeks? And for the Greeks of all eras?

Actually, for the fifth-century Greeks of Sophocles' audience it might have approximated the truth, since the decline of kinship-based groups and their replacement with voluntary associations and territorial units (*demes*) was well on its way after the reforms of Cleisthenes (Murray 1986). Even so, membership more often than not passed from father to son, and women were excluded. Sophocles himself eloquently describes the fate of women in their being "exiled" from their father's house on marriage (in a fragment—#583—from the otherwise lost play *Tereus*). A patriarchal, if not strictly patrilineal, ethos prevailed in Athens even when citizenship and contract had already displaced kinship and status to a large extent. But we must remember that Antigone and her people belonged to an older, aristocratic, and monarchical age when kinship, for the noble families at least, was more thoroughly patrilineal in the technical sense. This still remained in the Athens of Sophocles in the form of the *gennetai*—the aristocratic religious groups that monopolized the priesthoods and more important city cults. Sophocles' audience then would expect the *Antigone* to reflect the archaic and royal conceptions of kinship, not the vulgar, democratic concept that dominated the lives of most of them. Antigone was, let us remember, not a daughter of the people. She was a princess of a royal house only a few generations removed from the gods themselves, being a direct descendant (in the male line) of Cadmus, through his wife Harmonia of Ares and Aphrodite, and through Cadmus' father, King Agenor, of the unfortunate Io and Zeus himself. She was also, through another of Zeus' dalliances, a cousin of Dionysus at whose festival, and in whose theater, her story was being told.

Let us keep this in mind as we look at the disputed passage. It occurs during Antigone's sad and beautiful lament for her fate, so often quoted (lines 891-928). She interrupts the lament with a passage of bitterness and casuistry that seems so at variance with her high ethical position that many who have loved the play, from Goethe onwards, have insisted that it is an interpolation by some other hand.

Goethe prayed that some scholar would be able to prove once and for all that it was indeed an alien interpolation. None of the doubters, however, seem able to suggest why anyone should have wanted to insert the passage! But this lack of motive has not stopped the endless scholarly wrangling, with the "experts" variously dismissing it as not worthy of Sophocles or praising it as the essence of Sophoclean brilliance. Aristotle did not doubt its authenticity, and had a high regard for Antigone's casuistry. This alone should give us pause. If Aristotle of all people regarded it as "logical," then who are we to question it? And remember that he was working with an earlier and more authentic text than we possess. But Goethe continued with his prayers, and several scholars obliged with *obiter dicta*. Jebb, perhaps the greatest of the textual critics, feels that Sophocles' son Iophon, or some other "sorry poet," must have been responsible, but again, he never says why (Jebb 1902, 182). And why did Aristotle accept it? Could it again be our modern sensibilities getting in the way of what was, for Sophocles and his audience, and for Aristotle, a very straightforward statement of archaic, aristocratic fact?

I will give the original here for accuracy of reference, and then quote the translation of Fagles (in Fagles and Knox 1984) since it seems to me true to the original and does not present the same problems of translation as the first line. Antigone speaks of how she performed the obsequies for her father, mother, and brother Eteocles, but is now being punished for trying to do the same thing for Polynices. Then she launches into the disputed lines.

> οὐ γάρ ποτ᾽ οὔτ᾽ ἂν εἰ τέκνων μήτηρ ἔφυν,
> οὔτ᾽ εἰ πόσις μοι κατθανὼν ἐτήκετο,
> βίᾳ πολιτῶν τόνδ᾽ ἂν ᾐρόμην πόνον.
> τίνος νόμου δὴ ταῦτα πρὸς χάριν λέγω;
> πόσις μὲν ἄν μοι κατθανόντος ἄλλος ἦν,
> καὶ παῖς ἀπ᾽ ἄλλου φωτός, εἰ τοῦδ᾽ ἤμπλακον·
> μητρὸς δ᾽ ἐν Ἅιδου καὶ πατρὸς κεκευθότοιν
> οὐκ ἔστ᾽ ἀδελφὸς ὅστις ἂν βλάστοι ποτέ.

> Never, I tell you.
> if I had been the mother of children
> or if my husband died, exposed and rotting—
> I'd never have taken this ordeal upon myself,

never defied our people's will. What law,
you ask, do I satisfy with what I say?
A husband dead there might have been another.
A child by another too, if I had lost the first.
But mother and father both lost in the halls of Death
no brother could ever spring to light again.

What has upset the whole line of commentators from Goethe onwards is, in the first place, Antigone's seeming glaring inconsistency. Having been the high ethical defender of "familial values," she now seems to dump half the "family" she is supposed to be devoted to! Husbands and children don't count, it seems. Now, she has never, throughout the play, said they *did* count! She has only insisted that she has to bury her brother. It is the commentators, bringing to the lines their own notions of "family" and "familial" who scream "inconsistent." They are even more outraged by the "casuistry" in which she appears to justify her "inconsistencies." One can get another husband, she says, other children, but since her parents are dead, there can be no more brothers. Aristotle thought this a good defence and cited it as an example to follow. Personally, I see it as unnecessary. She did not need to defend her position. I suspect, however, that Sophocles felt that some of his audience might not fully grasp what she was saying, or might need to be reminded what the "familial values" were that she was defending, and so put in the "casuistry" to make her position clearer. It was not in fact casuistry at all, but simple clarification.

Patrilineal Ideology:
The Man Is Father to the Child

Even those who believe the lines to be genuine do not seem happy to take them at face value. Sophocles certainly wrote them, they say, but the lines *are* inconsistent, so we must explain with great subtlety the nature of the inconsistency, thus rendering it intelligible. Watling (1947, 167), in his notes, maintains that these lines are "possibly a spurious interpolation," but he doesn't say why anyone would have interpolated them in the first place. Some editors, he says, have considered them "logically and psychologically inappropriate." However, he argues, "on the supposition that Antigone, in her last despair, gives utterance to an inconsistent and even unworthy thought, the passage seems to me to be dramatically right." There we have it: the thought is inconsistent and unworthy, but Sophocles probably wanted us to realize that Antigone was breaking down under the strain. Why then, we might ask, did she utter such a seemingly cunning and casuistical argument, which impressed Aristotle with its cogency? Other commentators often come closer. Thus, Steiner, for example, stresses Antigone's "aloneness" and attributes her outburst to "shallow but momentarily dazzling rhetorical ingenuity which marked her father's style" (1984, 280). It is her "extremity" which forces her into this "Herodotean plea." It is "the sophistry whereby she would prove the unique status of a dead brother as against all other losses." But does she prove it against *all* other losses? Actually not: only against the loss of husband or children. She has already performed the lustrations for mother and father, and where it concerns males, she never excludes the father from consideration, only the husband and son. Even though Creon, for instance, is her mother's brother, it is clear she would never include him among those who deserve her "devotion unto death" in the matter of burial.

Unfortunately, her father Oedipus had no brothers or paternal nephews, or we could have clinched the argument if she had included (or not excluded) these. For, if we assume that she is here asserting a strict aristocratic-patrilineal view of kinship, it is indeed totally logical to exclude the husband and son. Neither of these are members of *her* royal patriline—of her own patrilineage. The lineage—or in the Greek usage, the "house"—in question is of course that of Labdacus and Laius (ultimately of Cadmus—back to the first line of *Oedipus Tyrannus* again), and Knox in one of the most perceptive contemporary commentaries recognized this:

> It is her fanatical devotion to one particular family, her own, the doomed, incestuous, accursed house of Oedipus, and especially to its most unfortunate member, the brother whose corpse lay exposed to the birds and dogs. (Fagles & Knox 1984, 49)

He points out that her repudiation of husband and son is not wholly hypothetical, since she has indeed sacrificed her marriage to Haemon and the children that might have issued from it. But even Knox sees this declaration as a "moment of self-discovery" when she realizes she is "absolutely alone." She identifies "the driving force behind her action, the private, irrational imperative," and so on. Although he comes close, Knox still feels some elaborate explanation is required. He cannot take her words at face value because, like the others, he does not know what that value is.

For those who are not anthropologists and for whom the transparency of patrilineal ideology may not be so obvious, let me simply diagram the relationships as they would appear patrilineally. (see diagram 3.1).

In diagram 3.1, the line of Laius, going back to Cadmus (the brother of Europa), is in "balanced opposition" to the line of Menoeceus, going back to Echion of the Spartoi (who sprang from the dragon's teeth sown by Cadmus). And indeed, the throne of Thebes has passed back and forth, by marriage and usurpation, between the two lines. As Bernal (1987) points out, in legend, accepted as based on historical truth by Hesiod and the Greeks generally, Kadmos (Cadmus) was a Phoenician who founded Thebes, bringing with him the Canaanite alphabet, which he taught to the Greeks. If we wish, we could take the Cadmean line back at least to Agenor, King of Argos, one of the sons

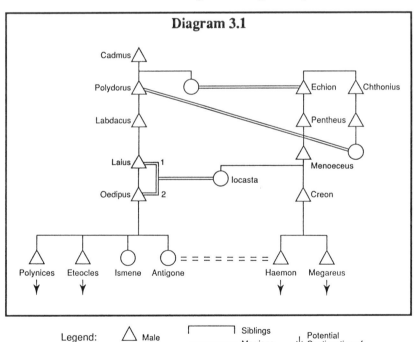

Diagram 3.1

of Io and Zeus. The Spartoi, springing from the ground, could well represent an autochthonous (Pelasgian?) lineage usurped by the immigrant line, or in turn usurping it.[39] There were a number of important marriages between the lineages, and the impending marriage of Haemon and Antigone would have been the last in the series. Its failure brought the dynastic story to a close in a sense wholly appropriate to tragedy: it was consummated in death and entombment. (We don't know what happened to Ismene, but there was no one of Creon's line left to marry her and carry on that lineage, so for purposes of this story she becomes sadly irrelevant.)

According to Antigone's theory (the ideology of patrilineal relatedness), Antigone herself would have been responsible for the children of her brothers, for example (except that they didn't have any), but not for those of her husband (i.e., her own children). None of this means she would not have *joined in* the lustral rites; she obviously would have. As we have seen, a wife was thoroughly incorporated into her husband's household and would have joined the women of the household in mourning the death of a member. Thus, Antigone had helped perform the rites for Iocasta, her mother. But what she is saying in her speech is that she would not have felt an obligation to defy the state unto death to perform such rites. That obligation she felt only for her patrilineal kin. In these matters, royal women in Greece were not nearly so isolated from their "houses" of origin as common women. No matter whom they married, they remained a "daughter" of their father's house first and foremost, and continued their attachments to it. As an example, think of the behavior of Olympias, the mother of Alexander the Great, who was constantly returning to her father's house to plot against her husband, Philip of Macedon (Lane Fox 1973).

What Antigone is saying, then, in her casuistry, is in effect: "there is no way in which the the royal line of Cadmus/Laius/Oedipus could be continued now that my brothers are dead. Polynices was the last male of that line and my duty was to him. Sons and husbands I could have had, but they would not replace him or continue the line; they would only perpetuate their own line. Therefore my duty to him was absolute and final." Thus, viewed as a statement of patrilineal ideology and its obligations, her "casuistry" is logical. It is a plain statement of the facts and can be taken absolutely at face value. And this patrilineal ideology, as we know, is deep-rooted not only in the Greek but in the general Indo-European past, as exemplified in the "Omaha" kinship terminology of proto-Indo-European (see Friedrich 1966; Benveniste 1969).

I was alerted to this issue in Greek tragedy by the more obvious case of Orestes in the *Eumenides* of Aeschylus. There, Apollo defends Orestes against the charge brought by the Furies that in killing his mother (Clytemnestra) in revenge for the murder of his father (Agamemnon), he laid himself open to death at their hands as the avengers of murdered kin. This was their job—a dirty one, but someone had to do it—since parricide could not go unpunished. Many anthropologists from McLennan in his *Studies in Ancient History* (1876) onwards have been fascinated by this passage. Let me quote it here since it is of obvious anthropological interest. Apollo has brought Orestes to Athens, where Athena has promised a fair trial. The Furies (Erinyes) are the accusers—the chorus in fact—and Apollo the defense counsel. Athena is the judge, and a jury of twelve Athenians has been empanelled. The Furies make their final accusation and Apollo makes his final clinching argument as follows (from Smyth 1926):

CHORUS: Mark now the meaning of thy plea for acquittal! Shall he who has spilled upon the ground his mother's kindred (homaimon) blood, shall he thereafter inhabit his father's house in Argos? To what altars of common worship shall he have access? What brotherhood (phrateron) will admit him to its lustral rite?

APOLLO: This too I will set forth, and mark how rightful shall be my answer. The mother of what is called her child is not its parent, but only the nurse of the newly implanted germ. The begetter is the parent, whereas she, as a stranger for a stranger, doth but preserve the sprout, except God shall blight its birth. And I will offer thee a sure proof of what I say: fatherhood there may be when mother there is none. Here at hand is a witness, the child of Olympian Zeus—and not so much as nursed in the darkness of the womb, but such a scion as no goddess could bring forth.

Smyth, in a footnote (number 334) makes two interesting comments. The Furies ask among what "kin," "clan," or "brotherhood" Orestes may perform the lustral rites. "Brotherhood" is the more correct translation of *phratria* since, apart from its etymological connections with the Indo-European root for "brother" (e.g., Latin frater), as Smyth observes, "kinsfolk, actual or fictitious, were united in *phratriai* with common worship, offerings, and festivals." But the *phratriai* were not descent groups in the anthropological sense. Kin of any connection could be inducted into them, and nonkin, upon adoption, became pseudokin—a kind of *compadrazgo* system: the first stirrings of the Godfather. Thus, the Furies here are asserting a kind of bilateral or cognatic or even fictive notion of kinship. This is interesting in view of Smyth's next note, where he gives examples of the patrilineal ideology of procreation in other Greek authors (especially Euripides) and says: "This passage in the play has been invoked as evidence that the Athenians of the fifth century B.C. were upholding some ancient mode of tracing descent from the mother (the argument of the Erinyes); others, the patrilinear theory advocated by Apollo."

Smyth obviously had McLennan and others of the "matriarchal origins" persuasion in mind, and indeed this is still alive and well in the works of Mary Renault (suitably seasoned with Frazer) and Robert Graves, to say nothing of its resurrection by some feminists. But there is no historical evidence for this, and indeed the internal evidence suggests that the Greek playwrights and audience expected the Erinyes to avenge *all* murdered parents—not just mothers. Why, it is asked, did they not visit vengeance on Clytemnestra for killing Agamemnon? Obviously, a husband is not kin to his wife, they reply. And note that Antigone invokes the same principle. But Apollo counters with the argument that neither is a son kin to his mother—for example, Athena, who sprang from the "head" (again) of Zeus without maternal intervention: a not too subtle attempt to sway the judge who had the deciding vote in the trial when the Athenian judges were deadlocked. Thus, according to Apollonian theory, it is only patricide, and not matricide, that has to be punished.

Looking ahead, we might note a peculiarity about interpretations of *Oedipus Tyrannus* that involve this point. Although commentators, and in particular Freud, have dwelt on the incestuous marriage of Oedipus and Iocasta, there is little in the original to suggest that this was nearly so important a "crime" as the murder of Laius; if indeed it was a crime at all as opposed to an unlooked-for disaster. What the oracle demanded in order to lift the plague from Thebes was the discovery of the murderer of Laius: the patricide. The incest was never mentioned. This is not to say that it was lightly regarded by the Greeks, but that it was not the cause of the misfortunes of the city, while the patricide was. In *Oedipus at Colonus*, we must remember, Creon, through the mediation of Ismene, begs Oedipus to return so that he may be buried just outside the boundaries of Thebes. This is in response to a prophecy promising victory in battle to those who honor the bones of Oedipus. But even though Thebes desperately wants to keep control of the tomb, it cannot allow it to be within the boundaries of the city because Oedipus' crime of patricide is too great. This is quite explicitly stated. It is not the incest, but the killing of his father, the Theban king, that prevents his native city from garnering the rich reward of burying him there. Oedipus of course refuses the offer and Athens gets the honor of his bones and ultimate victory. He had not slain his father in Athens, so there was no danger for the Athenians.

The quarrel in the *Eumenides,* as I read it, is not between a matrilinear (Erinyes) and patrilinear (Apollo) ideology, but between the aristocratic/royal/divine theory of the latter and a demotic notion of kinship based on the image of the *phratria*. After the reforms of Cleisthenes, the phratries took on greater importance, and the patrilinear *gennetai* declined. What Appolo, on Orestes' behalf, is saying, in essence, is what Antigone is saying on behalf of Polynices: whatever the notions of kinship that apply to the *demos* and are supported by the Erinyes, they do not apply to the royal/divine kinship, a kinship which is strictly patrilineal.

It is important to look back for a second to a point we flagged earlier. In all societies, "kinship" is cognatic in the sense that kin through both father and mother are recognized as such (the Roman *cognati*). But, as I said, different kin count differently for different purposes. Thus, Creon acknowledges that Antigone (as his sister's daughter) is his nearest kin except for his own family, but that brand of kinship does not count for purposes of succession, for example, or for the burial obligation. These are strictly a patrilinear matter, and that is what Antigone asserts. It is also what Apollo asserts: if you like to use the anthropological jargon, what they both assert is the aristocratic principle of *descent* as opposed to the Eumenidean/democratic principle of mere kinship.

Structuralist Challenge:
Who Saws the Jigs?

While I had often referred to the Aeschylean passage in discussing similar ideologies of procreation in patrilineal societies, I had not thought of applying it to the disputed passage in *Antigone* until I read Philip Bock's (1979) comments on the Theban plays. He was criticizing Michael Carroll's (1978) criticism of Lévi-Strauss's (1958) rendering of the Oedipus myth. Lévi-Strauss in his structural analysis of the myth sees two of the elements in opposition as "overvaluation of kinship" versus "undervaluation of kinship." Thus, in marrying his mother, Oedipus overvalues kinship, while in killing his father he undervalues it. Carroll, after a careful analysis in which he rejects the other opposition of "autochthonous origins" versus "natural origins," retains the undervaluation vs. overvaluation opposition but makes it "affirmation of patrilineal ties" versus "devaluation of patrilineal ties." He thinks this points to an "ambivalence towards patriliny" in the fourth- to sixth-century Greeks.

It is interesting to me to see the stress put on patriliny, which is certainly there. But I am not so sure about the particular case Carroll wants to make. He claims that the main evidence, in the sagas, for the "ambivalence towards patriliny" is the frequent killing of patrilineal relatives that goes on: Oedipus and Laius are one example; Eteocles and Polynices another. But does the killing of these relatives indicate an ambivalence towards patrilineal ties? Surely not. These killings occur in all patrilineal systems and in their legends, where struggles for succession and power are the issue. Patrilineal descent legitimizes claims to power/authority, but at the same time stands between individuals "down the line" and those further up. Alexander Pope advised, in *The Epistle to Dr. Arbuthnot*, that any man who wished "to rule alone/Bear, like the Turk, no brother near the throne." (The Sultan on ascending the throne was reputed always to have his half brothers by his father's other wives strangled.) The saga of the Zulu clan from even before Shaka to its eventual downfall (Ritter 1957; Morris 1965) is replete with murders of patrikin. But were any of those who were involved in the bloody histories and legends of patrimurder *ambivalent* about the principle of patriliny? I can't see this at all. The contrary, if anything, is true. The principle is so important that the principals are willing to kill for it. It is patrilineal descent that legitimizes their claim to authority; it is patrilineal kin who stand in their way. They never, never question the principle; to do so would be to question their own legitimacy. They simply object to the person of the incumbent and so get rid of him. (This is of course Max Gluckman's point [1963], in contrasting rebellion with revolution.)

In Greek (and other) legend, kin kill each other all the time (thus reflecting a common trend in all societies where, like our own, 80 percent of murders are "family affairs"). Wives kill husbands, sons kill mothers, mothers kill their children, fathers kill their daughters. Does this represent a "devaluation of marriage and the family" in fifth-century Athens? I doubt it. There is certainly no evidence of it. And while there is evidence—and Carroll is quite right—that the aristocratic patrilineal groups were not so powerful after the much-quoted reforms of Cleisthenes, it cannot be inferred that the Athenians were "ambivalent" about patriliny. They understood it to be a principle applicable to the nobility and particularly to the archaic/divine nobility represented in the dramas (much as we understand the principles of succession—e.g., from John of Gaunt—as central to the Shakespearean history plays, even though these principles have no part in our own democratic lives). But the killings of patrikin in fifth-century B.C. dramas cannot be adduced as evidence for the average Athenian's "devaluation" of the principle that scarcely applied to him anyway, at least in its strict form. (Greek society was, as we have said, still overwhelmingly patriarchal, if not strictly patrilineal.) As for Carroll's other point (borrowed without acknowledgement from Sir Henry Maine) that "territory" was replacing "kinship" as the basis for social organization in the Athens of the time, this may have been to some extent true (the combination of deme and phratry that was the peculiar genius of Cleisthenes), but it is not in any way reflected in the plays or legends. And in any case, the legends on which the plays were based long antedate these changes (on which see Murray 1986).

Thus, like Bock, I cannot see that replacing Lévi-Strauss's two "oppositions" with these two solves anything at all. It rather tends to confuse the whole matter and lose the point of the "patrilineal emphasis" in the plays. But there is a deeper principle at issue, and that is the nature and validity of any "structural analysis" of this kind. What guarantee do we have that any such analysis corresponds to any mental or social reality of the people who produced the plays and legends? It is claimed that the "real" message of the cycle, for example, is not something simple like "avoid incest and patricide at all costs," but rather the more subtle "do not overvalue or undervalue kinship." Now, at one level Lévi-Strauss's point is well taken. The "surface" tale, he tells us in a brilliant metaphor, is a jigsaw and often appears jumbled and arbitrary and inconsequential because we do not know how the pieces fit together. But what, he asks, if the shape of the pieces has been determined by some formula for regulating the cogwheels that turned the camshaft that drove the saw that cut the pieces that made up the final jigsaw? Then the only way we would know why the pieces had the shape they had would not be from studying the surface picture but from discovering the nature of the formula that produced it. Thus, in the Oedipus case, the "mythemes"—that is, the jigsaw pieces—are produced not by some simple moral about not sleeping with one's mother, but rather by a complex interplay of camshaft formulae to do with "overcoming contradictions" between overvaluation and undervaluation of kinship, and between autochthonous versus human origins.

This is all very ingenious, but it raises the problem: *how do we know that his definition of the jigsaw pieces is correct in the first place?* For that is the clincher. The pieces are not simply given to us as in a real jigsaw: we have to define them ourselves. And the argument that they are "sentences" does not inspire confidence. Whose sentences? They may be "sentences" in translation, but these may not relate isomorphically to the original. No. If we, the analysts, get to define the pieces, then this renders any determination of the camshaft formulae potentially tautological. And this can go back and forth forever. This, Carroll throws out one opposition, slightly amends a second, and suggests a third (kinship versus territory). Other structuralists have run it through their own imaginations and come up with other dichotomies. There is no end to it. An embarrassing air of casual arbitrariness pervades the whole enterprise.

Bock, on the other hand, takes the patrilineal issue, which is in the plays without a doubt, and looks for a "meaning" that is related to a solid social fact: the existence of two intermarrying patrilines. He is primarily concerned with how this affects the Oedipus myth, but we can see that his diagram (diagram 3.2) is very close to the one I used to stress the patrilineal issue in *Antigone*. (His numbers indicate the order of succession to the Theban throne.)

What Bock asserts, simply, is that what the whole Theban saga is "about" is the rivalry and intermarriage between the two patrilines that we have identified. Commentators as astute as Knox have "diagrammed" the "genealogy of Oedipus according to Sophocles as shown in diagram 3.3

Here, as you see, they have put Menoecceus as a direct descendant of Cadmus equal to Labdacus, making Laius and Creon equally his descendants. Such a geneology might have suited the Erinyes, but it hides the fact that Menoecceus was descended from a *daughter* of Cadmus, the mother of his father, Pentheus. This makes Menoecceus and Creon scions of the house of Ethion of the Spartoi, not the house of Cadmus. Such a small slip can make a huge difference when it comes to interpreting just what "doomed house" it was that Antigone

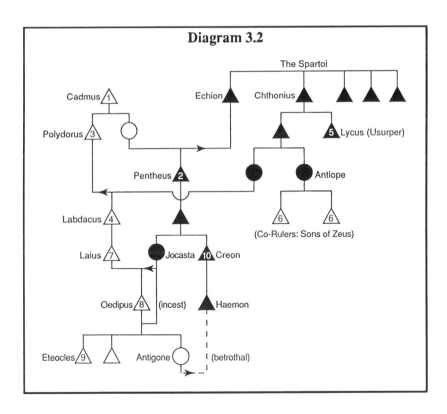

Diagram 3.2

(in her extremity of self-discovery, of course) was identifying with, and the logic of her exclusions.

Bock is much more accurate. There are a few differences of emphasis between us, but since there are many different versions of the myths, it is hard to settle on a definitive version. Bock does not include Haemon's brother Megareus, for example, and he is not relevant to the Oedipus story, certainly. But he is important in interpreting *Antigone*, since Creon is held responsible for his death, and this identification of Creon as "child-slayer" underlines his

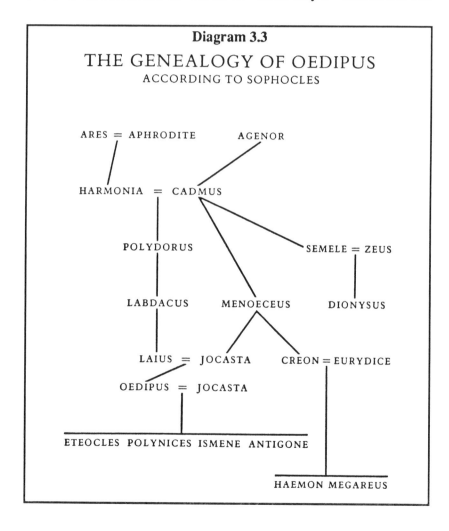

Diagram 3.3

THE GENEALOGY OF OEDIPUS
ACCORDING TO SOPHOCLES

ARES = APHRODITE   AGENOR

HARMONIA = CADMUS

POLYDORUS

SEMELE = ZEUS

LABDACUS   MENOECEUS   DIONYSUS

LAIUS = JOCASTA   CREON = EURYDICE

OEDIPUS = JOCASTA

ETEOCLES POLYNICES ISMENE ANTIGONE

HAEMON MEGAREUS

tyrannical nature and foretells his extermination of *all* the children, and hence of both lines. (Megareus appears in Euripides' *The Phoenician Women* as "Menoeceus"—named after his grandfather.) On the other hand, I have not included the two sons of Antiope, who indeed ruled Thebes for a while in the legends but do not appear in the trilogy. But if we take Bock's brilliant insight—that what we have here is a saga of two patrilines (houses) intermarrying and competing for the throne of Thebes, and apply this to the argument we have been making, then our interpretation of Sophocles' first line, Antigone's "inconsistency," and Apollo's defense of Orestes, makes great sense. It introduces a coherence to the use of the argument from patrilineal ideology in Greek drama that was not there before, and that probably gets closer to the "meaning" of the plays than arbitrary "oppositions" between elements that have been equally arbitrarily read into them.

Oedipus as Innocent:
The Sodomy of Laius

There is one loose end before we move on. We mentioned the importance of patricide, and how it took precedence over incest as a polluting "crime." Brother could kill brother, wife husband, and mother children, but none of these had the same polluting effects. Orestes did not commit patricide, and the matricide was declared of no account. Oedipus, on the other hand, albeit unknowingly, did commit patricide, and this was the source of the pollution. Although we have argued that the killing of patrilineal relatives (particularly brothers and half brothers) is part and parcel of the patrilineal game and reinforces rather than "devalues" the patrilineal principle, nevertheless, the killing of the father by his son was reckoned as striking at the heart of the principle; it was the worst crime of all—far worse than incest with the mother, which was, in its way, only a compounding of the offense against the father. But in the Oedipus story, as in all Greek tragedy, there is a theme of inevitability, of fate operating above and beyond the contingent affairs of mortals. Once the wheels are set in motion, fate grinds on to its grim conclusion. Somehow or other, Cadmus the Phoenician, the originator of both lines, made the initial fatal error— perhaps his refusal to search further for his brothers and sister Europa (which, contrary to Lévi-Strauss, we could see as an *undervaluation* of kinship!), and his angering of Ares by the slaying of the dragon whose teeth gave rise to the Spartoi when sown in the ground. Whatever. The curse continued down the line. One gets the feeling that nothing these people did would ever result in anything but tragedy. There was no way out.

Thus, Oedipus was doomed to commit patricide. Laius brought this upon himself in the first place by abandoning his son with crippled feet on the mountainside, thus setting himself up for a re-encounter at a later date. But more to the point, we must ask, why did Laius *deserve* to meet this terrible fate, which would then pollute the city of his fathers and lead to the further crime of incest and the products of incest, which would eventually end in the deaths of Antigone and Haemon? The legends never left such things to chance; there was no such thing as chance or accident in Greek theology, only fate (see Dodds 1951, 6). If Oedipus met his father on a lonely road and killed him in a quarrel, it was fated, as the oracle declared. Thus, Laius deserved to die, but in making his son the instrument of divine justice, fate contrived to compound the plot by making it inevitable that Oedipus himself would continue the saga of doom. But why the "punishment" of Laius and hence of his children and of his children's children? What had Laius himself done?

The answer to this "riddle of the Sphinx" is not to be found in Sophocles, who picks up the story with the reign of Oedipus. I had been too long away from Greek myth to remember, and so was puzzled until I came across a suggestion in Velikovsky (1960) that jogged my memory. He cites variations on the Oedipus legend that accuse Laius of the crime of introducing sodomy to Greece with his seduction of the youth Chrysippus. Laius had been banished from Thebes and taken refuge with Pelops at Pisa, whence he abducted the young boy charioteer. Hera, in fact, had sent the Sphinx to punish Thebes for just this crime. In one version, evidently, Oedipus kills his father while defending the youth from these unwonted advances. (Velikovsky cites E. Bethe, *Thebanische Heldenlieder* [1891], 23, 26. Robert Graves, in *The Greek Myths*, vol. 2, cites various classical sources to the same effect—the Scholiast, Apollodorus, Hyginus, Athenaeus, Plutarch. See Graves 1960.) This would indeed produce the cruel twist of fate the legend demands: in defending virtue, Oedipus commits the ultimate crime of patricide, for which he and the city and his offspring must then pay, not because of personal guilt, but because the taboo was broken and the inevitable punishment had to follow.

So it was with Oedipus. The original unnatural crime (not counting any of the offenses of Cadmus and his successors) was the sodomy of Laius, a crime Thebes compounded by instituting the famous Theban Three Hundred, a fighting body of homosexual lovers. In becoming the instrument of the gods (fate) in avenging this crime, Oedipus unwittingly breaks the taboo on patricide and thus brings down upon himself and his offspring the terrible fate that Sophocles documents in the Theban trilogy. Note here that the incest is simply a contingent and unfortunate consequence of the graver crime of patricide; it is not the cause of the pollution or anything of particular concern to the oracle and hence of the gods (fate). But it is certainly dealt with; and when Oedipus puts out his eyes, it is to hide from himself the memory of the incest, not of the patricide.

Why then does Sophocles not deal with the "crime of Laius" in the same brutal way that he deals with the incest? One must assume that he was aware of the legends; they were the source of his plots as much as Holinshed, Plutarch, or the Saxo Grammaticus were for Shakespeare. But Shakespeare edited the legends too, to suit the taste of his time. One can only assume that Sophocles was responding to a real change of values regarding sodomy in Greece. This is something that even the "devaluation of patriliny" theory has missed: one of the worst offenses against patriliny is a refusal to continue the line. Thus, patrilineal societies, while often recognizing sodomy for ritual or initiatory purposes, frown on it as a "lifestyle"—it strikes at the root of patrilineal succession and the need for sons. (We need not remind ourselves of the terrible fate of the Sodomites in the Old Testament—an archetypical patrilineal-patriarchal society. But we might remember that Cadmus was a Semite, or rather a mythologized memory of a Semitic colonization.) True, it can, as it eventually was in Greece (and certainly in Thebes), be incorporated into an overall sexual way of life that insists equally on procreation. That is, it is still frowned upon as an exclusive practice, but is allowed as "recreational sex" so long as the procreative functions are fulfilled. It can, as it was in fifth-century Athens, even come to be elevated to an aesthetically superior way of sex, once patrilineal succession has given way to partible inheritance and a balance between pleasure with boys and procreation with wives ensured. Thus, Sophocles would probably not have wanted to make a central theme of his drama the abhorrence of sodomy that went with the archaic patrilineal principle.

The consequence was that a gap was left in the story. The fate of Oedipus was made contingent: a matter of unfortunate coincidence rather than divinely cruel necessity. The truth is that Oedipus, as an instrument of divine justice, *had* to kill his father, and in doing so take upon himself, with Christlike innocence, the sin and its consequences. This is underscored in the last act of the trilogy, when, near his death at Colonus, he is indeed transformed into a divine figure who is taken into the underworld by the gods, and who brings, if not salvation (a much later concept) at least divine benefits on those who succored and believed in him (i.e., the Athenians under Theseus). But it is not really intelligible unless we know what sin he was atoning for in the first place. The terrible sacrifice of Oedipus redeemed the Greeks for their sin against natural procreation; and as in later Christian—although Greek-derived—theology, although they continued to sin, they continued to be redeemed. Was this hidden message perceived by the Athenian audience who watched the electrifying ending of the Oedipus saga at Colonus? We can never know for sure. But if it were so, would it not make a more convincing and astounding theory of the camshaft operation than "undervaluation of kinship" and the like? At the very least, whatever the sin of Laius, the preeminence of the patricide as the polluting element does something to reinforce the "ideology of patrilineal succession" argument, which is, after all, what is being promoted here.

As a "bridge passage" to the next stage of the argument, let us return to the Furies at the end of the trial of Orestes. They are not pleased. Not a bit. They complain bitterly to Athena of being slighted and threaten pretty terrible retribution on the Athenians. But the wise Athena is equal to the challenge. She offers them a place of honor as a kind of supernatural police force in Athens. From then on they will not just be the avengers of murdered kin but the guardians of the peace of the polis. Here is how Kitto (1951, 77) beautifully describes the denouement:

> So, to Aeschylus, the mature polis becomes the means by which the Law is satisfied without producing chaos, since public justice supersedes private vengeance; and the claims of authority are reconciled with the instincts of

humanity. The trilogy ends with an impressive piece of pagentry. The awful Furies exchange their black robes for red ones, no longer Furies, but "Kindly Ones" (Eumenides); no longer enemies of Zeus, but his willing and honoured agents, defenders of his now perfected social order against intestine violence. Before the eyes of the Athenian citizens assembled in the theatre just under the Acropolis— and indeed guided by citizen-marshals—they pass out of the theatre to their new home on the other side of the Acropolis.

The State Steps In:
The Church Steps Along

"Public justice supersedes private vengeance." Indeed it does, but here again our individualism creeps in, for what is superceded is not so much "private vengeance" as the automatic divine retribution meted out to the slayers of kin. In the clever action of Athena, the state takes over from supernatural sanction the right to settle disputes about slain kin. The purpose of the Furies is diluted to one of general protection of the state rather than specifically the avenging of murdered kin. In the future, juries will decide these things; bodies of citizens chosen by lot will determine what crimes against kinship deserve retribution. And the retribution will come from the state or its agents, and for its purposes. If "private" in Kitto's quote is read to mean "cosa nostra," then it is acceptable; that is, not vengeance as a matter for the individual, but vengeance as a matter for kin groups, or their divine surrogates. The taming of the Furies is a brilliant metaphor for the taming of kinship itself. Antigone and Orestes will, in future, have to deal with Creon's secretaries. The Furies now sit behind desks in government offices. You know they do; you have seen them.

My mention of "cosa nostra" was not just for effect. I promised to get from the virgin (Antigone) to The Godfather (Don Corleone), and this I cannot do except sketchily, for it would involve a rewriting of Western history and I am not equipped to do that. All I can do is make a few suggestions and hints that future rewriters might want to take into account. And my first suggestion concerns the endlessly fascinating Don—in some ways the most interesting Don since Quixote; a Don for our times, as it were. He too is tilting at windmills; he is tilting at Creon's secretaries in fact. He too is asserting anachronistic values in a hopeless battle against contemporary alienation. He even has a kind of gentleness that Mario Puzo portrays very lovingly and that Marlon Brando charmingly interpreted. Yes, he had people killed, but they by and large deserved it; and let us not forget that Quixote was a would-be knight, quite ready to slay his enemies if they had been real enemies. Both our Dons were warriors; it is just that we approve the warriordom of Quixote—because we know it was harmless and well intentioned—while we disapprove that of Corleone (or do we?). But in any case, let me recall for you a key moment in *The Godfather* where the old Don is being told of the deeds of valor performed in the war (World War II) by his eldest son, Michael. He is told of the citations for bravery, the purple hearts, the medals of honor, the courage over and above the call of duty, etc. He listens patiently, shakes his head, and says: "He does these things for strangers." As one who has lived for twenty-five years in New Jersey, and who has been if not on intimate, at least fairly close terms with members of several "families," I can vouch that Puzo's book is essentially documentary, not fiction. Most of the better stories he admits getting from his grandmother, and they were for real.

The Mediterranean cultures held onto their kinship values long after they had been at least officially abandoned in the North. They took them wherever they went and melded them with those of the locals. When I was in Colombia a few years ago, I was being taken round the estate of a friend whom we can, adding to our list of Dons, correctly call Don Mario (since that was what his tenants, servants, and employees called him). His majordomo, riding a mule with iron-clad (conquistadore) stirrups (to protect against cacti), and carrying a huge machete and rifle—looking in fact like a latter-day Quixote—introduced me to all the retainers. He ran through the list of all possible relatives: brothers, nephews, cousins, wives of cousins, sons-in-law, husbands of nieces, brothers-in-law, brothers of husbands of nieces of brothers-in-law, and on and on. Finally I stopped him and asked, in my bad Spanish, "Juan, do you never employ anyone who is not related to you by blood or marriage?" "But of course not, senor," he replied without hesitation. "They would steal from Don Mario, and what could we do?" In Colombia, we could not call the authorities, that's for sure. When the state fails to protect, people look longingly at the certainty of kinship. I did not say that idly: I have seen it in operation. I have seen it in South and Central America, in Italy (particularly Sicily, but not only there), in Ireland, in the Middle East, and even in Louisiana. (Those who saw that remarkable film about corruption in the New Orleans police department, *The Big Easy,* will not forget the dramatic ending. The Cajun cop hero, converted by the beautiful assistant D.A. to the side of right, surrounds himself with only those fellow Cajun cops who are uncles and cousins as he takes on the murderous drug dealers in the department in a fight to the finish.) But these represent areas where the state has not thoroughly established its rule over kinship; where it cannot guarantee order and hence must relinquish its monopoly over violence to groups that can, even in a limited way. These are the last outposts, for where the modern state is strong and centralized, it is the end process of that long struggle with kinship that is my theme, and that led us back to the Greeks to see its beginnings.

Through the Middle Ages, the church struggled to assert its temporal control of marriage and kinship, wresting this control from pagan-based custom. But as late as the nineteenth century, in many parts of Europe, this was still not totally in effect. The use of prohibited degrees, which were ever more widely extended, while partly a venal device to gain money from the sale of indulgences (as Luther complained) was also a way of forcing marriage outside the circle of kin. (The Napoleonic Code later reversed this trend by enforcing a modified form of partible inheritance. Napoleon, as First Consul, was unwilling to go all the way with the Revolutionary insistence on totally partible inheritance to promote "equality." He saw the need for strong nuclear families and the keeping intact of small family fortunes to promote business. But the results in the Code were essentially a compromise: inheritance was still partible, and most of what had been the privilege of the "family councils" was passed over to the state courts [see Fisher 1906]). By instituting celibacy, the church outlawed kinship from its own ranks (theoretically) and promoted a system of meritocracy, even if the term "nepotism" had to be invented later to cover the reproductive proclivities of various ecclesiastical dignitaries: kinship fights back. (This was beautifully satirized by Browning in "The Bishop Orders His Tomb at St. Praxed's Church.") And, of course, none of this prevented rich clerics from benefiting their relatives: "There is nothing," the Irish proverb has it, "as conceited as a Monsignor's niece." Nevertheless, the church, while promoting "the family," continued to carry on its own form of war against kinship. After the Merovingians, it persuaded the European monarchies and nobility to accept at least legal monogamy, although even here they fought back with, for example, the legitimization of bastards. But the church was on a winning ticket here, since increasing democratization always means a growing unpopularity with polygamy. Polygamy creates mate shortage with a more than fair share of brides going to the wealthy and powerful. Monogamy comes closer to ensuring fair shares, and is usually more popular with the people. The church's notion that marriage and kinship are incompatible with certain avocations persisted in many areas until very recently: fellows of Oxford and Cambridge colleges had to be celibate, and even the Royal Canadian Mounted Police required seven years' celibacy from recruits. (See Balch 1985 for an excellent discussion of these issues.)

What was happening throughout Europe, in varying degrees, was the growth of a now triangular struggle. Volumes have been written on the rise of individualism, as we have seen, and kinship has been seen as the enemy of the individual, as much as of the state. But very little has been written on the struggle of kinship with both these institutions. The state, despite its persecution of the individual from time to time, is much happier with individuals as units than with kinship groups for the simple reason that they are easier to control. If it wants to reduce kinship to the nuclear family (or less), then it wants to reduce its legal units to the individual voter of the eighteenth-century formula: the creature of the social contract, who rises yet again in the pages of Rawls' (1971) mammoth tome—kinless, sexless, ageless, and devoid of anything but a sense of personal survival. (Which leads rather amazingly to fair shares for all and a liberal democratic welfare state. One can take the social contract wherever one wants, it seems.) I think the real paradox here is that the state, at least in the bourgeois democracies, does not so much oppose individuals as promote them. It will, naturally, from time to time, persecute and repress certain individuals; it always has. But it prefers the individual contractors precisely for this reason: they are a lot easier to persecute and control than are large and powerful kin groups. Thus, it comes easily to the nation-state to promote the values of individualism while remaining totally suspicious of the claims of kinship. The law recently recognized the rights of a viable foetus as a "person" who could sue, at about the same time as it contemptuously turned down the rights of Mormon polygamists. On this score, at least, state and individual can been seen in league against kinship. (One of the few books to deal with this as an issue is, as one would expect, not by a social scientist, but by a talented amateur, Alex Shoumatoff [1985]. See especially his chapters 6, 7, and 8.)

The state, often using the celibate and meritocratic church as its agent, weighed in later than the church in the struggle, since it took longer to became effective and more centralized. The Tudors in England led the way in the taming of the noble houses (Henry VII was perhaps the first great "modern" king in this respect at least) and the setting up of a secular meritocracy of government: the beginning of the civil service, recruited from the ambitious bourgeoisie, themselves wedded to the small nuclear family, and decidedly anti-aristocratic. The Bourbons followed suit in France, and the height of royal power under the Sun King saw the abject surrender of the nobles to the demands of a court-centered charade brilliantly planned by Louis XIV to just that effect. Peter the Great, later but in the same vein, tamed the Boyars and pushed the state to the forefront, bringing in foreigners and Jews if necessary to forge an administration loyal to him rather than to its kin-based "houses." Areas in which the state could interfere with the family and override the *patria potestas* gradually increased with the growth of state power, although many anachronisms lingered. The taxing of large fortunes has proceeded to the point where the accumulation of wealth in powerful kinship groups is virtually impossible. The imposition of primogeniture mentioned earlier allowed single heirs to accumulate fortunes while sloughing off siblings and their descendants; the later taxing of these fortunes reduced even the remnants of wealthy kin groups, if not to genteel poverty at least to genteel political impotence. The Nixon government's attack on the large "foundations" was only one of the latest blows struck against private fortunes that could act as rival centers of power and influence. But it was not only the rich and powerful who were so reduced. The "policing of families" (to use the title of an interesting book on the subject [Donzelot 1979]) continued unabated until "family law" and public administration took over most of the functions of the family. Some critics have even seen the Reagan administration's indifference to the fate of the "family farm" and the "family business" as a latter-day example of the state's hostility to kinship in favor of agrobusiness and big business generally. The family farms almost always had an "extended" look, with at least two related adult males and their families involved in production. The latest developments in new "birth technologies" and the demand for their regulation is taking the state into the very act of procreation itself: not only the familial organisms but their genes are now matters for legislative control.

Socialist governments have been even less hospitable to kinship, for obvious reasons, and while communist experiments with the abolition of the family have not survived, very few functions are left to it. Yet even here, nepotism, however restricted, is evidently a plague of society. Kinship may be dead, but it won't lie down. I don't know enough about their history, but it is obvious that in China and Japan similar struggles between kinship and the state went on. In China the final solution has been to institute the nuclear family reduced to one child per couple, thus saying goodbye to the clans and to polygamy. In Japan, more interestingly, the integration of kinship values into managerial practice that has been so incredibly successful tells its own story. "If you can't lick 'em join 'em" seems to have been the Japanese response, and while the actual forms of traditional kinship diminish, its spirit lives in their form of industrial organization whose collectivism baffles our imaginations, so used are we to the linkage between industry and the "individual" contracting laborer and entrepreneur.

In America, where the hereditary principle was abolished with such ceremony two hundred years ago, the Kennedy "clan" continues to exercise its fascination. Bobby may well have been the best lawyer in the United States, but few people believe that this was the basis of his selection as attorney general; and whether Teddy would be a ranking senator without his family connections is, to say the least, an open question. The best way to get to the top, as some wag put it, is to start at the top. A fine kinship principle, but not one that in theory should operate in a democracy where all individuals are created equal. But then, we know that these individuals are not created equal. Apart from anything else, they each have a unique body of kin surrounding them, and that makes them different from each other. Hobbes was wrong: the state of nature was not, and the state of culture only struggles to be, a war of all against all. This is another blatant statement of individualist prejudice. The original social contract was not between individuals but between genes. There was never a war of all against all; it was always a war of some against others. And the some and the others, until the advent of the state, were always kin. Once the state emerged, the battle shifted; it continues now between kinship and the state itself. The final social contract will not be signed until the conditions dreamed of in most utopias are realized and the genes neutralized once and for all (Kummar 1987). It won't be in our lifetime, or in the lifetime of our kin.

Kinship in Legend Today:
All in the Family

As an epitaph, let me return to the notion that kinship is alive in legend. The immense popularity of Frank Herbert's *Dune* novels is not solely to do with ecology, as many commentators would have us think. Central to the ongoing complicated plot are the machinations of the Bene Gesserit, a strange order of far-from-celibate nuns whose purpose over the eons is to control breeding and blood lines in order to produce a messiah. (This backfires, but then he was an Atreidies—they should have known what they were messing with!) While this is a kind of eugenics program, it is in private hands (the order belongs to no government), and nobility of blood plays a central role in the dynastic quarrels that make up most of the plot (there is even a royal sibling marriage). Kinship and descent are central here, as they are in the conception of the monstrous Bene Tleilax, who combine a strangely one-sided (very few females) breeding system in which sperm is periodically "distributed," with a gruesome cloning mechanism, the secret of which is their power in the universe. They are all related and, it turns out, most appropriately, are all secret Muslims—of a suitably modified kind—bent on jihad against the infidels, i.e., the rest of the universe. The whole *Dune* series, in effect, could be looked at as a myth about the intermeshing of kinship and society.

And then there is the inimitable Kurt Vonnegut. He puts it in a nutshell in his novel suitably called *Slapstick* (1976). At some indistinct time in the future when the earth has been degravitated by miniaturized Chinese, the President of the United States, as one of his first acts of office, decides to restore kinship to its proper place by instituting an almost Chinese system of proper names. His campaign slogan is "Lonesome no more," and he assigns by computer ten thousand middle names based on a combination of objects and numbers. Everyone with the same middle name belongs to that "family" and has familial obligations to the others. Family clubs rapidly spring up, and people take to the whole scheme with great seriousness. Wars become harder to fight—the country has broken up into warring chiefdoms—because family members don't like to kill each other and they are scattered through the bellicose factions. "I realized that nations could never acknowledge their own wars as tragedies" says Vonnegut, "but that families not only could but had to" (page 214). Police forces are not needed because a rule springs up that if a family member commits a crime then whoever knows about it calls ten other family members and they settle it. The most moving and astonishing part of the book describes a "family meeting" of the Daffodils in Indianapolis (Vonnegut's President is a Daffodil from that city—Wilbur Daffodil-11 Swain.) The family becomes a little parliament, governed strictly by Robert's Rules of Order, which settles matters among its members in a charmingly pragmatic fashion. And, yes, Vonnegut deals with the issue of "relatives" possibly not liking each other. To end my point that kinship is alive and well in legend (and that these mythmakers may be the more acute sociologists of our time) let me quote from the President's comments on the essay he and his sister wrote as children when they first conceived the idea of the families.

> I found it absorbing. It said there was nothing new about artificial extended families in America. Physicians felt themselves related to other physicians, lawyers to lawyers, writers to writers, athletes to athletes, politicians to politicians, and so on. Eliza and I said that these were bad sorts of extended families, however. They excluded children and old people and housewives, and losers of every description. Also, their interests were so specialized as to seem nearly insane to outsiders. "An ideal extended family," Eliza and I had written, "should give proportional representation to all Americans according to their numbers. The creation of ten thousand such families, say, would give rise to ten thousand parliaments, so to speak, which would discuss sincerely and expertly what only a few hypocrites now discuss, which is the welfare of all mankind." (156-7)

I won't quote more, although there is much that is quotable and directly related to our theme, since I don't want to spoil the pleasure of those who haven't read it. I am just helping to make my point that kinship is indeed "alive in legend," which is where we should look for true insights, and not to the social scientists.

But to leave on an up note, in one of the most charming utopias of our own age—*Always Coming Home*—the daughter of a famous anthropologist, Ursula Kroeber Le Guin, envisages a postholocaust future somewhere in northern California where small and loosely allied villages, on the model of the Pueblos (particularly Zuni) that her father loved and studied, manage, with primitive electricity, a dash of geomancy, horse-drawn railways, and controlled literacy to live a pleasant and varied life allowing for the full range of human passions. And they are, of course, organized into exogamous matrilineal clans, themselves linked to occupational guilds. We should have expected nothing less from a close kinswoman of the great Kroeber. And she, along with many other observers, professional and lay, have noted a tendency to return to kinship after the hysterical tide of the narcissistic individualism of Tom Wolfe's "me-decade" has receded. Tiger (1978) even notes that the burgeoning of step-parenthood, seen as an attack on "family values" by the doomsayers, in fact creates large extended families where a child has double the number of parents and grandparents in each generation and a host of new cousins and half-siblings. Perhaps out of this side effect of the "breakdown of marriage" we may yet forge truly organic, kin-based social units. In years to come, another tragedy like *Antigone* may enthrall us with a sense of meaning as immediate to us as it was to fifth-century Athens—much as the tragedy of Mary Beth Whitehead, in her heroic struggle with the supremacy of contract over motherhood, has engaged us, on one or the other side of the battle, over the past years.

4

Sisters' Sons and Monkeys' Uncles: Six Theories in Search of an Avunculate

awos: mother's brother or mother's father
father and giver of my mother, or
her brother, avenger of her honor, my favoring "male mother"
you older men of her patri-clan
*I stand here, your *nepos, son of your sister/daughter*
give me presents
foster and raise me during summer visits

—Paul Friedrich
Kinship Alpha: Proto-Indo-European

Introduction

In departments of social anthropology in the United Kingdom in the 1950s there was a standard form of introduction to the subject. One pons asinorum after the other had to be crossed, and these were offered in order, starting with the "problem of the incest taboo." We read and criticized one or two of the standard declarations on the topic and, having settled *that* moved quickly on to "the mother's brother" issue: the question of the avunculate. The point here was to read Radcliffe-Brown's "The Mother's Brother in South Africa" and get

191

the truth, as opposed to the evolutionary error perpetrated by Junod—the object of Radcliffe-Brown's criticism. In this way the whole of nineteenth-century (indeed of pre-Radcliffe-Brown) anthropology could be rapidly dispensed with, and we could get on with "functionalism" and real science.

What never seemed to occur to anyone was to tie up the two things: incest taboo and avunculate. The next assignment was usually "the nuclear family," and by then we were far afield. Lévi-Strauss was not much taught in those days; he was as yet largely untranslated. It was later that I came across his interesting attempt to make this tie-in through the famous "atom of kinship," as shown in diagram 4.1 (Lévi-Strauss 1958, chap. 2).

Diagram 4.1

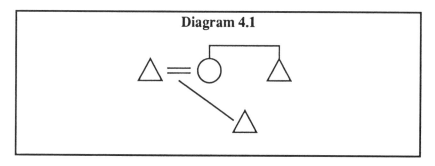

In the atom, the mother's brother was there to start with because the incest taboo between brother and sister ruled this pair out as parents. The sister was "released" to another man by this primary act of culture; her son was therefore the product, indirectly, of the brother's renunciation.

Well. This certainly got the incest taboo and the avunculate together, and even a shadowy nuclear family—or at least a pater/genitor person hovering on the edges. It is no secret that I have spent a lot of my time insisting that the incest taboo as such is not the appropriate cultural starting point, since avoidance of close inbreeding is common to most sexually reproducing organisms. Taboo certainly is unique to man since it involves language for interdictions, but avoidance is not unique. Without the taboo we would avoid anyway, so the taboo is not, as Lévi-Strauss insists, the voice of culture saying "No!" to Nature; it is saying, if anything, "OK!"

The next link in the chain—exchange—is surely important, but that has to do with marriage and hence exogamy, not incest. The argument is familiar. But it left me uncomfortable. If one takes the incest-taboo-as-prime-mover out of the atom, then what is left? Basically, mating and the avunculate. The primitive term is the in-law relationship and its derivative: that between mother's brother and sister's son. Mating clearly occurs in nature, as does incest avoidance, so we are left with the remarkable conclusion that only the avunculate is specific to culture. Or are we? It seemed to me worthwhile to review this relationship, which has been as important to anthropological theorizing as the incest taboo, and to ask just what it is and whether or not it is indeed the first true cultural incursion into nature that this logic suggests it must be. David Schneider once said to me: "If primates have kinship then I'll be a monkey's uncle." He spoke too soon—but thereby hangs a tale (and no pun is intended since old-world monkeys and apes—with which we shall be concerned—do not have prehensile tails to hang by). Let us first then canvass some anthropological thought on the avunculate and see where it gets us. I will give away the fact that we are going to come around full circle. But first to the beginning.

Since we shall be using it a lot, it is worth mentioning that the term "avunculate" derives from the Latin for mother's brother, *avunculus*, itself derived from *avus* (grandfather, ancestor) plus a diminutive suffix, *-unculus,*, as in, for example, *homunculus* (little man). Literally, then, avunculus means "little grandfather." It passed into English via Norman French, where only the suffix had been retained (*–oncle*). In calling someone "uncle," we are, etymologically, simply calling him little; the grandfather is forgotten. This equation of the maternal uncle with the grandfather is not uncommon in Omaha-type kinship terminologies, just as in the Crow opposites the maternal uncle is often equated with "elder brother." He is seen, that is, either as a reduced kind of grandfather or as an elevated kind of brother.

The reciprocal for the sister's son in Latin is, of course, *nepos* (our "nephew"), a word that originally simply meant "descendant" and then more specifically "grandson." It is, like the root for mother's brother (or mother's father) (*au-/*aw–), a very old Indo-European word, viz., Sanskrit *napat*. Roman kinship terms obeyed the "law of the reciprocal," which means that if I call my mother's brother "grandfather" then he will reciprocate by calling me "grandson." This is how the Latin for the latter became the term for "sister's son." But the older usage was astonishingly persistent. The *Oxford English Dictionary* records that as late as the seventeenth century, "nephew" was still being used to mean "grandson" as well as "son of sibling." (Our "niece" derives from late Latin *nepta*, again through Norman French, via Old English *nefa*.)

In normal English we meet the Latin original only in the adjective "avuncular." In anthropology, avunculate has come to mean any special relationship that exists between mother's brother and sister's son. This of course includes, in matrilineal societies, the right of the sister's son to succeed to the mother's brother's positions and titles as well as his wealth and often his wives. But ironically the issue was raised over the existence of a modified avunculate in patrilineal societies. Read on.

The Evolutionists:
Mothers Are the Necessity of Invention

Junod (1927) was not the first social evolutionist to fasten onto the avunculate as a survival of "matriarchy." But he became the focus of attention because Radcliffe-Brown singled him out. He was heir to the dispute between those, following Morgan and McLennan, who saw "matriarchy" or "motherright" as coming earlier in social evolution than "patriarchy" or "fatherright," and those, like Maine, who favored the opposite. There is no need to recapitulate the arguments here. Postfunctional anthropology finds them archaic and even laughable, although the primacy of matriarchy has had an embarrassing revival in some quarters.

This universal primacy of matriarchy was thought by some to rest on logical grounds: if savages were in doubt about the facts of paternity, then they would favor descent through females. On the other hand, matriarchy was thought to be basically biological, as in the cases of Bachofen (1861) and Briffault (1927), who saw its origins in nature—in the "matriarchal horde." (Durkheim's teacher Alfred Espinas [1878] saw most clearly that there was more balance in nature and that various family forms were found in varying conditions, but his interesting ecological views found no echo in the formulations of his favorite pupil. They were followed up by an interesting group of Belgian sociologists. But the First World War put a sharp stop to this development of ethological ideas. See Crook & Goss-Custard 1972.)

Junod was also heir to the doctrine of "survivals," again starting with McLennan and finding its strictest formulation in Tylor (1871). Present "anomolous" customs were leftovers from antiquity, and hence indicators of a past state of affairs. Thus, customs of symbolic "bride capture" were supposed to be a hangover from the days when brides were actually physically abducted, and so on. Putting the two things together, Junod came up with his classic interpretation of the avunculate among the BaThonga of South East Africa. The BaThonga were, like the other Southern Bantu, patrilineal: descent, inheritance, and succession went strictly in the male line. But the mother's brother was accorded a very special place in the life of his sister's son. He allowed privileges to his sister's son that seem outrageous. The boy could steal sacrificial meat from his mother's brother's altar—an act normally regarded as extreme sacrilege. He could take his mother's brother's goods and belongings without asking. He could even sleep with his mother's brother's wives—indeed, they were expected to initiate him. And, finally, he had the right to his mother's brother's daughter in marriage.

This latter form of marriage is common in Africa and in patrilineal societies generally. Often, in Africa, it goes along with marriage to the wife's brother's daughter, as shown in diagram 4.2. A man either marries his wife's brother's daughter or passes the privilege on to his son (at least this is one way of looking at it). In many societies it is simply a straightforward privilege to marry the mother's brother's daughter.

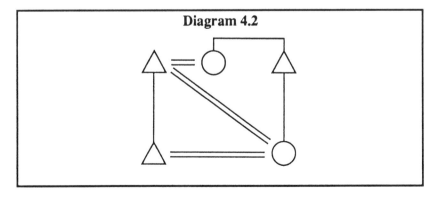

Diagram 4.2

Junod looked for an explanation of this seeming anomaly: in a patrilineal society, with "descent though males only," what was the mother's brother doing playing such a prominent part in the lives of his sisters' sons? The answer was that it was a "survival" of "motherright." The Thonga must once have been matrilineal and have passed through that stage (to patrilineal) while retaining traces (survivals) of their previous form of social organization, in particular the privileged relationship with the maternal uncle.

Junod accepted that patrilineal descent would have originated with the "discovery of paternity." This should be noted because there were really two views about the priority of matrilineal descent, and we should note them because they become important later. One insisted that savages lived in a state of promiscuity and hence could not know who their fathers were (McLennan). Under these circumstances, maternal kinship (descent through females only) was the only alternative. Thus, it was "uncertainty of paternity" that led to favoring descent through females, making the mother's brother and his sister's son the two most closely related males, as described by diagram 4.3.

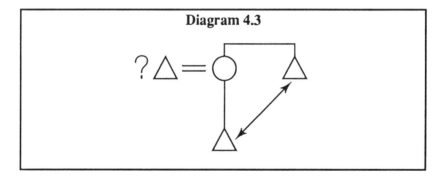

Diagram 4.3

Marriage could scarcely be allowed to exist. Only "group marriage" could handle the situation since it would be a wise savage who knew his own father under these circumstances. The most rudimentary form of social organization would probably have been one of matri-moieties (the tribe divided into two groups with children joining the group of their mother), with all the men of one, as a group, marrying all the women of the other, and vice versa. This view seemed to receive some support from statements of the natives themselves. When William

Penn enquired of the Delaware why they traced their descent through females, he was told "so that our offspring be not spurious" (Myers 1937). This kind of reasoning seemed to confirm the "paternity uncertainty" theory.

But this theory was strongly and convincingly attacked by others, notably Westermarck and Hartland. Westermarck (1891) concentrated his attack on demonstrating that primitive man was not promiscuous, and that regularized mating, families, etc. were universal. Hartland (1909-10) took a different tack and I want to quote him again for future reference. He wrote in the last paragraph of volume 1 of his prophetically titled *Primitive Paternity* as follows:

> Motherright then is found not merely where paternity in uncertain, but also where it is practically certain. Fatherright on the other hand is found not merely where paternity is certain, but also where it is uncertain and even where the legal father is known not to have begotten the children. Nay, the institutions of fatherright often require provision for, and very generally permit, the procreation by other men of children for the nominal father. It follows, therefore, that the uncertainty of paternity cannot be historically the reason for the reckoning of descent exclusively through the mother. Some other reason must be discovered.

He goes on, in volume 2, to examine this "other reason," which is of course the famous "sexual ignorance of savages." Savages, it seems, do not pay much attention to fatherhood, not because they are uncertain of it, but because they do not *know* about it. It is, after all, a rather hard deduction to make, in the absence of precise knowledge, that one act of intercourse out of many will result in a child appearing nine months later.

Today of course we would interpret these things differently. In the patrilineal case we know that the stress is on establishing the legal father,(pater) of the child, irrespective of the identity of the biological father (genitor). We also know that the supposed "ignorance of procreation" is better phrased as an ideology of the *irrelevance* of procreation. In other words, the ideology in either case *follows* from having different systems of descent. Matrilineal systems are less concerned as a rule with the identity of the genitor, since a child's clan is fixed by its mother. Usually, however, a pater is required so that the child can have a "father's clan" and so abide by the various rules of exogamy, preferential marriage, and moiety membership where this is patrilineal.

But for the moment let us take serious note of Hartland's pointed negative criticism of the "paternity uncertainty" principle as the basis for matrilineality and bracket it off for future reference. Junod didn't actively subscribe to either theory; it was enough for him that "fatherright" had been imposed on the Thonga and that the avunculate, as he found it, was a survival of motherright.

The Functionalists:
Getting Dad Back In (Auntie As Well)

Even before Junod, the evolutionist position was falling into disfavor. It has more recently been revived by Murdock (1949), who asserts that systems only change, if they change, in one direction—from matrilineal to patrilineal. This is not to subscribe, it should be noted, to a theory of universal matriarchy—according to Murdock's theory, most systems never were matrilineal; it is simply to assert a unidirectional pattern of change. In Murdock's specific reconstructions, he insists the BaThonga *were* originally matrilineal. I have argued as much for some types of African "double descent" (Fox 1967b). But between Junod and Murdock falls the shadow.

Radcliffe-Brown has taken something of a beating for not paying careful attention to the proper citation of his sources—or plagiarism as we sometimes call it (Needham 1971). Despite this, however, his peripatetic teaching career and strikingly authoritative manner entrenched his views as a "school" from Yenching to Capetown, and Sydney (via Chicago) to Oxford. His criticism of Junod remains the classic statement of the Functionalist disdain for Evolutionist arguments, or "conjectural history" as he preferred to call it (acknowledging, this time, Dugald Stewart).

His paper on "The Mother's Brother in South Africa" appeared first in 1924 (reprinted in Radcliffe-Brown 1952). He argued that the reason for the peculiar privileges extended to the sister's son had nothing to do with a supposed earlier state of matrilineality; in fact, they were incompatible with it. In matrilineal systems (and this was confirmed by Malinowski on the Trobriand Islanders), the role of the mother's brother, as a senior male of the matrilineage or clan, was essentially *authoritative*. The mother's brother in (central) African matrilineal societies, for example, could punish his sister's son, and even sell him into slavery. This contrasted with the role of the same relative in patrilineal societies like the BaThonga where it was indulgent or *affectionate*. What this difference represented, Radcliffe-Brown argued, was not evolutionary stages but complimentary opposites. Societies with great stress on the male line, male authority, and succession in that line, seemed at the same time to stress the affectionate relationship with the males of the mother's line. In many Bantu languages the mother's brother was a *malume*—a "male mother." In the bilateral, but definitely patriarchal Anglo-Saxon system, the mother's elder brother had an almost sacred position, and readers of *The Hobbit* will remember how the very Anglo-Saxon Fili and Kili fell in battle defending Thorin to the death "with shield and body because he was their mother's elder brother." The Latin reflects this principle in making him a diminutive grandfather—an affectionate person not involved in the *patria potestas* of the agnatic (patrilineal) line. In fact, among the northern BaThonga, he is known not as *malume* but as *kokwana* (grandfather)—interesting echoes of the Roman usage.

Radcliffe-Brown generalized this relationship system to a theory of sentiments in which "authoritative" sentiments on one side are always balanced by "affectionate" sentiments on the other. In patrilineal societies the authority is on the father's side, so the father, his brothers and sisters, and all his lineage and clan will be held in respect. The sentiment for the father will be "extended" to these others. In Oceanian patrilineal societies, for example, the father's sister is called by a term meaning "female father" and is accorded great respect. Her curse is the thing a man fears most, and he will do anything to avoid it. She can arrange his marriages and sexual affairs and takes his goods at will. (Just for the record, while we are in Oceania, let us note that Hocart had in 1915, in a paper titled "Chieftainship and the Sister's Son in the Pacific," also noted the privileged relationship of mother's brother and sister's son among the patrilineal Tonga [not to be confused with the African Thonga] and had dismissed the idea of a previous matrilineal stage, preferring a "symbolic" interpretation involving the idea of chiefs as gods. But this paper seems to have been forgotten, and certainly our attention was never drawn to it as undergraduates.)

Radcliffe-Brown was big on the "extension" of sentiments in this manner, something that Murdock picked up on, married to

Behaviorism, and trundled out under the banner of "stimulus generalization." Equally, then, the mother's line would be the subject of sentimental extensions from the mother herself. All the affection felt for her would be transferred to her relatives and hence to the indulgent, playful relationship with the mother's brother, and the marriage (often) with his daughter. The Functionalist theory then was, as Murdock correctly saw, a psychological theory—or more properly a social-psychological theory.

Radcliffe-Brown did not go into detail on the converse of his patrilineal case, but it logically follows that in matrilineal societies, if the locus of authority is in the mother and her brothers, then the father and his sisters must be the objects of affection and indulgence, and probably the father's sister's daughter should be the appropriate marriage partner. Again, Malinowski (1929) provided the type case here with his indulgent Trobriand father and father's sister, opposed to the authoritative and feared mother's brother. And, yes, marriage with the father's sister's daughter was preferred, especially for chiefs (see diagram 4.4).

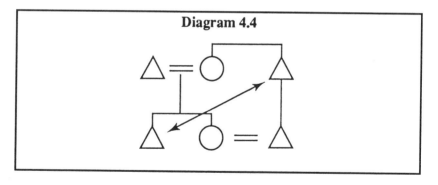

Diagram 4.4

The symmetrical nature of the system of sentiments should of course mean that the father's sister would be an indulgent figure in matrilineal societies, and an authoritative one in patrilineal. In fact this problem of the *amitate* (Latin *amita* = father's sister) had occupied a number of anthropologists, especially in Oceania where, as we have seen, the father's sister looms as large in a boy's life as the mother's brother does in South Africa.

Radcliffe-Brown's own teacher, W. H. R. Rivers, had in 1910 written his own classic paper on "The Father's Sister in Oceania" (much of which was incorporated into Rivers' *History of Melanesian Society*, published in 1914) which is full of interest since it hovers between a Junod-like and a Functionalist interpretation. (It is possible that Radcliffe-Brown might have consciously or unconsciously drawn on the title as a model for his own.) For example, the island of Mota (Banks Islands) has two hostile matrilineal moieties, and a pattern of privileged, including sexual, indulgence obtains between a boy and his father's sister, who is of course of the opposite (father's) moiety. Rivers at first advances the Junod-esque argument that this is a "survival" of a previous state of patrilineality. But he hastens to add that this argument is advanced "as a matter of form" and is not to be taken too seriously. He concentrates more on the business of the nail clippings. On Mota, the father's sister is the guardian of her brother's son's nail clippings (and his umbilical cord). This is not a small matter since the Mota live in fear of sorcery, especially from the opposite moiety, and nail clippings are the favorite tools of sorcerers. Whomsoever has your nail clippings has your life in her hands. Thus, it would be appropriate that the father's sister (his closest female relative in the opposite moiety) guard these precious objects for her favorite nephew. Then Rivers argues thus:

> *When relationship with the father begins to be recognized*, his sister is chosen as the receptacle of those objects by means of which the members of her division might injure the child, and she thus by their possession obtains a power over the child which makes her the most honoured relative. (Rivers 1910, 56, my emphasis)

Nail parings aside, Rivers even thanks Radcliffe-Brown for calling attention to the division of labor between kinsmen in this way. So he is fascinatingly hovering between the evolutionary tradition—the "discovery of paternity" syndrome—and the Functionalism being developed by Radcliffe-Brown. Thus, one of the arguments he considers seriously is that the real role of the father's sister is that of the mother's brother's wife. That is, previously the mother's brother married the father's sister, and the nephew was allowed to inherit his mother's brother's wife, or marry her daughter. He compares this with "cross-cousin marriage" on the same pattern among the Dravidians. The two possible systems are shown in diagram 4.5.

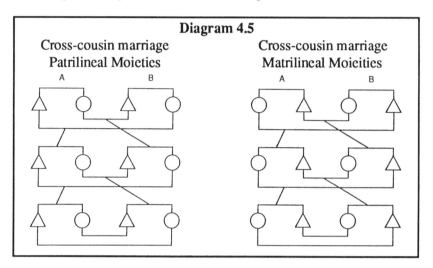

Diagram 4.5

Cross-cousin marriage
Patrilineal Moieties

Cross-cousin marriage
Matrilineal Moieities

The outcome described by Rivers would only be the case, of course, where this kind of "double cross-cousin marriage" was practiced: where the father's sister's daughter and the mother's brother's daughter are one and the same (because the mother's brother married the father's sister). While this is common enough, most of the examples that Radcliffe-Brown and Rivers studied involved marriage with either the one cross-cousin or the other: typically, father's sister's daughter in matrilineal and mother's brother's daughter in patrilineal societies.

Eggan, a student of Radcliffe-Brown at Chicago, helped clinch the Functionalist position with his own paper on "The Hopi and the Lineage Principle" (1949), where he describes for this Pubelo Indian matrilineal tribe the crucial role of the father's sister in the life cycle—particularly in the sexual and marital life—of her brother's son, as opposed to the authoritative role of the mother's brother. And, yes, at least formerly the father's sister's daughter might have been a preferred marriage partner.

The Functionalists quarreled over details. Fortes and his followers, for example, maintained that the role of the sister's son in patrilineal societies derived from his status as the son of a "residual sibling"—the sister. Sisters in patrilineal societies could not provide heirs for their lineages, so what was the status of their sons? Well, it was one of "complimentary filiation" to this "residual sibling" (Fortes 1959). That is, while the sister's son was not actually a member of his mother's brother's patrilineage, he had some status as the son of a woman of that lineage, and this is what gave him his privileged position. Proponents of this view (or versions of it), like Goody (1959), argued cogently that Radcliffe-Brown's "extensionist" theories only accounted for the behavior of the junior generation; they did not take account of the older generation: it mattered just as much how the mother's brother "felt" as it did how the nephew regarded him. Thus, the "privileged" stealing of ritual sacrifices from the mother's brother was seen purely from the point of view of the nephew; what was often ignored, as Goody points out, was the reciprocal obligation required of the nephew by the mother's brother: for example, his obligation to sacrifice the cow in the first place. (Goody's article contains a good summary of opposing views up to that date.)

The theory of sentiment extension was criticized also on logical grounds: in matrilineal societies mothers are just as indulgent of children as in patrilineal, so there is no reason why the sentimental attachment of sons to mothers should not be "extended" there also to mother's brothers. Also, in many patrilineal societies, as Hocart had pointed out, all this stealing business was anything but "indulgent" or friendly: there was often a considerable element of hostility and aggression in it. Talk then of "ambivalence" (as in Tax 1937) only complicated the situation further. Ambivalence characterizes all relationships.

As to the two kinds of cross-cousin marriage, Homans and Schneider in 1955 took the "extension of sentiments" theory to its extreme in examining why FZD (father's sister's daughter) marriage occurred mostly in matrilineal, and MBD (mother's brother's daughter) marriage in patrilineal societies. Where "jural authority" rested in one lineage, the relationship with the other lineage would be one of "affectionate indulgence," as Radcliffe-Brown had posited. Therefore, they argued, junior would be most likely to want to marry the girl with whom he had "extended sentiments" of affection: the FZD in the matrilineal, and the MBD in the patrilineal case. They clinched this with their own notion of "interaction"—the boy would interact differently with the two different cousins depending on the structure of authority-affection, and would marry the one with whom he had the most "sentimentally appropriate" interaction. (Remember Homans' famous "law" that "interaction produces liking if the propensity for liking was there in the first place.")

Criticism poured in, especially from Needham (1962), and most of it stressed the obvious fact that junior was usually the last person consulted in these marriage arrangements, which were fixed by custom and arranged by the older generation; that these marriages were often with classificatory relatives with whom junior had never interacted; that the preponderance of the matrilateral type (MBD) was easily explained by demographic arguments (Fox 1965), and so on. But it is worth noting that Homans and Schneider wrote their little effort as a critique of the "structuralism" of Lévi-Strauss, who had argued that MBD marriage was preponderant because, following Durkheim, it promoted greater "organic solidarity" than its opposite (FZD). Homans and Schneider wished to put an "efficient cause"— following Aristotle—in place of this "final cause," or teleological argument, and found it in Radcliffe-Brown's theory of sentimental extensions. This, then, is a natural bridge passage to the structuralists. (We might just note that an interesting insertion of the "symbolic" approach had appeared in 1971 in James J. Fox's essay, "Sister's Child as Plant." But, prescient as it was regarding the future course of anthropology, it didn't seem to help in these ongoing debates.)

The Structuralists:
Splitting the Atom of Kinship

We have already seen how Lévi-Strauss argues for the relationship between mother's brother and sister's son as a "primitive" term in the "atom of kinship." He states it as a four-role system of brother-sister-father-son, differing in emphasis from the Functionalists and others who want to start with the classic nuclear or elementary family: father-mother-brother-sister. In other words, the latter sees the mating relationship as primary while the former sees the incest taboo as primary: as logically coming first. In fact, Lévi-Strauss's atom is better stated as "brother, sister, brother-in-law, sister's son." In reality, to complete the picture, a second "atom" must be added since the brother himself must have a wife in order for the crucial mother's brother's daughter to enter the picture. What we get then, as the most "primitive" result of the primitive exchange, is as shown in diagram 4.6.

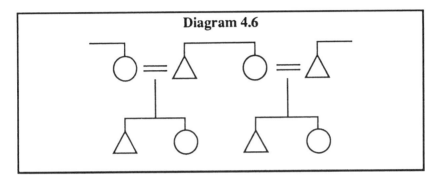

Diagram 4.6

In a sense, once the brother-in-law (sister's husband) is added, then logically so is his sister and hence his sister's daughter, thus bringing the FZD into play. This chain of atoms then forms the basic exchange system of human society, deriving, in Structuralist theory, from the incest taboo, which forces the brother to divest the sister (although this taboo in turn is seen as itself deriving from the benefits of exchange—all a bit circular, but press on.) Since the brother-sister tie is the one that in a sense sets all this in motion—the nucleus of the atom—and since the "sister's son" only exists thanks to the renunciation of the sister, then the maternal nephew is a kind of direct creation of his mother's brother, needing only the minor assistance of the father's sperm to be brought into being. Thus, the avunculate—the peculiar relationship between mother's brother and sister's son, is there from the beginning. It is not something that has to be activated by particular social circumstances; it is as primitive a term as the nuclear family itself, not some oddity of the perverse mentality of savages. We are bound to our mother's brothers as surely as to our mothers and fathers. Different social circumstances will of course "weight" this relationship differently, but in times of social crisis it will assert itself as a basic relationship. (Lévi-Strauss cites troubadour songs as evidence of this.)

What is more, the way it will be weighted, in this theory, is not directly correlated with the form of descent. Most of the world is not in fact governed by unilineal descent—which obsessed the Functionalists. It is not either matrilineal or patrilineal. But, as with the Anglo-Saxons, it can make much of the avunculate. If the Functionalist arguments exhausted the issue, this would be inexplicable. Homans had tried to deal with this by stressing the "locus of jural authority" (father versus mother's brother) rather than the form of descent. But this becomes confusing because, except in matrilineal societies, the locus of jural authority is rarely with the maternal uncle. For Lévi-Strauss the issue of cross-cousin marriage has nothing to do with the extension of sentiments but rather with the response to social requirements. "Direct" exchange—as in the double cross-cousin marriages in diagram 4.5—was "restricted"; there was no way it could expand except geometrically (splitting moieties into submoities; crossing patrimoities with matrimoities, etc.). Marriage with the MBD on the other hand was "generalized"—any number could play, adding infinitely to the basic A→B→C→A formula. Marriage with FZD lay in between producing only "short cycles" in alternate generations (see Fox 1967a, chaps. 6 and 7, for details). Thus, the preponderance of MBD marriage lay in the basic conditions of exchange, like the avunculate itself.

Even the "structure of sentiments" need not follow the unilineal pattern according to Lévi-Strauss. The main thing about sentiments was that they would be symmetrically distributed within the "atom." If one relationship was "positive" (warm, indulgent, friendly), its symmetrical opposite would be "negative" (stern, authoritarian, even hostile). Thus, in the Trobriand case for example, the relationship of brother and sister is negative; so that between husband and wife is

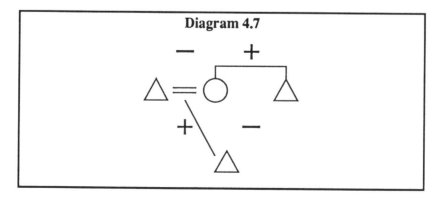

Diagram 4.7

positive. By the same rule the relationship between father and son will be positive and that between maternal uncle and nephew negative, as can be seen in diagram 4.7.

This is not necessarily correlated with rules of descent. Some wags pointed out that the only exception seemed to be the cranky islanders of Dobu where *all* relationships were negative. But this could have been a function of Fortune's (1932) own warped view of his dismal situation there.

Lévi-Strauss refers to the irreducible nature of the avunculate as reflected in the songs of the medieval troubadours. Certainly in many of the romances and epics there seems to be a stress on this relationship. In the Irish sagas we have the young Cuchullain as the sister's son of Conchobar, High King of Ireland. His early exploits concern his assertion of his right to a place in the king's retinue. Diarmud (under the influence of a spell) steals Grainne from his mother's brother, Finn MacCumhaill, thus sparking one of the great epic pursuits and the hero's Adonis-like death from the tusks of a great boar. In a derivation of this same tale, Tristan (under the influence of the love potion) likewise steals Isolde from his maternal uncle, King Mark, with the tragic consequences that form the basis of all modern "love romances." Parsifal is the sister's son of the wounded Grail King, Anfortas. Eventually he completes his task, allows the king, his uncle, to die in peace, and succeeds him as king and guardian of the Grail. (The Grail females, if they marry away, may reveal their origins, but not the males. Thus, Lohengrin, the son of Parsifal, has to return, by the next available swan, to Monsalvat when asked the forbidden question by his over-curious wife.)

In all this there is certainly rich material for theorists of "ambivalence." But for the moment let us simply note the ubiquity— and the reader will be thinking of many more examples—of this relationship which seems as "special" to the creators of these sagas as that between father and son. In fact the father in many cases is unknown or at least unmentioned; or the birth of the hero, as Hartland spelled out at length, is magical and divine, leaving the mother's brother as the nearest earthly male relative. Could the sagas indeed have this hidden meaning so close to Lévi-Strauss's own? Why not?

Followers of the Master added their own wrinkles. Leach (1961), for example, took up the question of "strong" versus "weak" patrilineal systems. Much had been made of this difference, but, Leach asked, how do you judge it? Functionalists like Fortes and Goody had, as we saw, made much of the sister's son as a child of a "residual sibling" in patrilineal societies. It was as if the patrilineage was reluctant to accept that it could not reproduce through its females, and so hung on to its "sisters' sons." But why should it? It should be much more concerned with getting hold of other people's sisters as wives to produce its heirs. Was a "strong" patrilineage one that gained absolute control over wives, detaching them thoroughly from their natal lineages, or one that kept control over sisters and hence the sons of the sisters? To accept the latter, said Leach, was to be obsessed with the importance of descent and consequently to overlook the importance of alliance—the marriage per se. Structuralists were to make this insistence, following Lévi-Strauss, on treating the marriage link as primary, not simply "the residue of exogamy" as Fortes had it. In their view, for example, the claim of a man on his MBD was simply a continuation of the alliance formed in the previous generation (see diagram 4.8). And a "mother's brother" was perhaps better regarded as a "father's wife's brother" (see Dumont 1953).

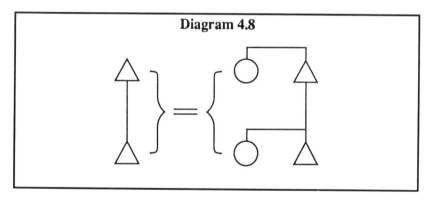

Diagram 4.8

All this—which in retrospect seems more to be a difference in emphasis than a different version of reality—stems from that original assumption of the incest taboo as the essential item in the "passage from nature to culture" that we have already questioned. So we go back to our original question: is the avunculate the basic social relationship created by "culture" or does it exist in some form in nature, like incest avoidance itself?

The Ethologists:
The Mother and Child Reunion

The central premise of the comparative ethological approach is that we must always treat the "cultural" status of social relationships as problematical. Thus, we cannot simply define any relationship as being purely cultural until we have examined the comparative evidence across species. Some relationships are going to be found, for example, across all mammalian species, and it is more logical therefore to start with these. Thus, instead of starting with the nuclear family or the atom of kinship or whatever, the comparative ethologist would start with the only universal mammalian relationship: that between mother and offspring.

Fox's "law of the dispensable male" (1985a) means that the relationship of males to this basic group is always up for grabs. There are four possible strategies: the units can congregate into herds; the genitor can stay with the mother-child unit or several such units; the males of the mother-child unit can stay with it and invest in the children of the females; or, the unit can fend for itself without male help. In many lower mammals the last alternative is common, and the unit itself breaks up regularly as the precocial young disperse. The "herd" solution is common among, for example, ungulates. But often there are subunits of ungulate herds which are males with "harems" of mother-infant units, a solution common to sea mammals as well. Where it pays a genitor to invest in his own offspring—or alternatively put, where it pays a female to get a genitor to so invest—and where harem formation is not possible (for ecological reasons), some form of

Diagram 4.9

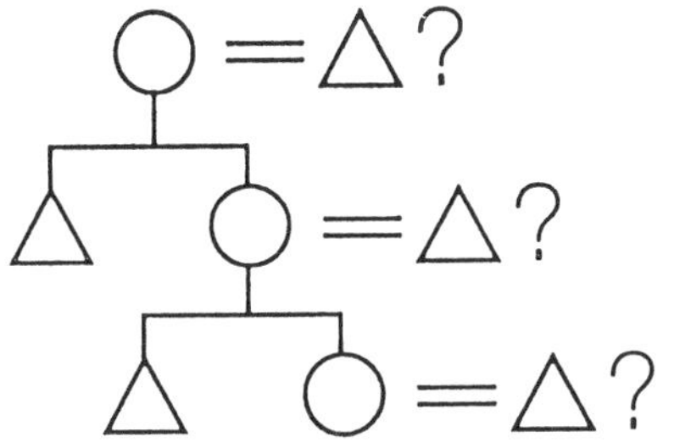

"pair-bonding" and a nuclear family will evolve. The last possibility is a kind of "group marriage," where all the males of a group stay with all the females and young without specific paring.

I suppose since we have diagrammed the other positions, this one needs its graphics too. Perhaps the simplest expression of it is the one described in diagram 4.9, where the mother-infant unit is stable and central, but the way males will relate to females as mates and parents is totally variable.

How do we state the uniqueness of the human situation given this perspective? The neatest statement of it was given by Tiger and Fox in *The Imperial Animal* (1971), and I paraphrase it here: mating consists of two phases, the courtship phase which brings the animals together, and the parental phase which keeps them there—at least until the offspring reach viability (i.e., are able to have their own offspring). The most logical way to produce a "parental" bond would seem to be to unite the genitor and his mate in a "pair bond," and this is indeed a common solution. But there is another possibility inherent in the situation: the children of the mother-infant unit, united by the common bond with the mother but having an asexual relationship because of (natural) incest avoidance, are available as a "pair" for parental purposes, even if not for "courtship" purposes. In other words, humans can and do separate the courtship bond from the parental bond, and assign parental duties to the noncourtship pair (as shown in diagram 4.10).

Obviously, this produces the basic "matrilineal" situation envisaged by theorists from Bachofen through Briffault to modern feminism. But we do not see it as a primary "stage" through which all human so-

Diagram 4.10

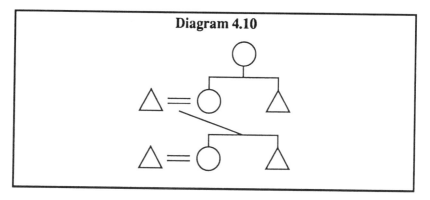

cieties must have passed; rather, it is viewed as an option open to human mating strategists—a neat alternative whereby males do their mating jobs with one set of women and their parental jobs with another. In the prototype situation, women remain "sisters" and "mothers" but are only peripherally "wives" if wives at all; men are "brothers" and "maternal uncles" but again, peripherally or not at all "fathers and husbands." This seems more in line with ethnographic reality in which the "matrilineal" solution—with its built-in avunculate—is a common but decidedly minority solution to the problem of how to attach males to the mother-child unit. (The "attachment" of the brother to the sister and her children, although "a-sexual" in the strict sense, may, under some circumstances, have strong sexual overtones. The exploration of this possibility would take us too far afield here, but is the subject of a long discussion in Fox 1980.)

But what about the avunculate in nonmatrilineal societies? Because of the common bond to the mother, the brother and sister always constitute a "reserve" unit of quasi-parental behavior even if the mating unit is husband-wife. There will therefore be a constant tug-of-war between the two "bonds" (the "husband-wife" bond and the "brother-sister" bond) generalized into a "consanguine versus affine" conflict. The mother-in-law joke *is* the world's oldest. It is not so much, as in the Structuralist version, that the brother "relinquishes" the sister to the husband, as that the "mother" relinquishes, often with great reluctance, both the brother and the sister to their spouses. There is always a strain towards reuniting the broken unit, the basic and fundamental unit, and this will "pull" the sister and her children—the new mother-infant unit—back into the consanguine fold: to the "mother's brother" in fact. For, although we speak of the mother-child unit as "basic," once the system is rolling, the mother will have a brother who will be the *responsable* as the French nicely put it: the closest responsible consanguine male. And this is as firmly built into the "atom" as it is in Lévi-Strauss's formulation, without having to do violence to the facts of human and animal behavior.

I have put "matrilineal" in quotes above quite deliberately, since the activation of the brother-sister bond for parental purposes is certainly not confined to matrilineal societies. The tug-of-war is always there in all societies (consanguine versus affinal bonds), and only circumstances will determine how this will turn out in terms of specific social institutions. True matrilineal descent groups can emerge, but also a balance-of-power situation can exist in which one bond takes over some functions and the other, others. Or at another extreme the brother-sister bond can be downplayed thoroughly at the expense of the husband-wife bond. I have expended a lot of ink describing these variations. The main point to note here is that the *possibility* of this variation exists in human mating strategies and that therefore the *probability* of the avunculate's cropping up in one form or another is high.

To illustrate the independence of the "brother-sister parental bond" situation from matrilineality, let me take an example from my own fieldwork on Tory Island. To set the scene, let us note that Fortes (1949), for example, in examining the consanguineal household among the Ashanti, had attributed the brother-sister parental bond to the matrilineality of these people (and by implication to matrilineal descent wherever it occurred). Thus, households of mothers and daughters, with the males of the households being the "sons" and "brothers," occur, according to Fortes, as a result of the power of the matrilineage in gathering together its members under one roof. But on Tory Island, in decidedly nonmatrilineal northwestern Ireland, such households formed a sizeable proportion of the total in traditional society, and even in the 1960s represented 20 percent of the total. Sisters, on marriage, did not leave their natal homes; neither did their brothers. Children stayed with their mothers, and thus the households were classical consanguineal setups, but with narry a hint of matrilineality. In fact, I concluded that the cart might have been put before the horse here and that matrilineality might more likely arise from the development of consanguineal households than vice versa.

This is an oversimplified description, and curious readers may consult the details for themselves. The point is simply to emphasize that the tug-of-war can result in very varied outcomes, even though it is based on the constants to which we have referred. It is also to show how we have in a sense shoved the issue of the avunculate further back into "nature" than Lévi-Strauss would have it. That is, the use of the sibling bond for parental purposes is "natural" in the human case in any situation where, for whatever reason, the mating bond is weak but there is still a need for males to be attached to the maternal unit. Cultural factors will determine how the "atomic" situation will manifest itself, but the atom, according to my theory, is not itself a cultural product—as with Structuralism—but entirely natural. This, however, still leaves open the question of how much further back into nature we can push the avunculate. It may be natural to our species as a result of our peculiar path of evolution, including the evolution of language that allows us to designate roles like "sister-in-law" and "mother's brother." But is it *unique* to us—or does comparative ethology, and particularly comparison with our closest evolutionary relatives, the primates, reveal anything that is, if nothing else, at least a plausible precursor to the avunculate in humans?

The Primatologists:
The Primate Baseline Drive

Is there an avunculate in nonhuman "nature"? The great humorist-anthropologist Weston LaBarre (1954) proclaimed definitively that "ducks don't have uncles." And, as we have seen, David Schneider would deny primates kinship at the risk of being a monkey's uncle! Well, as I remember, the world's most famous duck was in fact uncle (although I don't think it was specified that he was a maternal uncle) to Huey, Louie, and Dewey—nephews towards whom he certainly assumed, however frustratingly, a parental role. So let us take heart and go uncle hunting among our nearest relatives.

We have to start with the "discovery" of primate kinship. For many years it was not discovered, or thought not to exist. The notion that, even if "primitive man" was not randomly promiscuous his simian cousins were, died hard. Darwin, with Westermarck and Freud following him, tried to find some order in gorilla mating, but as late as 1932, Solly Zuckerman, in what was for years taken to be the last word, pronounced, on the basis of observations on overcrowded baboons with a preponderance of males in the London Zoo, that primate mating was indeed total chaos. Again, as late as 1960 Marshal Sahlins was repeating this as gospel, while Lévi-Strauss had made it a cornerstone of his nature-culture distinction in his great work in 1949. Primate mating was promiscuous, incestuous, and unordered; human mating was the absolute opposite in every respect.

Slowly, starting with the work of Japanese primatologists after World War II, and then with the students of Washburn at Berkeley, of

DeVore at Harvard, of Kummer in Holland, of Hall at Bristol (UK), and of Altmann on Cayo Santiago off Puerto Rico, the picture emerged of a much more ordered and structured primate group where mating was not randomized or incestuous, and kinship ties mattered a great deal. As groups of macaques and baboons were followed over several generations, and the importance of genealogical relationships became more and more obvious, the original picture of primate society based on male dominance and female subservience was considerably modified. In an attempt to put some order into this information—to try to establish what I called "the primate baseline"—I summarized it under two headings: kinship and mating in one-male groups, and the same in multi-male groups (see diagrams 4.11 through 4.13) ("Primate Kin and Human Kinship" in Fox 1975).

It had been observed—particularly in multi-male groups—that spatially the dominant (or alpha) males tended to stay in the center of the group, surrounded by the females and young, while the adolescent and subdominant males were always at the periphery, having been expelled from the center at puberty. I tried to outline this as in diagram 4.11. I then added the kinship relationships between all concerned (discovered as we have seen by diachronic studies) and came up with diagram 4.12. What this brings out is the "matrifocal" nature of primate kinship in such groups: it is based on the mother-daughter bond and persists through the mother-daughter tie. Mating tends to be on a "consort" basis: the dominant male or males will form a relationship with a female in estrus and guard her during this period, thus increasing the chances of adding the genes of the dominant male or males to the pool at the expense of less dominant males. Here, then, among (for example) our prototypical macaques and common baboons, we have kinship groups that endure for a time through the mother-daughter tie, and mating based on dominance.

The females too have a dominance hierarchy, and the fascinating thing that was discovered here was that a female passes on her dominance status to her offspring. Thus, the children and grandchildren (i.e., daughters' children) of high-ranking females are themselves also high ranking, and their offspring stand a better chance of becoming dominant than do those of low-ranking females. At first it seemed that the dominance of mating by high-ranking males was wholly to their own advantage; but it could also be seen as being to the

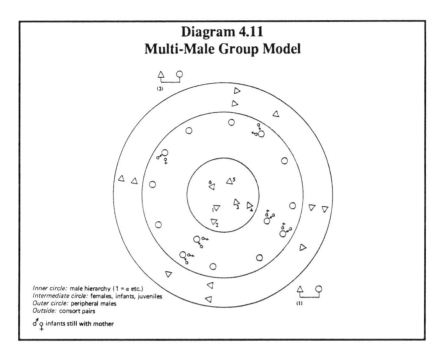

Diagram 4.11
Multi-Male Group Model

Inner circle: male hierarchy (1 = α etc.)
Intermediate circle: females, infants, juveniles
Outer circle: peripheral males
Outside: consort pairs

♂♀ infants still with mother

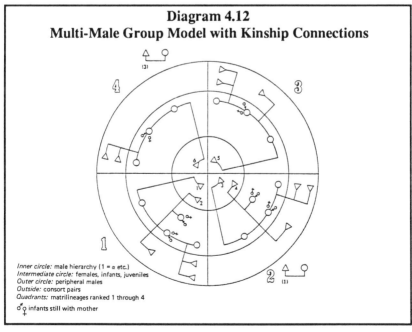

Diagram 4.12
Multi-Male Group Model with Kinship Connections

Inner circle: male hierarchy (1 = α etc.)
Intermediate circle: females, infants, juveniles
Outer circle: peripheral males
Outside: consort pairs
Quadrants: matrilineages ranked 1 through 4

♂♀ infants still with mother

mother's advantage in that her dominant sons would spread *her* genes disproportionately through the pool. This knowledge led to a little burst of aphorisms, with DeVore saying that males were "a breeding experiment run by females" while Fox announced that "males were the females' way of getting more females" (echoing the wisdom that a chicken was the egg's way of getting more eggs).

The alternative, "one-male group" structure is shown in diagram 4.13. This is the "harem" system of the hamadryas and gelada baboons, and to some extent the gorillas, for example. Here a male gathers, by various means, a harem of about six females to himself and guards these constantly. He either becomes an "apprentice" to a dominant male, tags along with him, and eventually takes over his females. Or he gathers young females, "fathers" them, and rears them to adulthood. Or he takes over the harem of another male after a fight. Or some combination of the above. In such a system, kinship seems to play little part, while mating is relatively permanent over the lifetime of the dominant male.

The concentric circles in these diagrams show the different ways in which males try to get from the periphery to the center. In the multi-

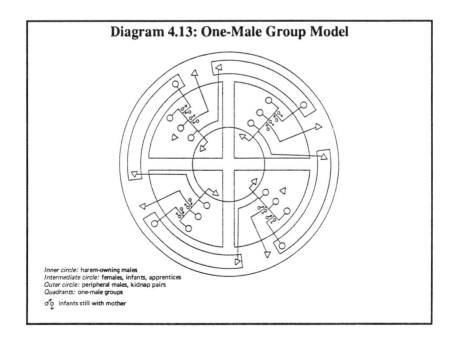

Diagram 4.13: One-Male Group Model

Inner circle: harem-owning males
Intermediate circle: females, infants, apprentices
Outer circle: peripheral males, kidnap pairs
Quadrants: one-male groups

♂♀ infants still with mother

male group, the son of a high-ranking female would eventually come to be accepted in the inner circle. In the one-male group he would work his way there through the accumulation of females for his harem. In the first case then, we can see that at least potentially the son of a high-ranking female would be depending on his maternal "lineage," which would include his mother's brothers. There is at least then the possibility of some sort of rudimentary "avunculate" in this type of system, particularly if there is little movement between groups. Any particular male's genitor would likely come from another lineage, while his maternal uncles would be part of his route to success, if they were high ranking, or peripheralization and possibly expulsion if they were low ranking. In the multi-male system this possibility seems likely.

I also dealt with the fact that, where it is possible, males seem to move a lot between groups. This movement is less likely, for example, in desert baboons where the groups are relatively isolated, and more likely in island-dwelling macaques, where groups are proximate. In some cases this movement bears a striking resemblance to human kinship systems. Thus, among Japanese macaques, the ranked lineages of an island group split into two groups, each with an equal number of lineages. Eventually all the males of group A moved to group B and vice versa. This is uncannily close to a human system of two matri-moieties where the males of one moiety marry the females of the other and vice versa, as in diagram 4.5. Here of course a male would end up mating where his mother's brothers mated. Even when it is not so neat as two groups, it has been shown that males are more likely to move where members of their natal groups have gone.

Diagrams 4.14 and 4.15 are taken from the work of Cheney 1983. (This paper is part of a collection of papers that is an excellent summary of current knowledge. See also Smuts et al. 1987.) Here we can see that males prefer to go to groups where others of their natal group have gone; and these were mostly the younger males. In a rough sense then we could see them as following their maternal kin: their brothers and mothers' brothers. Of course they could also be following their "fathers" and their "fathers' brothers," but as we have seen, the lack of a permanent pair-bond means that genitors are not traced or traceable in such groups. The only nearly related senior male kin of a young monkey would be its mother's brother.

More recent studies of hamadryas and gelada baboons (see summary in Rodseth et al. 1991) suggest that the harem-owning males may be linked in "clans" on a patrilineal basis. More recent work on chimpanzees suggests that while the matrifocal element is there as in the classic multi-male group, the males of the chimp group—more probably patrilineally related since among chimps, atypically, it is the females who change groups to mate—act together over long periods in a concerted way. Wrangham (1980) has even suggested a basis in dietary physiology for these different strategies.

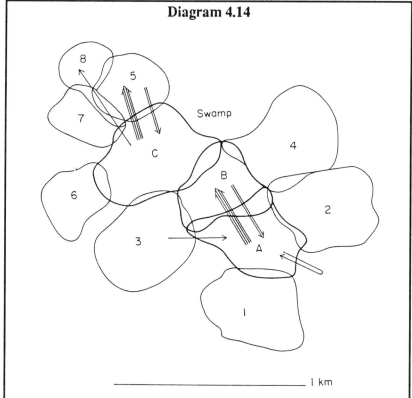

Diagram 4.14

Distribution of migration by natal and young adult males into and from the three study groups between March 1977 and March 1982. The arrows indicate the direction of movement and each line represents one male. The ranges of the study groups are lettered; the ranges of regularly censused groups are numbered. Only groups with ranges adjacent to the study groups are shown.

So reality presents a more mixed picture than my simple model of 1975 described. I had decided that both "descent" (the matrifocal kinship groups) and "alliance" (the one-male group harems) existed in nature but had never there been combined in one system. The human revolution had been to take these two natural elements and combine them; it invented nothing new, but the combination of two ancient systems was the new step into "culture." The human revolution was not the imposition of an incest taboo, as Lévi-Strauss and almost everyone else thought; that was there in the natural incest avoidance (see Bischoff in Fox 1975; Fox 1980). Rather, it was the combining of matrifocal kinship with relatively permanent mating, which gave rise to human kinship. This was the step beyond the primate baseline, and

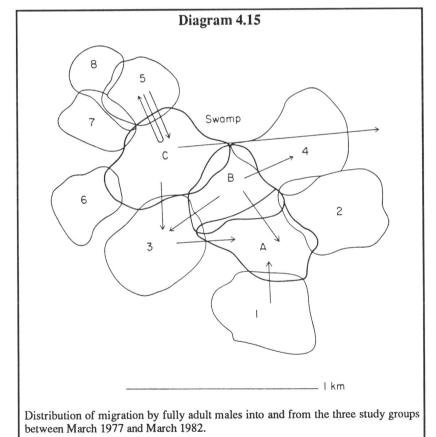

Diagram 4.15

Distribution of migration by fully adult males into and from the three study groups between March 1977 and March 1982.

a primitive avunculate was indeed built into it, but it was there before the formulation of the "atom of kinship." It was not a product, but a basic element.

If the gelada/hamadryas data are confirmed, however, then we may have an alternative route via patrilineally-related, harem-owning males. This is attractive since it represents the strategy of a large number of human societies, and seems something therefore that is "natural" to us. But of course all this is speculation. We are not baboons, macaques, or chimpanzees. We can only look to these for clues; for hints as to what is "in" nature; for the elements of the primate baseline. As I have continually stressed, we must have being doing something very *different* from these relatives in order to be where we are. But since we emerged from the same stock, it is plausible that we used elements that were common to the basic primate repertoire: we are able to form kin groups, possibly matrifocal with a "built-in" mother's brother, and we are able to form "alliances" (long-term mating arrangements of a polygynous nature). Thus, we became polygynous and avuncular, not because these were human cultural inventions, but because—*bricoleurs* that we are—we drew them from the ragbag of the primate repertoire and rearranged them to suit our own adaptive needs—or rather, nature in the form of natural selection did it for us.

If we don't use the precise language, we get dangerously close to saying that it happened "for the good of the group," when we should know that things do not happen for the good of the group but for the good of individual organisms and eventually individual genes. This is where selection takes place, and precisely in 1975, when I was debating these matters, a new subdiscipline was named and definitively formulated to analyze social behavior precisely from this point of view. Sociobiology was born, and one of its first ventures was a reanalysis of the avunculate.

The Sociobiologists:
It's a Wise Chimp That Knows Its Own Father

E. O. Wilson (1975) in developing "sociobiology" drew primarily on the theoretical work of Hamilton (1963 and 1964) and Trivers (1972). Hamilton had taken up the suggestions inherent in the work of

Fisher (1929) and Haldane (1932) that kinship in nature was important as a component of natural selection. It worked, if the anecdote is correct, on Haldane's principle that while he would not sacrifice himself for his brother, he would do so for two brothers or eight first cousins. This is the basic proposition of what came to be known as "inclusive fitness"—the principle that our relatives carry replicas of the same genes "identical by descent" as we do, and that therefore we can improve our "fitness"—i.e., the number of our genes in the gene pool—by promoting their reproductive success as well as our own. Since full brothers (or sisters) share 50 percent of our genes, to save two of them at our own expense fully replaces us, in a sense. First cousins share 12.5 percent of their genes with us, so we need eight to have the same effect. Genes, in this argument, are solely concerned with their own replication—they are ultimately "selfish" in Dawkins' usage (Dawkins 1976, the best popular introduction to this new thinking). Hamilton came up with his famous basic formula for inclusive fitness: $K > 1/\bar{\tau}$. K is the the ratio of cost-benefit in "fitness" to an altruist (one sacrificing himself for kin) and it must be greater than one divided by the average degree of relationship ($\bar{\tau}$) between the altruist and the recipients in order that the altruistic gene might be selected.

This process of selecting altruists, or more correctly of selecting genes for altruistic behavior, was christened "kin selection" to distinguish it from "individual selection" or "group selection." The ingenuity of the idea was that it left the "selfishness" of genes intact: even when acting in a self-sacrificing manner, the object was still the replication of genes, whose only purpose was indeed to replicate themselves. Thus, "kin altruism" was a by-product of genetic self-interest.

Trivers added a theory, dubbed "reciprocal altruism," to explain self-sacrificing acts towards non-kin, but that goes beyond our brief here. He did, however, add another crucial notion to the growing inventory of "sociobiological" ideas: that of "parental investment." Obviously, in species where parents invest a lot of time and effort in raising relatively few young—known as "K selected species" in the jargon—organisms would not be interested in raising young who were not related to them. The selfish genes were not interested in promoting the welfare of unrelated genes. Thus, where parental investment was high, mechanisms would evolve to ensure that organisms had a high degree of probability in "paternity certainty." Note that "maternity certainty" is not at issue: we always know who our mothers are and mothers know their children, since they produce them. But, as in the proverbs of many tribes and the statements of Roman law, paternity is only inferential. "It's a wise child that knows its own father," says our own version, which echoes a widespread uneasiness among fathers about their relatedness to their children; an uneasiness taken to its crazy extreme in Strindberg's disturbing play *The Father*, and in a lower key in Ibsen's *The Wild Duck*. The Scandinavians seem to have a particular problem in this respect.

But while they might have been outstanding in converting their obsession into great literature, the obsession seems pretty widespread—with many important exceptions, as we shall note. This was seized upon by a series of sociobiologists in the first major foray they undertook into the explanation of human behavior: an explanation of the avunculate. In fact, what they did was really to reinvent the wheel, since their theory took them right back into the heart of the nineteenth-century debate on the matriarchal and patriarchal origins of kinship systems that we have already canvassed earlier. Remember the debate between the "paternity certainty" and "paternity ignorance" factions in the origins of matrilineal descent? This was what was revived in its new, sophisticated, mathematical form by the sociobiologists. They plumped for the "paternity certainty" version, as one might expect, given their theories. And unlike Radcliffe-Brown and Junod, they were not much interested in the avunculate in patrilineal societies, but rather with the original question of the origins of matrilineal systems of descent, inheritance, and succession.

Alexander (1974) was the first to try this out, followed by Kurland (1979) and Hartung (1985). They differ among themselves somewhat, but let us try to state in a nontechnical way what they have in common. Their basic set of concepts are the aforementioned inclusive fitness, kin selection, altruism, and paternity confidence. To this they add "nepotism" in the sense of favoring relatives over strangers— although they don't seem to see the irony in that this literally means favoring the sister's son, which is what they are discussing. They address this largely in terms of "investment," and hence look more closely at inheritance than anything else, such as succession, seeing the latter as a form of inheritance, if they address the issue at all. They pose the question more or less like this: if a man is faced with the alternatives of "investing in" his own sons or his sisters' sons, why should he ever prefer the latter? Their answer is relatively simple if one leaves out the mathematics: he will prefer his sisters' sons when his confidence of paternity in his own sons is low.

The mathematics come in when we try to decide "how low?" But leaving that aside, let us look at the argument. Organisms, including human organisms, they say, wish desperately to avoid the "cuckoo effect." They do not want to be tricked into raising unrelated genes, so to be "cuckolded" is the worst thing that could happen. If, however, they live in a relatively promiscuous society, with few checks on who is the genitor of a child, then they constantly face the prospect of having to invest in children not related to them. Thus, the higher the level of adultery and promiscuity, the more likely they are to feel a low confidence of paternity and turn to alternatives. The probability of their genetic relationship to their own sons varies from 100 percent to 0 percent. They may then have a .5 genetic relationship, or a 0. But their genetic relationship to their sisters' sons remains constant (100 percent) at .25. Better, it is argued, to settle for a certain .25 relationship than a possible 0. Over time, you are better off with the steady .25. Much of the argument has rested on where exactly the "paternity threshold" lies. Hartung puts it at a probability of 46 percent. Below this, it will pay a man to invest in his sisters' sons rather than risk the unrelatedness of his own.

It is an attractive argument. It would, with precision and economy, account for matrilineal inheritance practices and hence the origins and persistence of matrilineal systems. And indeed, these systems often do seem to report loose or nonexistent marriage practices, a high independence of women that goes with greater promiscuity, and so on; not universally, but in a preponderance of such societies. So the sociobiologists, invoking the notions of genetic nepotism and parental investment, calculate that these conditions would force men to choose sister's children over their own. Where are the women in all this? Are they merely pawns in male schemes? It would seem so. For example, in very few places are women the sole heirs; it is always men who inherit (although the sociobiologists have not really faced up to the not inconsiderable number of systems where inheritance is partible and women get some of the patrimony, even if only in the form of dowries). But Hartung at least argues that matrilineal inheritance is a better long-term strategy for women and that this may have a lot to do with its acceptance.

But does the argument hold up? For a start, there is a logical flaw in it. If the society is really promiscuous and the confidence of paternity low, then a man cannot be sure that his sister is a full sister. In fact, logically, the lower the confidence of paternity, the better the chance that she is a half-sister. Thus, her children would not be related by a factor of .25, but only .125—no better than first cousins. In small communities with high levels of endogamy (marriage within the community), after a few generations everyone is related to everyone else within the range of second cousins (.0625)—genetically a very low level of relationship. Deciding then between those related by a possible .125 and .0625 and beyond becomes a very fine point and almost not worth bothering with. We are a long way from the firm and tempting .25 of the theory.

Another point to notice is that a causal direction is assumed by the theory, but not proved by it. That is, it is assumed that low levels of paternity confidence will "cause" men to decide on investment in the sister's sons. But the only systems we know of are systems in which this decision was taken possibly millenia ago. Men for countless generations have grown up in systems that were already matrilineal. They go on "investing" in sisters' children, often reluctantly, because the laws and customs of their societies demand this of them. The literature is replete with examples of the tug-of-war we described in section four of this chapter ("The Ethologists") between the brother-sister tie and the husband-wife tie, in which "sisters" compete with "wives" for the investment of the brother, and in which the brother would rather invest in his wife's children than his sisters', but is constrained by law and custom to favor the latter. I have argued that Central African systems of "double descent," where one finds strong matrilineal clans crosscut by cattle-owning patrilines, may well have originated this way, with patrilineal inheritance pushing aside the older matrilineal system when men favored their sons in cattle inheritance (Fox 1967b). Thus, rather than following smart evolutionary promptings when investing in sisters' sons, men in matrilineal societies are often seen to be acting against their own genetically better judgement. (It is also worth noting that promiscuity—and hence low paternity confidence—far from causing matrilineal descent is more likely a consequence of it. As we have seen, the identity of the genitor is considered irrelevant in matrilineal ideologies.)

I would suggest that, even if there is some truth to the hypothesis of "low paternity confidence = matrilineal investment," it is perhaps best tested under circumstances where men have a *choice* in their investment decisions, rather than where they are forced to invest by law in one way or another. I have pointed out that our own contemporary society in fact offers such a testing ground (Fox 1985b). Since the sixties, and the rise of divorce and the sexual revolution, paternity confidence should be at an all time low. And here we can make wills in favor of any heir. We should, according to the theory, be rushing to favor sisters' children. I see no evidence of this. But if we are talking about *behavior* rather than custom—and we should be if we are really taking evolutionary behavioral genetics seriously—then we should be comparing individual behavior within societies, and not comparing the customary usages of whole societies.

This of course raises the whole question of what individuals are in fact motivated to do. Are they really motivated to "maximize their inclusive fitness," as the sociobiological formula has it? (That is, to maximize their own fitness plus that of those who share genes identical by descent.) As we saw in chapter 2, there is reason to doubt this. Of course, the theory can hold that this is rarely a *conscious* motivation but that unconsciously this is what they strive to do. But again we must apply Occam's razor: do we need to posit more explanatory entities when less will do the job? Do we need to posit hidden motives which, like the conspiracies of conspiracy theories, can explain, but whose existence cannot be refuted? I don't think so. Is it not enough to say that we have a number of simple and observable motives, and that if we act on these then there is a strong likelihood that we shall achieve that maximization? Thus, obviously we are motivated to have sex, to accrue wealth, to enjoy children, to achieve status, to help relatives, etc. If we get all these right, then "maximization of inclusive fitness" will follow. We do not have to posit hidden and unconscious motives that go directly to maximization choices (Fox 1986).

And then there is the basic objection of Hartland's that we spelled out at the beginning of this chapter. There are plenty of patrilineal societies in which not much attention is paid to the identity of the genitor so long as the "wife's" children become the legal offspring of her husband. Indeed, Radcliffe-Brown pointed out, as we saw in section 2, that much of Bantu law was concerned with establishing that regardless of the identity of the genitor, a woman's children belonged to her legal husband—a basic tenet of Anglo-Saxon and Roman law also, and one that intruded itself into the peculiarities of the surrogate mother case as well. African patrilineal tribes practice, among other things, ghost marriages and woman marriages. In the former, a woman bears children to the name of her dead husband and they are "his" children and belong to his lineage and clan. In the latter, a woman marries "wives," who bear children to the name of her clan. In both these cases, it is the continuity of the clan as a social group that is at issue. The patriclan or patrilineage will "invest" in these children regardless of who the genitor is. The same is true in those patrilineal societies practicing wife lending (in some ways a more drastic assertion of male patriarchal power over women than is their claustration). Paternity certainty becomes irrelevant in these societies, which are as "strongly patrilineal" as any Functionalist could wish. Equally, we can find numerous examples of matrilineal societies with lasting marriages and high confidence of paternity.

As Hartland saw, the issue is not really the certainty of paternity at all, but "something else." He thought it was "ignorance of paternity," but I would rather label it "paternity irrelevance" (Fox 1985b). It is not that these people are necessarily ignorant of the facts of paternity, but that they regard it as irrelevant. In a matrilineal society, if a child has a mother it has a clan, and the identity of the genitor is irrelevant. This irrelevancy is often elaborated in ideological doctrines of virgin birth, or conception by clan spirits, or anything that underscores the irrelevance of the genitor. Thus, the so-called "ignorance of paternity" more often turns out to be an ideological denial of the relevance of physical paternity.

Almost always, however, in matrilineal societies, there is a definite acceptance of the need for a pater: a social father who will fulfil the necessary obligations of the "father's clan" towards his wife's offspring. Correct marriages between clans are often of great importance in the social system, and as we have seen, marriages into the father's clan (FZD) or even the mother's father's clan (MFZDD) are required marriages. But these are social positions. Thus, in the Pueblo of Cochiti, New Mexico, which I studied in the 1950s when a large part of its traditional matrilineal culture was still intact, if a girl had a child before marriage, which was not uncommon, and she was not married when this child was of marriageable age, then where did the "father's clan" come from that was so necessary to a proper marriage (and also to the assignment of a boy to a patrilineal moiety)? The answer was that her elder sister's husband's clan, and failing that the clan of any husband of an elder clanswoman, would serve. In short, the clan of a man who had "married into" her clan was, for social purposes, a "father's clan." The genitor here is wholly irrelevant. (In the Crow-type system of kinship terminology, all these men would be called "father" or "grandfather" anyway, a seeming genetic anomaly which in fact makes great sociological sense, as social anthropologists have been at pains to point out.)

The theory of a direct causal relationship between low paternity certainty and matrilineal descent, and hence of the special role of the mother's brother in inheritance and succession, has been stoutly argued and stoutly criticized. But at least it has done one thing: it has raised the issue of the avunculate to a central place in theories of what it means to be human—of what it means to be cultural as opposed to natural. As I predicted, it would be the avunculate and not the incest taboo that would become the defining principle of humanity and culture. I am not sure that "investment in the sister's son" exhausts the meaning of the avunculate, especially in patrilineal societies. But it is certainly one thing to consider. Animals don't do it, even if they may occasionally, as with the primates, end up in a "special relationship" with the maternal uncle. It seems to be a peculiarly human thing to allow the asexual brother-sister tie to take over certain aspects of the parental role from the husband-wife tie. This gives rise to avuncular responsibilities that may flower into full-blown matrilineal succession and inheritance, or to the classical indulgences of the patrilineal avunculate, or to the sacred duties towards mothers' brothers in bilateral systems, or even to the "love triangle" conflicts with them where the power of the maternal uncle threatens to rob the young males of their breeding preferences.

Malinowski first saw the real Oedipal ambivalence of the sister's son towards the mother's brother in the matrilineal Trobriands, and although this particular interpretation has been recently challenged (see Spiro 1982—it was always regarded with suspicion by the die-hard Freudians), it is widespread enough to be convincing. The maternal uncle is, as Lévi-Strauss saw, in some sense a primitive given in the kinship equation. My own bet is that our attitudes are indeed deeply atavistic and reflect as much the hangover of the primate baseline as our fear of snakes and dreams of falling. Knowing our fathers and developing Oedipal ambivalences to *them* probably came relatively late in our primate history, and this innate knowledge, however extensively elaborated by culture and patrilineal/patriarchal institutions, has never erased the ineluctable species memory of the monkey's uncle. He crops up like other atavistic memories, sometimes friendly, sometimes frightening, but always a powerful potential lurking behind our rational calculations and cultural certainties. In cultures that turn him into an authority figure, he can even be hated; in those where he is not he can be the refuge from paternal hates. But he is always there, if only in the shadowy background, waiting to step forward when social systems decay and we are forced back to those primitive equations of kinship that are as much our creators as our creations. And it is, as Freud saw so clearly, the curse of our humanity, constantly to recreate that which created us.

Conclusions

What then of the anthropological obsession with the maternal uncle? Is it merely a piece of tribal or historical exotica? Is it solely to do with the statistically small incidence of matrilineal succession? We can answer no on both counts. If the Structural-Ethological position is correct, he is there in the primitive equation of kinship more surely than fathers and fathers brothers are. When these emerge, as in systems of patrilineal succession, the maternal uncle does not disappear. Far from it: he emerges strongly as the counterbalance to the *patria potestas*. He is, in Paul Friedrich's words, the connection through the mother to the "wife-giving" males of her patriclan, like the mother's father with whom he is often terminologically equated. He is there, too, often more strongly, in bilateral (non-unilineal) systems of succession, where as the senior male on the "distaff side" he often achieves almost sacred status as against the pragmatic status of the males on the "spear side"—to use the Anglo-Saxon distinctions.

Whether we regard his special status as purely a result of the incest taboo and the benefits of exchange as the Structuralists did, or as built into the dynamics of the mother-child (son and daughter) bond as the Ethologists (at least this one) might prefer, the outcome is the same: the mother's brother is one of the "primitive" terms of the kinship equation. Fathers and fathers' brothers merge, like mothers and mothers' sisters; terminologically, they are often identical. But the mother's brother stands out as distinctive and important, balanced by his symmetrical opposite: the father's sister. These two are the product of the "opposite sex" sibling bond rather than the "same sex" bond, and this ensures their distinctiveness. While the mother's brother may be there in "nature" (at least primate nature) in a shadowy form, the father's sister is not. She is indeed a product of the human innovation, but not of the Structuralists' primary incest taboo. Rather, along with her brother, she is the product of the human working out of the logic of succession stemming from the mother-child unit. (The brother and sister would, like their primate cousins, usually avoid sexual relations anyway without the taboo being needed.) Mother's brother and father's sister are the "brother and sister/son and daughter" of the aboriginal mother-child triad whose fate is bound to be different because of the sex difference but whose fate is also a unity because of the link to the mother. The human bricolage is to take the logic inherent in this situation and to actualize it: to try constantly to reunite the children of the brother and sister who must mate elsewhere than in the maternal nest. Their asexual (if not unsexy) relationship stands always as a kind of magnet drawing their children back together, either in direct relationships of the kind we have explored in the avunculate and the amitate, or in the kinds of cross-cousin marriage (which is of course marriage of the children of brother and sister) we have hinted at and which are so widespread in kinship systems. The consummation that is not open to the parents can still be achieved by the children, and the unity of the group can be restored in the next generation. The variations on the way this can be achieved are what delight (or at least once delighted) social anthropologists and we have run round some of them here. But we should not allow the ethnographic dazzle to blind us to the constants that lie beneath the surface variations. To go back to Lévi-Strauss's haunting metaphor: what are the instructions in the cam shaft that produce these dazzling pieces of the ethnographic jigsaw?

If we do not ask this question then we end up treating the variations as local contingencies based on various local "causes" or "variables." These contingent influences are certainly important in determining the form of the variations, but they do not explain why we should be playing variations on *this* tune (and in this way) and not some other. Again, as Lévi-Strauss has pointed out, there is not logical reason why we should not get societies in which kinship is ignored altogether, or totally arbitrary relationships designated by custom, much as Vonnegut envisioned in his society of the future. But this we do not get. What we do get are a series of very tight variations with a logical relation and internal consistency as intricate as Bach's *Musical Offering* or a Euclidian theorem. And this only works, in all these cases, because of the original axioms and what is built into them. Here I have tried to get at the axioms both as logical premises of the systems and as chronological premises arising in the course of natural selection.

The Evolutionists saw the importance of the mother's brother but assigned him to an early "stage" in social development (motherright), seeing his later appearance in the stage of fatherright as a kind of cultural hangover from which we eventually recovered. The functionalists rescued him from this sequence of stages and placed him, and the father's sister, in the context of power and sentiment relations between unilineal groups. But they did not see him as more than the product of the situations created by the existence of these groups. The Structuralists pushed him one stage further back into nature by recognizing him as part of the primitive kinship atom where he was there *ab origino* as a result of the "renunciation" of the sister. The Ethologists moved him even further back, rejecting the incest taboo as the starting point and seeing him built into the mother-son-daughter triad as part of the potential quasi-parental brother-sister pair, always ready to act since the attachment of males to the mother-child group was never certain. This was bolstered by the Primatologists, who both confirmed the incest avoidance in nature and found that kinship was strongly established in the primate baseline with even a potential in some systems for matrilines and mother's brothers as nearest recognized kin (in a behavioral sense). The Sociobiologists revived the evolutionist interest in paternity certainty—or rather, paternity uncertainty—as a basis for the mother's brother's "investment" in his sister's child. This position though, like that of the Evolutionists and the Functionalists still views the avunculate as a contingency produced by variable circumstances. The Ethological-Structural position sees it not as an event to be caused but rather, in the Aristotelian sense, as a potential to be evoked. It is always "there," only in some cases more visible than others. Thus, there is really no conflict between the positions properly regarded. The Structural-Ethological-Primatological position tells us why the *potentia* exists: the Evolutionist, Functionalist, and Sociobiological positions suggest some reasons for particular forms of actualization. (To be fair, early Evolutionists did see the roots of the avunculate in nature, and the Sociobiological position too could be interpreted as positing an actualization of a potentiality given by the logic of degrees of genetic relatedness.) And if the Ethological position is correct, then our conclusion stands that the avunculate is indeed the most primitive term of the cultural equation (not the incest taboo, not the nuclear family, and not reciprocal exchange).

But where then are maternal uncles today? Of course they are still there in the family equation, but they have suffered along with every other kinship bond in the war we have described between kinship and the state, between status and contract, between collectivism and individualism, between kinship law and state law. If even the privilege of the mother-child bond cannot be assured—if we are willing to buck over 120 million years of mammalian evolution—then what chance has the more fragile avunculate? Actually, more than one might expect. This has not been systematically observed by sociologists whose turf it is, obsessed as they are with "the family" and its "decline," but changing kinship circumstances consequent on the sexual revolution, divorce, and remarriage and the rise of single-parent families, constitute a fertile breeding ground for a re-emergence of the avunculate. As spouses become less reliable, and even as the "state avunculate"—Uncle Sam as surrogate parent through welfare—becomes a less popular option, then the tie between brothers and sisters may well become more attractive as a quasi-parental option. In some ex-slave societies, where marriage has never been thoroughly institutionalized, this seems to be a real trend, and in societies where marriage becomes fragile, optional, and even devalued, the proverbial certainty of the brother-sister bond might well emerge as an attractive alternative to the anomie that threatens rampant individualism when applied to the inherently collectivist scheme of kinship. Of course, this will always be rendered difficult by the extremes of mobility that our industrial society fosters. But even these might be ameliorated in the postindustrial phase with its computer links and home-based work situations. We are returning to the cottage industry situation of the early industrial revolution, which, as we know, fostered the unity of the nuclear family rather than its destruction. The new cottage industries might well make single parenting with sibling cooperation a very attractive option. Kinship is indeed subversive, and before the law joins in with the sociologists in celebrating (or lamenting) its demise, let us be cautious. If kinship itself is resilient and capable of protean adaptations, then the most basic term of the cultural kinship equation, the avunculate, is perhaps the most resilient of all. When the State Uncle fails, the Maternal Uncle is there in the wings, waiting to step forward. And should this happen, we shall see the lawyers rushing to be educated in the arcana of matrilineal succession; trying to pick up where their colleagues in Iowa left off nearly half a century ago.

Notes, References, and Acknowledgments

General Acknowledgments

Thanks for specific help is recorded in the notes for each chapter. Here I would like to thank Irving Louis Horowitz, who had the idea for this book and helped to determine its theme and contents. Also I would like to thank Mary Curtis, Esther Luckett, and the staff of Transaction Publishers, and especially Arri Parker, every author's dream of the perfect editor. Margaret Gruter, and the institute that bears her name, have been a constant source of help and inspiration.

Chapter 1
The Case of the Polygamous Policeman

Notes

1   See Mark P. Leone, *Roots of Modern Mormonism* (Cambridge: Harvard University Press, 1979), and works cited therein, pp. 242-44. See especially Fawn M. Brodie, *No Man Knows My History* (New York: Knopf, 1945). On Mormon polygamy, see Jessie L. Embry, *Mormon Polygamous Families: Life in the Principle* (Salt Lake City: University of Utah Press, 1987); Richard Van Wagoner, *Mormon Polygamy: A History* (Salt Lake City: Signature Books, 1986). On Mormon legal history see Edwin B. Firmage and Richard C. Mangrum, *Zion In the Courts: A Legal History of the Church of Jesus Christ of Latter-Day Saints, 1830-1900* (Urbana: University of Illinois Press, 1988), especially part 2. On economic history, see Leonard J. Arrington, *Great Basin Kingdom: An Economic History of the Latter-Day Saints* (Cambridge: Harvard University Press, 1958).
2   *Cantwell v. Connecticut* (310 U.S. 296 [1940]); *West Virginia State Board of Education v. Barnett* (319 U.S. 624 [1943]); *Hamilton v. Regents of the University of California* (293 U.S. 245 [1934]); *Braunfeld v. Brown* 366 U.S. 599 [1961]); and *Sherbert v. Verner* 374 U.S. 398 [1963]).
3   On the relation of the right to marry issue and polygamy, see G. Keith Nedrow, "Polygamy and the Right to Marry: New Life for an Old Lifestyle," *Memphis State University Law Review* 11: 1 (1981), 303-49.
4   Frank Murphy was a stout defender of civil liberties on the bench, and one of the clearest thinkers in the Supreme Court during the 1940s. See Harold Norris, *Mr. Justice Murphy and the Bill of Rights* (Dobbs Ferry, NY: Oceana Publications, 1965).
5   For example, Australia, The South Seas, Micronesia, Melanesia, New Guinea, Native North and South America, etc., to say nothing of European Muslims in the Balkans.
6   See George Stocking, *Race, Culture and Evolution* (New York: Free Press, 1968).

7 For a concise historical treatment of English and European marriage laws and practices, see Mary Ann Glendon, "Legal Concepts of Marriage and the Family," in *Loving, Parenting and Dying: The Family Cycle in England and America Past and Present*, edited by V. C. Fox and M. H. Quitt (New York: Psychohistory Press, 1980). See also John R. Gillis, "Conjugal Settlements: Resort to Clandestine and Common Law Marriage in England and Wales, 1650-1850," in *Disputes and Settlements*, edited by John Bossy (Cambridge: Cambridge University Press, 1984).

8 References to the church's attitude to sexuality are too numerous to cite. The following are a few general works with their own excellent bibliographies: Reay Tannahill, *Sex in History* (New York: Stein and Day, 1980); G. Rattray Taylor, *Sex in History* (New York: Thames and Hudson, 1954); Denis de Rougement, *Passion and Society* (London: Faber, 1940) (originally *L'Amour et l'Occident* [Paris: Plon, 1934]). Still the standard work on the early period is W. E. H. Lecky, *History of European Morals from Augustus to Charlemagne* (London: Longmans Green, 1869). For possible early alternatives to the Christian tradition that was finally enforced see Elaine Pagels, *The Gnostic Gospels* (New York: Random House, 1979).

9 On the Merovingians see J. M. Wallace-Hadrill, *The Long-haired Kings, and Other Studies in Frankish History* (London: Methuen, 1962) and S. Dill, *Roman Society in Gaul in the Merovingian Age* (London: Macmillan, 1926).

10 On polygyny after the Thirty Years' War see E. Westermarck, *A Short History of Marriage* (New York: Macmillan, 1926), p. 236: "In 1650, soon after the Peace of Westphalia ... the Frankish *Kriestag* at Nuremburg passed the resolution that thenceforth every man should be allowed to marry two women." On the Russian case, see Paul Friedrich, "Semantic Structure and Social Structure: An Instance in Russian," in W. H. Goodenough (ed.), *Explorations in Cultural Anthropology* (New York: McGraw-Hill, 1964). On the seventeenth-century sects, see Christopher Hill, *The World Turned Upside Down: Radical Ideas During the English Revolution* (Harmondsworth: Penguin, 1976); also J. Cairncross,

After Polygamy Was Made a Sin: The Social History of Christian Polygamy (London: Routledge, 1974). On the Medieval period, see J.A. Brundage, *Law, Sex and Christian Society in Medieval Europe* (Chicago: University of Chicago Press, 1987); G. Duby, *Medieval Marriage* (Baltimore: Johns Hopkins University Press, 1978); F. Gies and J. Gies, *Marriage and the Family in the Middle Ages* (New York: Harper and Row, 1987); D. Herlihy, *Medieval Households* (Cambridge: Harvard University Press, 1985).

11 On the legitimation and entitlement of bastards among the nobility (and consequently de facto polygyny), see J. F. Cooper, "Patterns of Inheritance and Settlement by Great Landowners from the Fifteenth to the Eighteenth Centuries," in *Family and Inheritance: Rural Society in Western Europe 1200-1800*, edited by J. Goody, J. Thirsk, and E. O. Thompson (Cambridge: Cambridge University Press, 1978).

12 See Jerzy Peterkiewicz, *The Third Adam* (London: Oxford University Press, 1975), ch. 7.

13 F. Engels, *The Condition of the Working Class in England*, translated by W. Henderson and W. H. Chaloner (Stanford: Stanford University Press, 1958) (originally published in Germany in 1845); B. Disraeli, *Sybil, or, The Two Nations*, 3 vols. (London: Colburn, 1845).

14 Professor Lieber, on whose erudite opinion the court leans heavily, as we shall see, had the following observations to make on women: "The nature and consequent duties of woman exclude her from public life. Her timidity, bashfulness, delicacy, and inferior grasp of mind, as well as those sacred duties more especially assigned to her, require her being more retired than the other sex. A woman loses in the same degree her natural character, as a woman, as she enters into publicity" (*Manual of Political Ethics* [Boston: Little Brown, 1839], 124-5).

15 See, e.g., N. W. Thomas, *Kinship Organization and Group Marriage in Australia* (Cambridge: Cambridge University Press, 1906).

16 L. H. Morgan, *Ancient Society* (New York: Holt, 1877); J. F. McLennan, *Primitive Marriage* (Edinburgh: Black, 1865); Herbert Spencer, *Principles of Sociology* (London and Edinburgh:

Williams and Norgate, 1876-1896), vol. 1, part 3. To be fair, the justices would have had to have been pretty on the ball to have assimilated any of this by 1878! They might, however, have been acquainted with some of the work of the German comparative ethnologists like Bastian and Humboldt, or with the Jesuit Relations, etc.

17 R. D. Alexander, J. L. Hoogland, R. D. Howard, K. M. Noonan, and P. W. Sharman, "Sexual Dimorphisms and Breeding Systems in Pinnipeds, Ungulates, Primates and Humans," in *Evolutionary Biology and Human Social Behavior*, edited by N. Chagnon and W. Irons (North Scituate, MA: Duxbury, 1979).

18 G. P. Murdock, *Social Structure* (New York: Macmillan, 1949); G. P. Murdock, "World Ethnographic Sample," *American Anthropologist* 59 (1957): 604-87; C. S. Ford and F. A. Beach, *Patterns of Sexual Behavior* (London: Eyre and Spottiswoode, 1951); E. Bourguignon and L. S. Greenbaum, *Diversity and Homogeneity in World Societies* (New Haven: HRAF Press, 1973).

19 See Robin Fox, *The Keresan Bridge: A Problem in Pueblo Ethnology* (London: Athlone, 1967).

20 See C. M. Arensberg and S. T. Kimball, *Family and Community in Ireland* (Cambridge: Harvard University Press, 1940). For an alternative Irish lifestyle reflecting prefamine conditions more closely, see Robin Fox, *The Tory Islanders: A People of the Celtic Fringe* (Cambridge: Cambridge University Press, 1978).

21 See for example the classic discussions of the Tallensi by Fortes and the Nuer by Evans-Pritchard in M. Fortes, *The Dynamics of Clanship among the Tallensi* (London: Oxford University Press, for the International African Institute, 1945); M. Fortes, *The Web of Kinship among the Tallensi* (London: Oxford University Press, for the International African Institute, 1949); E. E. Evans-Pritchard, *The Nuer* (Oxford: Clarendon Press, 1940); and E. E. Evans-Pritchard, *Kinship and Marriage among the Nuer* (Oxford: Clarendon Press, 1951).

22 A. R. Radcliffe-Brown and D. Forde, eds., *African Systems of Kinship and Marriage* (London: Oxford University Press for the International African Institute, 1950); Nur Yalman, *Under the Bo*

Tree: Studies in Caste, Kinship and Marriage in the Interior of Ceylon (Berkeley: University of California Press, 1971); M. Freedman, *Chinese Family and Marriage in Singapore* (London: HMSO, 1957); W. Shapiro, *Miwuyt Marriage: The Cultural Anthropology of Affinity in Northeast Arnhem Land* (Philadelphia: Institute for the Study of Human Issues, 1981); P. Bohannan and J. Middleton, eds., *Marriage, Family and Residence* (Garden City, NY: Natural History Press, 1968); Denise Paulme, ed., *Women of Tropical Africa* (Berkeley: University of California Press, 1971); I. Schapera, *Married Life in an African Tribe* (London: Faber, 1940).

23 See: W. N. Stephens, *The Family in Cross-cultural Perspective* (New York: Holt, Rinehart and Winston, 1963).

24 M. Daly and M. Wilson, "Abuse and Neglect of Children in Evolutionary Perspective," in *Natural Selection and Social Behavior*, edited by R. Alexander and D. W. Tinkle (New York: Chiron Press, 1981).

25 Richard F. Burton, *The City of the Saints* (London: Longman Green, 1861), appendix 4.

26 See L. L. Betzig, *Despotism and Differential Reproduction: A Darwinian View* (New York: Aldine, 1986). For the Mormons specifically, see L. Mealey, "The Relation Between Social Status and Biological Success: A Case Study of the Mormon Religious Hierarchy," *Ethology and Sociobiology* 6 (1985): 249-57.

27 This objection has been stated by Richard D. Schwartz, "Using Sociobiology in Shaping the Law," *Journal of Social and Biological Structures*, special issue entitled "Law, Biology and Culture" 5: 4 (1982): 325-33. He uses as a reference W. J. Goode, *World Revolution and Family Patterns* (New York: Free Press, 1963), but the point is made in almost every sociological and anthropological text on the family. Schwartz also raises the point about the postindustrial society but gives no reference. The standard work is of course Daniel Bell, *The Coming of Post-Industrial Society* (New York: Basic Books, 1973). Schwartz also interestingly uses the *Reynolds* and subsequent polygyny cases to make his point about the problems of introducing sociobiological reasoning into legal matters.

28 Robin Fox, *The Red Lamp of Incest: A Enquiry into the Origins of Mind and Society* (New York: Dutton, 1980; 2nd ed. Notre Dame: Notre Dame University Press, 1983); see particularly chapters 6 and 8 and the notes and references thereto. For the author's more general opinions on kinship and marriage systems, see Robin Fox, *Kinship and Marriage: An Anthropological Perspective* (Harmondsworth: Penguin, 1967; reprint, New York: Cambridge University Press, 1989).

29 See the contrasting findings, for example, of Gary R. Lee, "Marital Structure and Economic Systems," *Journal of Marriage and the Family* 41 (1979): 701-707, and Jack Goody, "Polygyny, Economy and the Role of Women" in *The Character of Kinship*, edited by J. Goody (Cambridge: Cambridge University Press, 1973), 175-190.

30 L. Tiger and R. Fox, *The Imperial Animal* (New York: Holt Rinehart and Winston, 1971; reprint, New York: Henry Holt, 1989).

31 See Robin Fox, "Fitness By Any Other Name," *The Behavioral and Brain Sciences* 9 (1986): 192-3; a response to D. R. Vining, "Social versus Reproductive Success: The Central Problem of Human Sociobiology," *The Brain and Behavioral Sciences* 9 (1986): 167-216.

32 Carol S. Bruch, "Nonmarital Cohabitation in the Common Law Countries: A Study in Judicial-Legislative Interaction," *American Journal of Comparative Law* 29 (1981): 2, 217-45.

33 For an excellent account of the adoption issue, see R. Michael Otto, "Wait 'Til Your Mothers Get Home: Assessing the Rights of Polygamists as Custodial and Adoptive Parents," *Utah Law Revue* 4 (1991): 881-931.

Acknowledgments

I would like to thank Richard Alexander, Roger Masters, Warren Shapiro, and Paul Bohannan for useful observations; Dennis Haslam, attorney-at-law, Salt Lake City, for guidance on Utah law; Carol Sanger for encouraging my foray into legal reasoning; Carol Bruch for trying to explain the true implications of *Marvin v. Marvin*; Michael

Wald and E. Donald Elliott for general encouragement and their assurance that legal scholars would be interested. A preliminary version was presented at the Fourth Monterey Dunes Conference of the Gruter Institute for Law and Behavioral Research. I am grateful to Margaret Gruter and the participants for their input. All errors, omissions, and overall conclusions are my own responsibility.

Chapter 2
The Case of the Reluctant Genetrix

Since I was writing an amicus brief, I had access to all the trial documents including transcripts, copies of other amicus briefs, copies of all judgements and motions, and copies of all documents (e.g., the contract) submitted in evidence. In addition I have a daily file of press clippings for the whole of the proceedings. I attended several days of the trial in the Superior Court, and represented the Gruter Institute as amicus curiae at the Supreme Court hearings, and at the press conferences after both the Superior and Supreme Court judgements. When I quote from nonpublished documents in this chapter, I am quoting from those in my possession as a result of this participation.

Acknowledgments

I have obviously incurred a lot of debts in the process of writing and researching the chapter. The two most basic are those owed to Donald Elliott, for guiding me through the thickets of contract law and for sticking with the grueling task of preparing a brief, which was indeed brief but which packed the needed punch, and to Michael McGuire, who gave me a mini-course in endocrinology to make up for what I had forgotten since I studied it briefly (as an NIMH Fellow) at Stanford Medical School in 1970. Margaret Gruter, as president of the foundation which bears her name, made most of this cooperation possible, and along with the other members of the Gruter "team" had a great deal of input. That leaves the rest of the team, Paul J. Bohannan, and Joan Hollinger to be thanked for their numerous criticisms and comments. Finally I should like to thank Mary Beth Whitehead herself. I never got to know her well—she was naturally shielded as much as possible during the trials—but I knew enough of her to know that the Supreme Court was absolutely right to rebuke the lower court's treatment of her. She is, as one press commentator had the courage to say, the stuff of heroines; and we lack them today, lord knows. She is a good mother and a brave woman. I wish her and all her children well; I regret we could not do more.

A summary of some of the material used in this chapter appeared first in R. Fox, "In the Matter of Baby M: Report from the Gruter Institute for Law and Behavioral Research," *Politics and the Life Sciences* 7 (1988): 1, 77-85.

References

Amiel-Tison, Claudine. 1985. "Pediatric Contribution to Present Knowledge on the Neurobehavioral Status of Infants at Birth." In *Neonate Cognition*, edited by J. Mehler and R. Fox. Hillsdale NJ: Erlbaum.

Bateson, P.P.G. 1976. "Rules and Reciprocity in Behavioural Development." In *Growing Points in Ethology*, edited by P.P.G. Bateson and R.A. Hinde. Cambridge: Cambridge University Press.

Blum, B.L., ed. 1980. *Psychological Aspects of Pregnancy, Birthing and Bonding.* New York: Human Sciences.

Blurton Jones, N. 1972. "Comparative Aspects of Mother Child Contact." In *Ethological Studies of Child Behavior*, edited by N. Blurton Jones. Cambridge: Cambridge University Press.

Blurton Jones, N. 1985. "Anthropology, Ethology and Childhood." In *Biosocial Anthropology,* edited by R. Fox. London: Malaby Press.

Bowlby, John. 1951. *Maternal Care and Mental Health.* Geneva: WHO.

Bowlby, John. 1969. *Attachment and Loss.* Vol. 1, *Attachment.* London: Hogarth Press.

Bowlby, John. 1973. *Attachment and Loss.* Vol. 2, *Separation.* London: Hogarth Press.

Bowlby, John. 1980. *Attachment and Loss.* Vol. 3, *Loss.* London: Hogarth Press.

Brazelton, T.B. 1973. "Effect of Maternal Expectations on Early Infant Behavior." *Early Child Dev. Care* 2: 259-273.

Brown G.W., and Harris, T. 1978. *Social Origins of Depression: A Study of Psychiatric Disorder in Women.* London: Tavistock.

Campbell, B., and Peterson, W.E. 1953. "Milk Let-down and Orgasm in the Human Female," *Human Biology* 25: 165-68.

Chesler, Phyllis, 1988, *Sacred Bond: The Legacy of Baby M.* New York: Times Books.

Chisholm, J.S. 1983. *Navaho Infancy: An Ethological Study of Child Development*. New York: Aldine.

Chrichton, M. 1990. *Jurassic Park*. New York: Knopf.

Cloninger, C.R., Sigvardsson, S., Bohman, M., and van Knoring, A. 1982. "Predisposition to Petty Criminality in Swedish Adoptees: II Cross-fostering Analysis of Gene-Environment Interaction." *Archives of General Psychiatry* 39: 1242-7.

Condon, W.S., and Sander, L.W. 1974. "Neonate Movement is Synchronized with Adult Speech: Interactional Participation and Language Acquisition." *Science* 183: 99-101.

Corbin, A. 1960. *Treatise on the Law of Contracts*. St. Paul, MI: West Pub. Co.

Count, Earl W. 1973. *Being and Becoming Human*. New York: Van Nostrand.

Daly, M., and Wilson, M. 1987. "Evolutionary Psychology and Family Violence." In *Sociobiology and Psychology*, edited by C. Crawford, M. Smith, and D. Krebs. Hillsdale, NJ: Erlbaum.

DeCasper, A.J., and Fifer, W.P. 1980. "Of Human Bonding: Newborns Prefer Mother's Voices." *Science* 208: 1174-1176.

DeMott, Benjamin. 1990. *The Imperial Middle: Why Americans Can't Think Straight about Social Class* New York: Morrow.

Department of Health and Social Security. 1984. *Report of the Committee of Inquiry into Human Fertilization and Embryology*. London: HMSO.

Deykin, E.Y., Campbell, L., and Patti, P. 1984. "The Postadoption Experience of Surrendering Parents." *Amer. J. Orthopsych.* 54: 271-280.

Dunn, J. 1976. "How Far Do Early Differences in Mother-Child Relations Affect Later Development?" In *Growing Points in Ethology,* edited by P.P.G. Bateson and R.A. Hinde. Cambridge: Cambridge University Press.

Eibl-Eibesfeldt, I. 1970. *Ethology: The Biology of Behavior*. New York: Holt, Rinehart and Winston.

Ekman, P., Friesen, W.V., and Ellsworth P. 1972. *Emotion in the Human Face*. Elmsford, NY: Pergamon Press.

Fox, Robin. 1960. "Therapeutic Rituals and Social Structure in Cochiti Pueblo." *Human Relations* 13: 4, 291-303. Reprinted as "Witches,

Clans and Curing" in *Encounter with Anthropology* (New York: Harcourt Brace Jovanovich, 1973). 2nd. ed. published by Transaction Books, New Brunswick, NJ, 1991.

Fox, Robin. 1967. *Kinship and Marriage: An Anthropological Perspective*. Harmondsworth: Penguin. 2nd ed. published by Cambridge University Press, New York, 1985.

Fox, Robin. 1973. "Comparative Family Patterns." Chap. 3 of *Encounter with Anthropology*. New York: Harcourt, Brace, Jovanovich. 2nd. ed. published by Transaction Books, New Brunswick, NJ, 1991.

Freedman, S.B., et al. 1963. "Behavioral Observations on Parents Anticipating the Death of a Child." *Pediatrics* 32: 610-625.

Friedman, Lawrence M. 1985. *A History of American Law*. 2nd. ed. New York: Simon and Schuster, 1973.

Gellner, E. 1981. *Muslim Society*. Cambridge: Cambridge University Press.

Goodall, Jane. 1971. In *The Shadow of Man*. New York: Dell.

Hall, F., et al. 1980. "Early Life Experiences and Later Mothering Behavior: A Study of Mothers and Their 20-week Old Babies." In *The First Year of Life*, edited by D. Shaffer and J. Dunn. New York: Wiley.

Hamburg, D.A. 1974. "Coping Behavior in Life-Threatening Circumstances." *Psychotherapy and Psychosomatics* 23: 13-25.

Hamburg, D.A., et al. 1968. "Studies of Distress in the Menstrual Cycle and the Postpartum Period." In *Endocrinology and Human Behaviour*, edited by R. Michael. Oxford: Oxford University Press.

Hamilton, W.D. 1963. "The Evolution of Altruistic Behavior." *American Naturalist* 97: 354-56.

Hansen, E.W. 1966. "The Development of Maternal and Infant Behavior in the Rhesus Monkey." *Behavior* 27: 107-149.

Harlow H.F., and Harlow M.K. 1965. "The Affectional Systems." In *Behavior of Nonhuman Primates*, vol. 2., edited by M. Schrier, H.F. Harlow, and F. Stolnitz. New York and London: Academic Press.

Harlow, Harry F. 1959. "Love in Infant Monkeys." *Scientific American* June: 1-8.

Harlow, Harry F. 1974. "Induction and Alleviation of Depressive States in Monkeys." In *Ethology and Psychiatry*, edited by N.

White. Toronto: Toronto University Press.

Harlow, Harry, F. 1961. "The Development of Affectional Patterns in Infant Monkeys." In *Determinants of Infant Behavior*, edited by B.M. Foss. London: Methuen. Vol. 1.

Herbert, M., Sluckin, W., and Sluckin, A. 1982. "Mother to infant 'bonding'." *Journal of Child Psychology and Psychiatry* 23: 205-221.

Hinde, R.A., and Spencer-Booth, Y. 1971. "Effects of Brief Separation from Mother on Rhesus Monkeys." *Science* 173: 111-18.

Hofer, Myron A. 1972. "A Psychoendocrine Study of Bereavement, Part 1." *Psychosomatic Medicine* 36(6): 481-491.

Hollinger, Joan H. 1985. "From Coitus to Commerce: Legal and Social Consequences of Noncoital Reproduction." *Journal of Law Reform* 8(4): 865-932.

Huxley, A. 1932. *Brave New World*. London: Chatto and Windus.

Kagan, J. 1981. "Universals in Human Development." In *Handbook of Cross-cultural Human Development*, edited by R.H. Munroe, R.L. Munroe, and B.B. Whiting. New York: Garland STPM Press.

Kagan, J., Kearsley, R.B., and Zelazo P.R. 1980. *Infancy: Its Place in Human Development*. Cambridge: Harvard University Press.

Katz, A. 1986. "Surrogate Motherhood and the Baby-Selling Laws." *Columbia Journal of Law and Social Problems* 20(1): 1-53.

Keane, N., and Breo, D. 1981. *The Surrogate Mother?* New York: Everest House.

Klaus, M.H., and Kennell J.H. 1982. *Parent-Infant Bonding*. 2nd. ed. St. Louis: Mosby.

Konner, M., and Worthman C. 1980. "Nursing Frequency, Gonadal Function and Birth Spacing among !Kung Hunter Gatherers." *Science* 207: 788-91.

Konner, Melvin. 1982. *The Tangled Wing: Biological Constraints on the Human Spirit*. New York: Holt, Rinehart and Winston.

Lamb, M.E., and Hwang, C.-P. 1982. "Maternal Attachment and Mother-neonate bonding: A Critical Review." In *Advances in Developmental Psychology*, vol. 2, edited by M.E. Lamb and A.L. Brown. Hillsdale, NJ: Erlbaum.

Lorenz, Konrad. 1970. *Studies in Animal and Human Behavior*, vol. 1, translated by Robert Martin. Cambridge: Harvard University Press.

Mackey, W.C. 1979. "Parameters of the Adult Male-Child Bond: A Cross-Cultural and Cross-Species Analysis." *Ethology and Sociobiology* 1: 59-76.

Mackey, W.C., and Day, R. 1979. "Some Indicators of Fathering Behaviors in The United States: A Cross-Cultural Examination of Adult Male-Child Interaction." *Journal of Marriage and The Family* 4: 287-299.

Maine, Sir Henry. 1861. *Ancient Law*. London: John Murray.

Mehler, J., Bertoncini, J., and Barrière, M. 1978. "Infant Perception of Mother's Voice." *Perception* 7: 5.

Mehler, Jacques, and Fox, Robin, eds. 1985. *Neonate Cognition: Beyond the Blooming Buzzing Confusion*. Hillsdale, NJ: Erlbaum.

Mehler, Jacques. 1985. "Language Related Dispositions in Early Infancy." In J. Mehler and R. Fox, eds. *Neonate Cognition*. Hillsdale, NJ: Erlbaum.

Miles, M., and Melhuish, E. 1974. "Recognition of Mother's Voice in Early Infancy." *Nature* 252: 123-24.

Newton, Niles. 1973. "Interrelationships Between Sexual Responsiveness, Birth and Breast Feeding." In *Contemporary Sexual Behavior: Critical Issues in the 1970s*, edited by J. Zubin and J. Money. Baltimore and London: Johns Hopkins University Press.

Parker, Phillip J. 1983. "Motivation of Surrogate Mothers: Initial Findings." *Amer. J. Psychiatry* 140(1): 117-18.

Querleau, D., and Renard, K. 1981. "Les Perceptions Auditives du Foetus Humain." *Medicine et Hygiène* 39: 2102-2110.

Rheingold, H.R., ed. 1963. *Maternal Behavior in Mammals*. New York: Wiley.

Robertson, J. 1986. "Embryos, Families and Procreational Liberty: The Legal Structure of the New Reproduction." *Southern California Law Review* 59: 939-1041.

Rossi, Alice. 1977. "A Biosocial Perspective on Parenting." *Daedalus* 106: 1-33.

Rynearson, E.K. 1982. "Relinquishment and its Maternal Complications: A Preliminary Study." *Amer J. Psychiatry* 193(3): 338-40.

Sameroff, A. 1978. "Summary and Conclusions: The Future of Newborn Assessment." In *Organization and Stability of Newborn Behavior*, edited by A. Sameroff. Monographs of the Society for Research in Child Development 43(5-6): 102-17.

Schwartz, A. 1979. "The Case for Specific Performance." *Yale Law Journal* 89: 271-289.

Seay, B., Alexander, B.K., and Harlow, H.F. 1964. "Maternal Behavior of Socially Deprived Rhesus Monkeys." *J. Abnormal Soc. Psych.* 69: 345.

Seligman, M., and Maier, S. 1976. "Failure to Escape Traumatic Shock." *J. Exp. Psych.* 74: 1-9.

Sorosky, A.D., Baran, A., and Pannor R. 1978. *The Adoption Triangle*. Garden City, NY: Anchor Press/Doubleday.

Stanworth, M., ed. 1987. *Reproductive Technologies: Gender, Motherhood and Medicine*. Cambridge: Cambridge University Press.

Suomi, Stephen J. 1975. "Depressive Behavior in Adult Monkeys Following Separation from Family Environment." *J. Abnormal Soc. Psych.* 84: 576-78.

Temple, G. 1984. "Freedom of Contract and Intimate Relationships." *Harvard Journal of Law and Public Policy* 8(1): 121-173.

Tiger, L. 1969. *Men in Groups*. New York: Random House.

Tiger, L., and Fox R. 1971. *The Imperial Animal*. New York: Holt, Rinehart and Winston. (2nd ed. New York: Henry Holt, 1989)

Trivers, R. 1972. "Parental Investment and Sexual Selection." In *Sexual Selection and the Descent of Man, 1871-1971*, edited by B. Campbell. Chicago: Aldine.

Tulchinsky, D., and Ryan, K.J. 1980. Maternal-Fetal Endocrinology. Philadelphia: Saunders.

Weber, Max. 1930. *The Protestant Ethic and the Spirit of Capitalism*. Translated by Talcott Parsons. New York: Scribner; London: Allen and Unwin, 1904-5.

Weiss, J., Glazer, H.I., and Pohorecky, L.A. 1976. "Coping Behavior and Neurochemical Changes in Rats: An Alternative Explanation for the Original Learned Helplessness Experiments." In *Animal Models in Human Psychobiology*, edited by G. Servan and A. Kling. New York: Plenum.

Whitehead, Mary Beth (with Loretta Schwartz-Nobel). 1989. *A Mother's Story*. New York: St Martin's Press.

Yakovlev, P., and Lecours, A.R. 1967. "The Myelogenetic Cycles of Regional Maturation of the Brain." In *Regional Development of the Brain in Early Life*, edited by A. Minowski. Oxford: Blackwell.

Young, L., Suomi, S.J., Harlow, H.F., and McKinney W. 1973. "Early Stress and Later Response to Separation in Rhesus Monkeys." *Amer. J. Psychiatry* 130: 400-405.

Part 2
Introduction: The Lineal Equation

References

Beckstrom, J. 1985. *Sociobiology and the Law*. Chicago: University of Illinois Press.

Chase, A.H., and Phillips, H. 1982. *A New Introduction to Greek*. 3rd. ed. Cambridge: Harvard University Press.

Engels, F. 1905. *The Origins of the Family, Private Property, and the State*. Translated by E. Untermann. Chicago: Kerr. (Originally published as *Der Ursprung der Familie, des Privateigenthums und des Staats im Anschluss an Lewis H. Morgans Forschungen*. Zurich: 1884.)

Fox, R. 1967. *The Keresan Bridge: A Problem in Pueblo Ethnology*. London: Athlone.

Fox, R. 1978. *The Tory Islanders: A People of the Celtic Fringe*. Cambridge: Cambridge University Press.

Harrison, J.E. 1927. *Themis: A Study in the Social Origins of Greek Religion*. Cambridge: Cambridge University Press.

Jenkyns, R. 1980. *The Victorians and Ancient Greece*. Cambridge: Harvard University Press.

Jenkyns, R. 1982. *Three Classical Poets*. Cambridge: Harvard University Press.

Krader, L., ed. and trans. 1972. *The Ethnological Notebooks of Karl Marx*. Netherlands: Van Gorcum.

Maine, H.S. 1883. *Dissertations on Early Law and Custom*. London: Murray.

Maine, H.S. 1884. *Ancient Institutions*. London: Murray.

McLennan, J.F. 1865. *Primitive Marriage: An Enquiry into the Origins of the Form of Capture in Marriage Ceremonies*. Edinburgh: Black.

McLennan, J.F. 1876. *Studies in Ancient History*. London: Quaritch.

Morgan, L.H. 1877. *Ancient Society: Researches into the Lines of Human Progress from Savagery through Barbarism to Civilization*. New York: Holt.

Murdock, G.P. 1949. *Social Structure*. New York: Macmillan.

Radcliffe-Brown, A.R. 1952. *Structure and Function in Primitive Society*. London: Cohen and West.

Chapter 3
The Virgin and the Godfather

Acknowledgments

The original version of this chapter was delivered to a seminar at the University of Virginia. I would like to thank David Sapir, Richard Handler, and the other members of the Department of Anthropology for their lively and stimulating comments. For particular insights and criticisms I am deeply grateful to Paul Friedrich, Dell Hymes, Phillip Bock, Peter Kibby, Robert Fagles, Robert Storey, Felix Browder, and especially Lowell Edmunds and Paul Benson. The original printed version of the chapter appeared in *The Journal of the Steward Anthropological Society* 17: 1 & 2 (1987-1988), 141-192; copyright © The Steward Anthropological Society. Diagram 3.2 is reproduced by permission of the American Anthropological Association from Bock 1979. Diagram 3.3 is reproduced by permission of Viking Penguin, a division of Penguin Books USA, Inc., from Fagles and Knox 1984, © 1982 by Robert Fagles.

Notes

34 He actually seems to have made a habit of it as regards burial, since he denied burial to the fallen Argives, sparking heroic deeds of cadaver rescue by Theseus, King of Athens, who was later to give shelter to the wandering blind Oedipus. See Jebb 1902, 201-202.

35 Three of the above I took from the notorious Cliff Notes which I had picked up in the bookstore in order to observe the received wisdom that was being transmitted to students. (It was the "Antigone-as-individual" line, of course.) But interestingly, the author, to illustrate the problems of translation, had included a few samples of attempts at the opening lines.

36 Several critics, including a smart graduate student at the University of Virginia, have insisted that I give the second and subsequent lines so that this discussion of the first line might have a context. Here is the original with Jebb's translation:

ἆρ' οἶσθ' ὅ τι Ζεὺς τῶν ἀπ' Οἰδίπου κακῶν
ὁποῖον οὐχὶ νῷν ἔτι ζώσαιν τελεῖ ;
οὐδὲν γὰρ οὔτ' ἀλγεινὸν οὔτ' ἄτης ἄτερ
οὔτ' αἰσχρὸν οὔτ' ἄτιμόν ἐσθ', ὁποῖον οὐ
τῶν σῶν τε κἀμῶν οὐκ ὄπωπ' ἐγὼ κακῶν.

Knowest thou what ill there is, of all bequeathed by Oedipus, that
Zeus fulfills not for us twain while we live? Nothing painful is
there, nothing fraught with ruin, no shame, no dishonour, that I
have not seen in thy woes and mine?

37 It is one of Steiner's great contributions to take us beyond the
well-known passages from Hegel in the *Philosophy of Religion*
into other sources of his opinions on Antigone and tragedy
generally. Of other commentators, Kojève (1947) and Derrida
(1974) seem to come close to a good understanding of the nature
of the conflict, insofar as one can extract the sensible from the
fanciful in the latter and plough through the neo-Hegelian density
of the former.

38 For the record, in answer to the old anthropological chestnut "is
the family universal?" one can respond that two things are
universal but not necessarily isomorphic: the household, and the
kinship roles indicated by the terms for primary kin.

39 Velikovsky (1960) adds to the complications the theory that
Egyption Thebes might have been the source for the whole
Oedipus legend via the real story of Akhnaton, who married his
mother and destroyed at least the memory of his father, and
brought about the destruction of his line. Sphinxes were, after all,
Egyptian, not Greek, mythological creatures. There is also the
burial alive of a princess in there somewhere, which could be the
source of the whole Antigone episode.

References

Balch, Stephen H. 1985. "The Neutered Civil Servant: Eunuchs,
Celibates, Abductees and the Maintenance of Organizational
Loyalty." *Journal of Social and Biological Structures* 8: 313-328.

Benveniste, E. 1969. *Le vocabulaire des institutions indo-européenes.* 2 vols. Paris: Minuit.

Bernal, M. 1987. *Black Athena: The Afroasiatic Roots of Classical Civilization.* Vol. 1, *The Fabrication of Ancient Greece 1785-1985.* New Brunswick, NJ: Rutgers University Press.

Bock, Philip. 1979. "Oedipus Once More." *American Anthropologist* 81: 905-6.

Bradley, A.C. 1909. "Hegel's Theory of Tragedy." In *Oxford Lectures on Poetry.* London: Macmillan.

Carroll, Michael. 1978. "Lévi-Strauss on the Oedipus Myth: A Reconsideration." *American Anthropologist* 80: 805-14.

Derrida, Jacques. 1974. *Glas.* Paris: Gallimard.

Dodds, E.R. 1951. *The Greeks and the Irrational.* Berkeley and Los Angeles: University of California Press.

Donzelot, J. 1979. *The Policing of Families.* New York: Pantheon.

Dumont, Louis. 1986. *Essays on Individualism: Modern Ideology in Anthropological Perspective.* Chicago: Chicago University Press.

Fagles, R., and Knox, B. 1984. *Sophocles: The Three Theban Plays.* New York: Penguin Books (Penguin Classics Edition). First published 1982.

Finley, M.I. 1979. *The World of Odysseus.* 2nd rev. ed. London: Penguin. First published 1954.

Fisher, H.A.L. 1906. "The Codes." In *Cambridge Modern History,* edited by A.W. Ward, G.W. Prothero, and Stanley Leathes. Vol. 9, *Napoleon.* Chap. 6. Cambridge: Cambridge University Press.

Fox, R. 1967. *Kinship and Marriage: An Anthropological Perspective.* Harmondsworth: Penguin Books.

Fox, R. 1983. *Kinship and Marriage: An Anthropological Perspective.* 2nd North American ed. New York: Cambridge University Press.

Friedrich, P. 1966. "Proto-Indo-European Kinship." *Ethnology* 5: 1-36.

Friedrich, P. 1977. "Sanity and the Myth of Honor: The Problem of Achilles." *Ethos* 5: 281-305.

Gellner, Ernest. 1981. *Muslim Society.* Cambridge: Cambridge University Press.

Gluckman, Max. 1963. *Order and Rebellion in Tribal Africa.* London: Cohen and West.

Graves, Robert. 1960. *The Greek Myths*. Vol. 2. Rev. ed. Harmondsworth: Penguin. First published 1955.

Havelock, Eric. 1978. *The Greek Concept of Justice*. Cambridge: Harvard University Press.

Jebb, Sir Richard C. 1902. *The Antigone of Sophocles: with a Commentary*, edited by E. Shuckburgh, Cambridge: Cambridge University Press. First published 1900.

Kitto, H.D.F. 1951. *The Greeks*. Harmondsworth: Penguin Books.

Kojève, A. 1947. *Introduction à la lecture de Hegel*. Paris: Galilée.

Kummar, K. 1987. *Utopia and Anti-Utopia in Modern Times*. Oxford: Basil Blackwell.

Lane Fox, Robin. 1973. *Alexander the Great*. London: Allen Lane.

LeGuin, Ursula K. 1985. *Always Coming Home*. New York: Harper and Row.

Lévi-Strauss, Claude. 1958. *Anthropologie structurale*. Paris: Librairie Plon.

McFarlane, A. 1978. *The Origins of English Individualism*. Oxford: Basil Blackwell.

McLennan, J.F. 1876. *Studies in Ancient History*. London: Quaritch.

Morris, D.R. 1965. *The Washing of the Spears: The Rise and Fall of the Zulu Nation*. New York: Simon and Schuster.

Morris, I. 1987. *Burial and Ancient Society: The Rise of the Greek State*. Cambridge: Cambridge University Press.

Murray, Oswyn. 1986. "Life and Society in Classical Greece." In *The Oxford History of the Classical World*, edited by J. Boardman, J. Griffith, and O. Murray. Oxford: Oxford University Press.

Parsons, Talcott. 1937. *The Structure of Social Action*. New York: McGraw Hill.

Partridge, Eric. 1983. *Origins: A Short Etymological Dictionary of Modern English*. New York: Greenwich House.

Puzo, Mario. 1969. *The Godfather*. New York: Putnam.

Rawls, John. 1971. *A Theory of Justice*. Cambridge: Harvard University Press.

Redfield, James. 1975. *Nature and Culture in the Iliad: The Tragedy of Hector*. Chicago: Chicago University Press.

Ritter, E.A. 1957. *Shaka Zulu*. New York: Putnam.

Roche, Paul. 1958. *The Oedipus Plays of Sophocles*. New York: New

American Library.

Schoumatoff, Alex. 1985. *The Mountain of Names: A History of the Human Family.* New York: Simon and Schuster.

Smyth, W.S. 1926. *Aeschylus: Vol. II.* (Loeb Classical Library) Cambridge: Harvard University Press/London: Heineman.

Steiner, George. 1984. *Antigones.* Oxford: Clarendon Press (Oxford University Press).

Storr, F. 1912. *Sophocles: Vol. I.* (Loeb Classical Library). Cambridge: Harvard University Press/London: Heineman.

Tiger, Lionel. 1978. "Omnigamy: Towards a New Kinship System." *Psychology Today* July.

Tönnies, F. 1887. *Gemeinschaft und Gesellschaft.* Leipzig: Fues Verlag.

Velikovsky, I. 1960. *Oedipus and Akhnaton.* New York: Doubleday.

Vonnegut, Kurt. 1976. *Slapstick.* New York: Dell.

Watling, E.F. 1947. *Sophocles: The Theban Plays.* Harmondsworth: Penguin Books.

Chapter 4
Sisters' Sons and Monkeys' Uncles

Acknowledgments

Diagrams 4.14 and 4.15 are reproduced by permission of Blackwell Scientific Publications, publishers of R. Hinde, ed., *Primate Social Relationships* (Oxford, 1983). I am grateful to my grandson, Michael Khater, six, for correcting my spelling of the names of Donald's nephews. "Kinship Alpha" appeared originally on pages 74-78 of *Bastard Moons* by Paul Friedrich (Chicago: Waite Press) and is reproduced by permission of the author.

References

Alexander, R.A. 1974. "The Evolution of Social Behavior." *Annual Review of Ecology and Systematics* 5: 325-383.

Bachofen, J.J. 1861. *Das Mutterrecht.* Basel: Schwabe.

Briffault, R. 1927. *The Mothers: A Study in the Origins of Sentiments and Institutions.* New York: Macmillan.

Cheney, D.L. 1983. "Proximate and Ultimate Factors Related to the Distribution of Male Migration." In *Primate Social Relationships*, edited by R. Hinde. Oxford: Blackwell Scientific Publications.

Crook, J.H., and Goss-Custard, J.D. 1972. "Social Ethology." *Annual Review of Psychology* 23: 277-312.

Dawkins, R. 1976. *The Selfish Gene.* Oxford: Oxford University Press.

Dumont, L. 1953. "The Dravidian Kinship Terminology as an Expression of Marriage." *Man* (o. s.) 54.

Eggan, F. 1949. "The Hopi and the Lineage Principle." In *Social Structure,* edited by M. Fortes. Oxford: Oxford University Press.

Espinas, A. 1878. *Des Sociétés Animales.* Paris: Baillière

Fisher, R.A. 1929. *The Genetical Theory of Natural Selection.* Oxford: Clarendon Press.

Fortes, M. 1949. "Time and Social Structure: An Ashanti Case Study." In *Social Structure,* edited by M. Fortes. Oxford: Oxford University Press.

Fortes, M. 1959. "Descent, Filiation and Affinity: A Rejoinder to Dr.

Leach." *Man* (o. s.) 59.

Fortune, R. 1932. *Sorcers of Dobu*. London: Routledge.

Fox, J.J. 1971. "Sister's Child as Plant: Metaphors in an Idiom of Consanguinity." In *Rethinking Kinship and Marriage*, edited by R. Needham. London: Tavistock.

Fox, R. 1965. "Demography and Social Anthropology." *Man* (o. s.) 65.

Fox, R. 1967a. *The Keresan Bridge: A Problem in Pueblo Ethnology*. London: Athlone.

Fox, R. 1967b. *Kinship and Marriage: An Anthropological Perspective*. Harmondsworth: Penguin. (2nd. North American Edition, New York: Cambridge University Press, 1983.)

Fox, R. 1978. *The Tory Islanders: A People of the Celtic Fringe*. Cambridge: Cambridge University Press.

Fox, R. 1980. *The Red Lamp of Incest*. New York: Dutton. 2nd ed. Notre Dame: Univ. of Notre Dame Press, 1983.

Fox, R. 1985a. "The Conditions of Sexual Evolution." In *Western Sexuality*, edited by P. Ariès and A. Béjin. Oxford: Blackwell. Originally published as a special edition of *Communications* (Paris: Editions Seuil, 1982).

Fox, R. 1985b. "Paternity Irrelevance and Matrilineal Descent." *The Behavioral and Brain Sciences* 8(4): 674-5.

Fox, R. 1986. "Fitness by any other Name." *The Behavioral and Brain Sciences* 9(1): 192-3.

Fox, R., ed. 1975. *Biosocial Anthropology*. London: Malaby Press.

Goody, J. 1959. "The Mother's Brother and the Sister's Son in West Africa." *Journal of the Royal Anthropological Institute* 89: 61-88.

Haldane, J.B.S. 1932. *The Causes of Evolution*. London: Arnold.

Hamilton, W. 1963. "The Evolution of Altruistic Behavior." *American Naturalist* 97: 354-56.

Hamilton, W. 1964. "The Genetical Evolution of Social Behavior." *Journal of Theoretical Biology* 7: 1-52.

Hartland, E.S. 1909-10. *Primitive Paternity*. 2 vols. London: David Nutt.

Hartung, J. 1985. "Matrilineal Inheritance: New Theory and Analysis." *The Behavioral and Brain Sciences* 8(4): 661-88.

Hocart, A.M. 1915. "Chieftainship and the Sister's Son in the Pacific."

American Anthropologist 17: 631-46.

Homans, G.C., and Schneider, D.M. 1955. *Marriage, Authority and Final Causes.* Glencoe, IL: Free Press.

Junod, H. 1927. *Life of a South African Tribe.* 2 vols. Revised and enlarged. London: Macmillan. Originally published in 1913.

Kurland, J. 1979. "Paternity, Mother's Brother and Human Sociality." In *Evolutionary Biology and Human Social Behavior,* edited by N. Chagnon and W. Irons. North Scituate, MA: Duxbury.

LaBarre, W. 1954. *The Human Animal.* Chicago: Chicago University Press.

Leach, E.R. 1961. *Rethinking Anthropology.* London: Athlone.

Lévi-Strauss, C. 1949. *Les Structures Elémentaires de la Parenté.* Paris: Presses Universitaires de France.

Lévi-Strauss, C. 1958. *Anthropologie Structurale.* Paris: Plon.

Malinowski, B. 1929. *The Sexual Life of Savages in North-western Melanesia.* London: Routledge.

Murdock, G.P. 1949. *Social Structure.* New York: Macmillan.

Myers, A.C., ed. 1937. *William Penn: His Own Account of the Lenni-Lenape or Delaware Indians 1683.* Philadelphia: Published by the editor.

Needham, R. 1962. *Structure and Sentiment.* Chicago: Chicago University Press.

Needham, R., ed. 1971. *Rethinking Kinship and Marriage.* London: Tavistock.

Radcliffe-Brown, A.R. 1924. "The Mother's Brother in South Africa." *South African Journal of Science* 21: 542-55.

Radcliffe-Brown, A.R. 1952. *Structure and Function in Primitive Society.* London: Cohen and West.

Rivers, W.H.R. 1910. "The Father's Sister in Oceania." *Folk-Lore* 21: 42-59.

Rivers, W.H.R. 1914. *The History of Melanesian Society.* 2. vols. Cambridge: Cambridge University Press.

Rodseth, L., Wrangham, R.W., Harrigan, A., and Smuts, B. 1991. "The Human Community as a Primate Society." *Current Anthropology* 32(3): 221-254.

Sahlins, M. 1960. "The Origins of Society." *Scientific American* 203: 76-86.

Smuts, B.B., Cheyney, D.L., Seyfarth, R.M., Wrangham, R.W., and Struhsaker, T.T., eds. 1987. *Primate Societies.* Chicago: Chicago University Press.

Spiro, M.E. 1982. *Oedipus in the Trobriands.* Chicago: Chicago University Press.

Tax, S. 1937. "Some Problems of Social Organization." In *Social Anthropology of the North American Tribes*, edited by F. Eggan. Chicago: Chicago University Press.

Tiger, L., and Fox, R. 1971. *The Imperial Animal.* New York: Holt, Rinehart and Winston. 2nd. ed. New York: Henry Holt, 1989.

Trivers, R. 1972. "Parental Investment and Sexual Selection." In *Sexual Selection and the Descent of Man 1871-1971*, edited by B. Campbell. Chicago: Aldine.

Tylor, E.B. 1871. *Primitive Culture.* 2 vols. London: John Murray.

Westermarck, E. 1891. *The History of Human Marriage.* London: Macmillan.

Wilson, E.O. 1975. *Sociobiology: The New Synthesis.* Cambridge: Harvard University Press.

Wrangham, R.W. 1980. "An Ecological Model of Female-Bonded Primate Groups." *Behaviour* 75: 262-300.

Zuckerman, S. 1932. *The Social Life of Monkeys and Apes.* London: Routledge.

Index